FIRST EDITION

STRATEGIC MANAGEMENT FOR RESULTS

PRACTICAL STRATEGIES FOR SUSTAINABLE OUTCOMES

WRITTEN AND EDITED BY
LINDA L. BRENNAN
AND
FAYE A. SISK

cognella™
San Diego, CA

Bassim Hamadeh, CEO and Publisher
Michael Simpson, Vice President of Acquisitions
Jamie Giganti, Managing Editor
Jess Busch, Graphic Design Supervisor
Zina Craft, Acquisitions Editor
Natalie Lakosil, Licensing Manager

ISBN: 978-1-62131-053-2 (pbk) / 978-1-62661-359-1 (br)

www.cognella.com 800.200.3908

CONTENTS

SECTION I: CHARTING THE DIRECTION OF THE ORGANIZATION

1. Understanding the Strategic Management Process   3
   Reading: A Business Plan? Or a Journey to Plan B?

2. Defining a Meaningful Vision   17

Closing Case   23

SECTION II: UNDERSTANDING THE ORGANIZATION IN CONTEXT

3. Addressing the Governance and Social Responsibilities of the Organization   27
   Reading: Strategic Responsibility: Technology Management for Corporate Social Responsibility

4. Assuring Corporate and Resource Sustainability   47
   Reading: The Business of Sustainability: What It Means to Managers Now

5. Surveying the External Environment   63

Closing Case   71
   Reading: The Library Rebooted

SECTION III: CONSIDERING STRATEGIC OPTIONS

6. Assessing the Organization's Capabilities   83

7. Evaluating the Value Chain   93
   Reading: "Greening" Transportation in the Supply Chain

8. Identifying the Paths to Take Toward the Vision   111

9. Taking a Deeper Look at Innovation   121
   Reading: Excerpt from 12 Different Ways for Companies to Innovate

Closing Case   131
   Reading: Intel Corporate Venturing

SECTION IV: MANAGING FOR RESULTS

10. Ensuring Your Strategy is Complete and Clear   143
    Reading: Are You Sure You Have a Strategy?

11. Considering Strategies in a Global Context   161
    Reading: The China and India Strategy

12. Leading Strategically   173

Closing Case   179
    Hong Kong Disneyland

ABOUT THE AUTHORS   199

REFERENCES   203

ACKNOWLEDGMENTS

I am deeply grateful for my family's support and encouragement during the process of developing this textbook. Working on a book while teaching a crazy schedule was not easy, but my husband, son, mother, and father made it possible. I want to thank my students of strategy over the years for helping me to refine my thoughts. Faye has been a terrific accountability partner with a pragmatic perspective. Finally, I'd like to acknowledge the enthusiasm and support of Jessica Knott and the team at Cognella.

—*LLB*

Thanks go to my students for providing the insight as well as serving as a sounding board to verify and expand the topics we discuss in this book. Teaching primarily graduate MBA students who are employed in a variety of industries provides a rich source of current information from which to gather current and timely information to complement the more theoretical basis of the content. Of course, I thank my co-author for her initiative and skill in driving this book to completion.

—*FAS*

Section I
Charting the Direction of the Organization

To paraphrase Lewis Carroll's Cheshire Cat, "if you don't know where you are going, it does not much matter how you get there." In the same way, strategic management starts with defining a target.

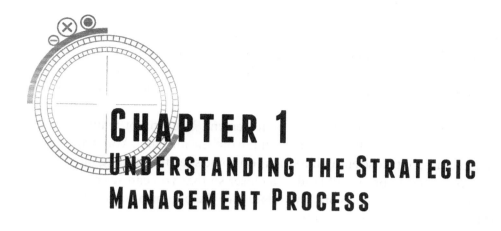

CHAPTER 1
UNDERSTANDING THE STRATEGIC MANAGEMENT PROCESS

"The great virtue of free enterprise is that it forces existing businesses to meet the test of the market continuously, to produce products that meet consumer demands at lowest cost, or else be driven from the market. ... Naturally, existing businesses generally prefer to keep out competitors in other ways."

—*Milton Friedman*

OPENING VIGNETTE

Richard Branson, the British billionaire, is arguably a man with style and vision who understands free enterprise and market forces. He recently dedicated Virgin Galactic's Spaceport America in New Mexico. The facility will be used as the base for his new space tourism venture. The plan is to conduct test flights through 2012, and begin offering commercial suborbital flights once the testing is completed and the Federal Aviation Administration licenses the company.

Branson knows how to leverage resources to build a business model and create a competitive advantage. He negotiated with the State of New Mexico to build the $209 million taxpayer-financed spaceport. Tickets, selling for $200,000 for a two and a half hour flight, are already being sold. And NASA has already signed a $4.5 million contract for up to three chartered research flights.

Based on a report from the Associated Press, reported on October 18, 2011, in *The Wall Street Journal*. Accessed November 4, 2011, at http:online.wsj.com.

It seems fitting that a book about strategy should provide a vision of the journey you will take through its pages. Ultimately, this is a book about achieving desired results in the market-place, setting targets and reaching them in a competitive environment. If you want a theoretical perspective of strategy, you have the wrong book. *Strategic Management for Results* is designed to be a practical guide.

We will begin with a "helicopter view" of strategic management. You do not want to be in the clouds and only have a vague idea of what you are seeing from the airplane. You want to be high enough to get the big picture, but close enough to focus on some specific building blocks. As you proceed through the book, the chapters will land you closer so that you can see the details.

Now we want to establish a general framework and relate it to the organization of the book. Successful mastery of this material will enable you to:

- identify characteristics of a strategy
- describe the strategic management process
- understand the economics underlying competition
- define a business model
- identify different types of business models

INTRODUCTION

The term "strategy" is an endangered word. Unlike endangered animals that are over-hunted and are becoming scarce, endangered words are overused and are becoming vague. Go through a typical day and you will hear it used for a range of applications, e.g., "what's your strategy for getting this stain out," or "what's your strategy for finishing the report," or "what's your strategy to hire more people?" "Strategy" has been diluted to be synonymous with "plan."

Here is a simple definition: a strategy is a plan that creates or sustains a competitive advantage. Strategies are plans, but not all plans are strategies. The key difference is the focus on competition. If you are ahead of the competition, how are you going to stay (i.e., sustain) that way? If you are not, how are you going to create a strategy that meets the competition and creates an advantage?

Getting a stain out of your favorite jeans is probably not creating a competitive advantage. Finishing a report may be important, but generally does not create or sustain a competitive advantage. Likewise, hiring more people might be a good thing—and yes, you might be competing for scarce resources—but just hiring more people is not a good or a complete strategy.

Strategies are important. Not all important activities are strategic. For example, to be on an approved vendor list, your company might have to be ISO 9000-certified. That certification is certainly important, but is it strategic? To enter certain markets it may be, or it may not be, since your competitors can become (and possibly, already are) certified.

A strategy is a plan to create or sustain a competitive advantage. The plan may be long-term but does not have to be. In sports, competition is at the heart of any game. If you are a coach you may have a particular strategy going into a game, but as the team or individual faces the competition and deploys the strategy, you may find that you have to adjust it during a thirty-second time out.

Market conditions can also change quickly. It is not enough to just have a plan; the plan needs to be part of an overall process whereby the plan is developed, executed, adjusted, and evaluated. That process is what we call "strategic management."

Figure 1-1. Example of different smartphones

Effective strategic management is characterized by 4 Ds: it is a Dynamic, Data Driven process, led by Determined leaders.

Illustration

An example of a dynamic company that is driven by data and sets the market through determination is Apple. Steve Jobs had the ability to "see" the future and set a strategy before major competitors could respond. A specific example was the ability of Apple with its iPhone to use technology and strategic partnerships with cell phone companies to usurp RIM, the leader in "smart phone" technology, and to replace the Blackberry as the singular choice in the wave of intelligent devices in cellular phones. The responses by both RIM and Google with alternative technologies and devices failed to offset the wave of consumer allegiance and the technological criteria established by Apple.

THE STRATEGIC MANAGEMENT PROCESS

A process is a sequence of activities intended to produce a desired result. Sometimes the sequence is straightforward and linear. Sometimes a sequence may be iterative, or require several repetitions and reworks, before it is successful. A good process has feedback mechanisms in place to ensure that the process is working.

In the same way, strategic management is a sequence of activities intended to produce a desired result. In general, the first activity is to define the desired result, or your vision of a successful state. As you improve your organization's competitive ability, what will that look like?

The next step is to put your vision in context. There are a lot of things, current and future, known and unknown, which can have a bearing on your ability to achieve your vision. You will want to survey the external environment to reduce the uncertainty in your planning.

Before you start identifying strategies, you will want to understand your starting position. That may sound unimportant, but if I want to drive cross-country to San Francisco, it makes a big difference if I am starting in Miami or if I am starting in Boston. You cannot develop strategies until you understand your current capabilities as well as your future needs, while recognizing what is happening around you.

Now you can start discussing strategies. You may have some over-arching, company-wide strategies; you may have divisional or departmental initiatives that may or may not be strategic for the whole company. Strategies can be simple or can be quite complicated. Global efforts are complex. Stakeholder expectations can complicate matters.

You weigh your options and select your strategies. Now it is time for a reality check—do you really have a strategy? Will it work?

STRATEGIC EXECUTION

After you have validated the completeness of the strategy, it is time to start leading strategic execution. It takes a special kind of leader to get an organization mobilized for change, to execute the plans. A big part of execution is communication.

One way to clearly communicate is to be specific and to develop metrics or measurements. Measurement systems help employees to understand the vision in more concrete terms. They also help management to determine how well the organization is progressing toward the vision. Through measurement, you may determine that adjustments to the strategy are warranted, and you may need to reassess the environment, or use a different approach, or adjust the measurement system.

As we said before, strategic management is dynamic, it is data-driven, and it is intense. While the chapters of the book are presented in the sequence we have just described, the process does not always flow that smoothly. Before we begin the next chapter with defining the vision, we want to emphasize an important fundamental.

THE ECONOMICS UNDERLYING COMPETITION

One of the key components of a sound strategy is its economic logic, or business model. In the end of chapter reading, "A Business Play? Or a Journey to Plan B?" you will learn about different business models, or economic logic that answers the question, "how can we make money and compete by doing this," or "does the strategy make economic sense?"

Some of the best strategic ideas, although good ideas, are just not successful because the environment in which the company finds itself and the resources it possesses along with shareholder expectations simply do not provide an opportunity for the strategy to work and for the company to make money. The business model simply does not work, and as the reading illustrates, many successful businesses are different from what their founders originally envisioned.

Creating and sustaining a competitive advantage in business means that you need to make money now and in the future (Goldratt and Cox 1984). Understanding the economic logic to your company's ability to compete is a pre-requisite for strategic management. In the abstract, competitive advantage arises from an imperfection in the market system—either on the production or consumption side. The imperfections can be categorized as: information economics, inimitability considerations, preemptive conditions (e.g., lock-in), regulatory barriers, or market size versus investment cost (i.e., scale) (Goodman and Lawless 1994, pp. 29–31).

Anyone who has purchased a car has a sense of information economics. The more a buyer knows about the dealer's cost structure, the better the deal that the buyer is able to negotiate. In the case of home electronics (e.g., trying to figure out how to stream movies from the Internet onto my television), the harder or more costly it is for a consumer to get information about a desired capability, the more important firm reputation and friends' recommendations become. Some companies compete by making information readily available, such as Sears.com offers options to compare refrigerators side-by-side (and they do not have to be side-by-side refrigerators!). In this vein, Google has made a lot of money by selling the top of its lists' results. Its clients want to gain a competitive advantage by being at the top of the list.

Information imperfections can be a competitive advantage when one company knows how to do something valuable that its competitors do not. Patents or copyrights might protect this information. Sometimes the information asymmetry is also manifest as a first-mover advantage, as in the case of Apple Computer's iPhone; it might also make the company "in-the-know" harder to imitate, i.e., inimitable.

Inimitability arises from other situations as well. Instead of information, an organization might have exclusive access to a particular resource, such as land or mineral rights. Wal-Mart started by providing access to low-cost goods in remote locations. Oil-producing nations exert a great deal of power in this way.

Alternatively, the sequence of developments that led to inimitability might be hard to replicate, creating path dependency. One example might be the Walt Disney Company, which started as a couple of artists making animations, one frame at a time, gradually building to full-length feature films that provided material for theme parks and merchandise. This subsequently generated enough cash to buy other media companies to create cross-marketing synergies.

Casual ambiguity is another source of inimitability: it may be unclear as to how a certain advantage was created. This is often the case when a strong corporate culture undergirds the delivery of goods and services. Southwest Airlines provides a distinctive flying experience, due in some part to the personality of its founder.

The economic logic behind preemptive conditions is essentially interfering with free markets. This might result from a contractual agreement, e.g., iPhones were only available for use on the AT&T network for the first five years of their availability. Preemptive conditions can also result from a "lock-in" situation, which makes switching to a competitor costly. In the information technology industry, companies create lock-in by having proprietary technologies, i.e., certain types of software only work with certain types of hardware. With open source code, international standards, and industry conventions, this type of lock-in is gradually declining.

Similarly, government regulations interfere with free markets. There are numerous ways in which this can happen. For example, tariffs might be used to create a domestic advantage over foreign imports. Government subsidies can make local products artificially more affordable, as has been the case with cotton in the United States and Africa.

Economies of scale are an easily identified source of competitive advantage. It can be too expensive to profitably enter a market and vie against existing competitors. We see this in capital-intensive industries, such as steel production. Pharmaceutical companies also face this challenge; as expensive as it is to develop a new drug or treatment, will there be enough of a demand to recoup the costs?

Illustration

The Coca-Cola Company, arguably the world's most recognized brand, has leveraged several different market imperfections in its history. The "secret formula" is an example of information asymmetry. The inimitability of the company is somewhat path-dependent (Carpenter and Sanders 2009, pp. 82–83):

> in order to build troop morale during World War II, General Dwight D. Eisenhower requested that Coca-Cola be available to all American servicemen and service women. To ensure that GIs could buy Coke for five cents a bottle, the government and Coca-Cola cooperated to build 64 bottling plants around the world.

This unusual set of circumstances was amplified by the government subsidy that created an extensive international presence. Coke has continued to leverage this advantage and enjoys economies of scale against its competitors, even PepsiCo, on a global scale.

APPLICATION AND REFLECTION

- You, Inc. is an important organization of one. Describe how the strategic management process would be applied for you to develop a life/career plan.

- The economic logic of competition is that it arises from market imperfections. Identify an example of your own for each type of imperfection described.

- In more concrete terms, you would describe competitive advantage in terms of a business model. In the following reading, you will learn about the importance of a business model in planning. If your friend, a starving artist, asked you what you learned today, how would you describe a "business model?" How might that apply to his/her business?

A BUSINESS PLAN?
OR A JOURNEY TO PLAN B?

John Mullins and Randy Komisar

From Apple to Twitter, some of the most successful businesses are not what their inventors originally envisioned.

In March 2006, Biz Stone, Evan Williams, and Jack Dorsey were working on a new venture called Odeo, a podcasting service. Odeo was in something of a creative slump, and Dorsey wondered if a short messaging service that would enable everyone in the company to communicate with others in the group might be of some help.

Their solution, which the world now knows as Twitter, Inc., was to build a simple Web application that would let the team stay in touch by sending short 140-character messages to the rest of the group. It wasn't long before they realized that the new application held considerably more promise than the original podcasting idea on which they had been working.

The rest of the story is history. Twitter reached its tipping point at the South by Southwest festival in 2007, where the number of tweets per day jumped to 60,000 and it won the festival's Web Award. Whether or not Twitter will develop a viable business model remains in question, but the Twitter story is a powerful reminder that an entrepreneur's main job is not to flawlessly execute the business idea so lovingly articulated in his or her business plan. It's to embark on a learning journey that may, on occasion, reach the destination that the initial plan had in mind. More commonly, though, for open-minded entrepreneurs and innovators in large companies, the surprises that arise on this journey lead to a very different destination, which we call Plan B.

So, What's the Problem?

Nearly every aspiring entrepreneur or innovator has a business plan, and virtually all of these individuals believe that *their* business plan—what we call Plan A—will work. They can probably even imagine how they'll look on the cover of *Fortune* or *Inc.* And they are usually wrong. But what separates the ultimate successes from the rest is what they do when their first plan sputters. Do they lick their wounds, get back on their feet, and morph their new insights into great businesses, or do they stick to their original plan? If the founders of Google, Starbucks, or PayPal had stuck to their original business plans, we'd likely never have heard of them. Instead, they made radical changes to their initial models, became household names, and delivered huge returns for themselves and their investors. How did they get from their Plan A to a business model that worked? Why did they succeed when most new ventures crash and burn?

First, an uncomfortable fact: The typical startup process, whether in nascent entrepreneurial ventures or in the innovation units of established businesses, is largely driven by poorly conceived business plans based on untested assumptions. This process is seriously flawed. Most new ventures, even those with venture capital or corporate backing, share one common characteristic: They fail. There is a better way to launch new ideas—without wasting years of time and loads of investors' money. This better way is about *discovering* a business model that really works: a Plan B, like those of Google, Inc. and Starbucks Corp., which grows out of the original idea, builds on it, and once it's in place, helps the business grow rapidly and prosper.

Most of the time, breaking through to a better business model takes time. And it takes errors, too—errors from which you learn. For Max Levchin, who wanted to build a business based on his cryptography expertise, Plans A though F didn't work, but Plan G turned out to be PayPal, Inc.

Getting to Plan B at Apple

Were Sergey Brin and Larry Page of Google, Howard Schultz of Starbucks, or PayPal's Max Levchin simply lucky? Or is there something rigorous and systematic about their successes that any entrepreneur can learn? Indeed, there is. Let's let the story of Apple, Inc.'s transition from a creative but struggling maker of personal computers to a consumer electronics and music phenomenon show us the way.

While the iPod and the iTunes store have no doubt revolutionized how people listen to and approach music—not to mention TV and movies—are they really all that new after all? Consider Sony Corp.'s Walkman: It made music personal and portable back in 1979! By 2000 Sony had sold more than 300 million Walkmen. Then there was Napster, Inc., another analog, whose 26 million users were downloading music one tune at a time (illegally, as the courts eventually decided). But analogs—predecessor companies that are worth mimicking in some way—are only part of the Apple story. For Apple there were antilogs, too: predecessor companies compared to which you explicitly choose to do things differently, perhaps because some of what they did was unsuccessful. For the iPod and the iTunes store, there were several important antilogs. There were MP3 players like the Rio, which sported clunky user interfaces. There were online music stores like MusicNet and Pressplay, whose very limited music selection and limited rights limited their appeal to music lovers.

For Apple, there was one more analog that put all the pieces together, courtesy of The Gillette Co.'s razors and razor blades. Gillette sold razors at low break-even prices and made its money selling the blades. Ingeniously, Apple's Steve Jobs flipped the model. Jobs's hypothesis was that people would pay for easy-to-use, licensed downloadable music and that a business model of high gross margins on the iPod with razor-thin margins in the iTunes store would be profitable, while keeping the music industry off his back. Jobs showed how well he understood the value of applying an existing idea to his business: "Picasso had a saying: he said good artists copy, great artists steal ... and we have always been shameless about stealing great ideas."

Apple's revenue on iPod sales in the first year alone was $143 million. When the iTunes store was launched in April 2003, over 1 million songs (at 99 cents each) were downloaded the first day. In 2007, Apple's music business passed $10 billion in annual revenue, and by 2008, 6 billion tunes had been sold to 75 million customers through the iTunes store. Paying for downloaded music had become cool.

GETTING TO PLAN B IN YOUR BUSINESS

How can you break through to a business model that will work for your business? First, you'll need an idea to pursue. The best ideas resolve somebody's pain, some problem you've identified for which you think you have a solution. In Apple's case, the pain of music composers and artists and their publishers was both tangible and real. Consumers were enjoying their music but not paying for it!

Next, you'll need to identify some analogs, portions of which you can borrow or adapt to help you understand the economics and various other facets of your proposed business and its business model. And you'll need antilogs, too. As we have seen from the Apple story, analogs and antilogs don't have to be only from your own industry. Sometimes the most valuable insights come from rather unusual sources.

Having identified both analogs and antilogs, you can quickly reach conclusions about some things that are, with at least a modicum of certainty, known about your venture. But it is not what you know that will likely scupper your Plan A, of course. It's what you don't know. The questions you cannot answer from historical precedent lead to your leaps of faith—beliefs you hold about the answers to your questions despite having no real evidence that those beliefs are actually true.

TAKING THE LEAP

To address your leaps of faith, you'll have to leap. Identify your key leaps of faith and then test your hypotheses that you believe hold the answers. That may mean opening a smaller shop than you aspire to operate, just to see how customers respond. It may mean trying different prices for your newly developed gadget to see which price makes sales pop. By identifying your leaps of faith early and devising ways to test hypotheses that will prove or refute them, you are in a position to learn whether or not your Plan A will work before you waste too much time, and money, too!

But what do you actually need to consider when developing your business model? What is it that you hope your analogs, antilogs, and some judiciously chosen hypothesis tests will tell you? Every business model needs to quantitatively address five key elements. (See "Ready to Embark? A Business Model Framework.")

READY TO EMBARK? ABUSINESS MODEL FRAMEWORK

Your current idea and the customer pain that it resolves:

EXAMPLE: APPLE'S ITUNES PRE-ENTRY

Business model element	Relevant analogs and the numbers they give you	Relevant antilogs	Leaps of faith around which you will build an initial dashboard	Your hypotheses that will prove or refute your leaps of faith
Revenue model	Napster	MusicNet and PressPlay	Consumers will pay for at least some of their downloaded music; music publishers will 'play ball'	99 cent price
Gross margin model	Gillette razors and blades, turned upside down		None	
Operating model	Napster		None	
Working capital model	Other online digital providers		Music publishers will provide suitable terms	Consumer cash paid on delivery via PayPal; vendors will take 60-day terms
Investment model				

- **Your revenue model:** Who will buy? How often? How soon? At what acquisition cost? How much money will you receive each time a customer buys? How often will they send you another check?
- **Your gross margin model:** How much of your revenue will be left after you have paid the direct costs of what you have sold?
- **Your operating model:** Other than the cost of the goods or services you have sold, what else must you spend money on to keep the lights on?
- **Your working capital model:** How early can you encourage your customers to pay? Do you have to tie up money in lots of inventory waiting for customers to buy? Can you pay your suppliers later, after the customer has paid?
- **Your investment model:** How much cash must you spend up front before enough customers give you enough business to cover your costs?

Uncovering useful analogs and antilogs, identifying your most important leaps of faith, and testing a series of hypotheses to inform all five elements of your business model will give you much of the data you need to craft a possibly compelling business model, at least for Plan A. But a truly viable business model is unlikely to arise in a single "eureka" moment. Getting from Plan A to a viable Plan B, as PayPal's Max Levchin discovered, is a journey that can take months, even years.

GUIDING YOUR JOURNEY

Like any journey that wants to get somewhere, this journey needs a tool to point the way and track your progress, something we call a dashboard. (See "Guiding Your Journey: Your

GUIDING YOUR JOURNEY: YOUR DASHBOARD

A DASHBOARD FOR JOHNNY'S LEMONADE STAND

Hypotheses	Metrics	Actual period 1	Actual period 2	Actual period 3	Insights obtained, course corrections needed
Leap of faith 1: Commuters will stop and buy a refreshing drink					
Hypothesis 1: At least 10 customers per day	Customer count	2 customers	No one stopped in the rain	6 customers	High pricing deters sales, they look, don't buy; no point in setting up if it rains; seems like demand is somewhat less than Johnny thought.
Leap of faith 2: People will pay a premium price					
Hypothesis 2: $1.50 per glass will be accept-able	Total sales, price paid	$3.00 total sales, $1.50 per glass		$5.50 in sales (1@ 50 cents, 5@ $1)	$1.50 too high, based on Monday sales; pricing then reduced; $1 looks about right based on Wednesday's lower pricing.

Dashboard.") A dashboard drives an evidence-based process to plan, guide and track the results of what you learn from your hypothesis testing. In part, it highlights key indicators of your progress, much as the dashboard in your car tracks key information about your holiday trip to Grandma's house. But dashboards as entrepreneurs use them are much more than the dashboard in the family car. A dashboard in this sense is also a trip planner to help you determine the best route. It provides a detailed map of the hypothesis-testing journey you will take, as well as making clear the need for any necessary midcourse corrections as your journey unfolds.

Your dashboard serves four key roles:

It forces you to think strategically about the most crucial issues presently on the table that can—quickly and inexpensively—answer the all-important question, "Why won't this work?"

It forces you to think rigorously about how you can examine your leaps of faith by testing hypotheses whose results can be measured quantitatively, most of the time. Numbers are more persuasive than naive hopes or dreams.

If one or more of your leaps of faith are refuted by the evidence you collect, the results displayed on your dashboard are visible and dramatic indicators of the need to alter your Plan A and move toward Plan B.

A dashboard is a powerful tool for convincing others—whether members of your management team, investors, or others, even yourself—of the need to move from Plan A to Plan B. If your tenacity or perseverance is questioned, you can point to the evidence to support the move toward Plan B. You are not being erratic or flighty. You are systematically testing hypotheses to prove or refute your leaps of faith, and you are listening to what the data tell you.

A dashboard is a flexible tool for addressing your leaps of faith. It forces you to keep track of the most crucial questions you have about your venture, while keeping your assumptions (often guesses, really) in mind. It focuses your attention and more efficiently deploys your precious time and resources to remove the critical risks. And it provides a way to respond to the real-life data you generate. Moving into the dashboarding stage in developing your business model means moving from *spectator*—observing others as you gathered analogs and antilogs—to *doer*.

While all successful business models address each of the five elements, for many great companies, just a single element holds the key. The key element for Google was its eventual revenue model, but initially there wasn't a revenue model—just a free search engine. Plan B, to license its engine to other portals, wasn't much better. In order to bring money in, Google's Plan C—as anyone with an Internet connection knows—provided paid search listings alongside the "objective" ones. Google's even more successful Plan D built on its proprietary search algorithms to deliver targeted ads to other Web sites, which has generated more than half of Google's revenue since 2004.

For Ryanair Holdings, Inc., the low-cost European airline based in Dublin, the key was its operating model. The Ryanair operating model utilized only one type of aircraft, no free in-flight meals, direct-to-consumer online ticket booking to cut out travel agent commissions, and even got rid of window shades and seat back pockets to decrease the time on the ground between flights. This incredibly efficient operating model has allowed Ryanair to soar past all other European airlines and become Europe's largest in passenger traffic.

There are many more examples of businesses around the world that have revolutionized their industries by hanging their hat on one key element of their business model. Some of these companies include:

- China's Shanda Interactive Entertainment Limited: Revenue model
- Japan's Toyota Motor Corp. and the United States' eBay, Inc.: Gross margin models
- India's Oberoi Hotels & Resorts: Operating model
- The United States' Costco Wholesale Corp. and Dow Jones & Co., Inc.: Working capital models
- Luxembourg's Skype Technologies S.A.: Investment model

For others, such as Spain's Zara International, Inc., combining two or more elements has made their business models particularly difficult to imitate, creating sustainable competitive advantage and an ability to grow rapidly even in challenging industries like retailing. Zara's is a story of how a carefully crafted combination of sourcing, merchandising, and distribution strategies created a unique new pattern of revenue, gross margin, and working capital models that enabled Zara to grow like wildfire and take its young fashion-forward customers by storm.

The Zara model revolves around four processes, all tailored for speed—design, production, distribution, and sales—resulting in so-called "fast fashion," where an article of clothing can go from design sketch to the store in less than two weeks.

- **Revenue model:** Small production runs create scarcity and encourage shoppers to visit Zara often and purchase quickly, before its fast-moving styles disappear.
- **Gross margin model:** The number of unpopular items is minimized, so markdowns are rare, providing one of the highest gross margins among apparel retailers.
- **Working capital model:** In return for predictable high-volume business with Zara, its suppliers gave it favorable 60-day terms. With customers buying their clothes with cash or credit cards, Zara has its customers' cash in hand in less than a week. Fast-turning inventory paired with quick customer cash and slow payment for its merchandise produces an attractive working capital model indeed!

Most business plans assume that almost everything is already known up front—but that is not the case, as our examples have now shown. As the famed American general in World War II, Douglas MacArthur, is reputed to have said, "No plan ever survives its first encounter with the enemy."

The process articulated here is a healthy alternative to the straightjacket of today's business planning practices—enabling you to anticipate and move beyond a failing or suboptimal Plan A. It is a process designed for learning and discovering, rather than pitching and selling. It's a process that may enable you to discover the next Twitter. Most importantly, it's a process that recognizes and embraces the cold, hard facts: Most often, what ultimately works is not the Plan A that was so persuasively articulated in the original plan. Instead, it's the unexpected surprise that we call Plan B.

About the Authors

John Mullins is an associate professor of management practice and the David and Elaine Potter Foundation Term Chair in Marketing and Entrepreneurship at London Business School. **Randy Komisar** is a partner at Kleiner Perkins Caufield & Byers in Menlo Park, California. Their latest book, from which the ideas in this article are adapted, is *Getting to Plan B: Breaking Through to a Better Business Model* (Harvard Business Press 2009). Comment on this article or contact the authors at smrfeedback@mit.edu.

CHAPTER 2
DEFINING A MEANINGFUL VISION

Begin with the end in mind.

—*Stephen Covey*

OPENING VIGNETTE

Take a simple idea, prompted by a vision for social good, add entrepreneurial energy, stir gently, and soak overnight, and you have a recipe for a successful enterprise. TOMS Shoes started as such an idea. Blake Mycoskie, an entrepreneur from Texas, returned from a trip to Argentina where he witnessed poverty and the surprising number of people who were "shoeless," particularly children. Why did this trouble him?

From www.toms.com/our-movement/:

- A leading cause of disease in developing countries is soil-transmitted diseases, which can penetrate the skin through bare feet. Wearing shoes can help prevent these diseases, and the long-term physical and cognitive harm they cause.
- Wearing shoes also prevents feet from getting cuts and sores. Not only are these injuries painful, they also are dangerous when wounds become infected.
- Many times children can't attend school barefoot because shoes are a required part of their uniform. If they don't have shoes, they don't go to school. If they don't receive an education, they don't have the opportunity to realize their potential.

Founded in 2006, TOMS Shoes manufactures shoes inspired by the Argentine alpargata design. Through its *One for One* program and its nonprofit subsidiary and with the help of 501©

Based on B. Mycoskie and T. Schweitzer. "I'm so used to traveling that I can sleep anywhere." *Inc.* 32 no. 5 (2010): 112–114.

nonprofits, for every pair of shoes sold, the company donates a pair of shoes to someone who is shoeless. The goal is not only to provide shoes but also to educate concerning shoes' health benefits. The company has given away 600,000 pairs of shoes, which sell from 45–65 USD in upscale stores.

In chapter 1, we saw that the strategic management process begins with defining a vision. In order to have "strategic management for results," you must know what results you want. In this chapter, we focus on vision statements. Successful mastery of this material will enable you to:

- distinguish between vision and mission statements
- explain what meaningful vision statements should and should not contain
- evaluate others' vision and mission statements
- define your desired end results

INTRODUCTION

When you plan a vacation, how do you start? If you are like most people, you start with an idea of the kind of vacation you want and refine that idea by selecting a destination. You have to know where you are going in order to figure out how to get there.

In the same way, in order to create and sustain a competitive advantage, an organization needs to define a future state that describes its ideal competitive position. Then the organization will be better situated to determine how to get to there by developing strategies that will move the organization in the right direction.

Meaningful visions provide coherence across an organization. A vision statement is a unifying concept for employees, managers, and executives to understand the strategic direction of the organization.

Collins and Portas (1991) emphasize the importance of a vision to unify a company and provide direction. In their work "Organizational Vision and Visionary Organizations," they identify the differentiation between companies that are driven by their visions from those that are not. They identify two components of a vision: a guiding philosophy and a tangible image. They credit Thomas Watson, former CEO of IBM, with first understanding the importance of a guiding philosophy. These are Watson's words:

> I firmly believe that any organization, in order to survive and achieve success, must have a sound set of beliefs on which it premises all its policies and actions. Next, I believe that the most important single factor in corporate success is faithful adherence to those beliefs. And, finally, I believe [the organization] must be willing to change everything about itself except those beliefs as it moves through corporate life. (p. 35)

The tangible image provides a picture of what the company will look like when the vision is achieved. This image makes the intangible a tangible that once conceptualized can be achieved. The mission of a company should be more than the who, what, where, and why. It should also distinguish the firm and how it makes a *fundamental* difference in the lives of others, thus the difference between organizational vision and visionary organizations.

Illustration

Leadership is crucial in setting the direction of a company and in achieving the vision. When leaders fail in this very important objective, they sometimes "have to go." An example of this is the termination of Yahoo's CEO Carol Bartz, even though she had more than a year remaining on her contract. The reason given by the Board of Directors was that Ms. Bartz failed to accomplish the vision to reestablish Yahoo's predominance on the Internet (*Daily Technician* 2011).

Figure 2-1. Carol Bartz, former Yahoo! CEO

DEFINING VISIONS AND MISSIONS

Like strategy, "vision" is also becoming an endangered word, often overused and vague. Naysayers think defining a vision is a waste of time. If it is not done well, than it probably is a waste of time!

So, let's start with distinguishing between a vision and a mission. A vision is a desired future state. For an organization, that state describes its competitive position at some time in the future.

A mission statement describes the organization's current state. It defines what the business is, not necessarily what it will become. In essence, a mission statement describes the scope and purpose of the organization, as it is, in terms of what it does in the present, for whom and where.

Illustration

Netflix, Inc., in their 2010 proxy statement for the Securities and Exchange Commission (SEC), described their vision in terms of the future and their mission in terms of the business's scope:

> We believe delivery of entertainment video over the Internet will be a very large global market opportunity, and that our focus on one segment of that market—consumer-paid, commercial-free streaming subscription of TV shows and movies—will enable us to continue to grow rapidly and profitably.
>
> With 20 million subscribers as of December 31, 2010, Netflix, Inc. ("Netflix", "the Company", "we", or "us") is the world's leading Internet subscription service for enjoying TV shows and movies. Our subscribers can instantly watch unlimited TV shows and movies streamed over the Internet to their TVs, computers and mobile devices and, in the United States, subscribers can also receive standard definition DVDs, and their high definition successor, Blu-ray discs (collectively referred to as "DVD"), delivered quickly to their homes.

What makes something meaningful to you? The way it is presented or how you experience it? That it is heartfelt? How it influences your thinking or actions?

A vision statement is meaningful if it matters to the organization. For it to matter, it should be clear, compelling, and concise to everyone in the company. The vision should also be complete enough to guide decision-making and operational activities, and it must be to the point. Increasingly, vision statements also address the social responsibility of the organization to its stakeholders and the environment. This is a topic that we will explore in later chapters.

To be *clear*, the vision should be communicated frequently, in a variety of media, to all levels of the organization. Clarity also comes from the use of concrete language, not from abstract ideas. Vagueness sands the clarity off of a vision (Stanley 2006). For a vision to be clear it must be understood and stated in a way that is easily understood. It cannot be vague or subject to interpretation.

To be *compelling*, a vision statement should be aspirational and attainable. Too much ambition is daunting. Not enough ambition supports inertia.

To be *complete*, there should be ways to gauge progress toward the vision. Sometimes, the vision is accompanied with goal statements that have measurable outcomes. They can also contribute to the clarity of the vision.

And to be *concise*, a meaningful vision contains only words that are necessary for it to matter. Sentence structure should be simple. Concise does not prescribe a specific length, although shorter statements tend to be more memorable.

Illustration

According to Amazon.com (*see* www.amazon.com Investor Relations—referred to as their mission):

> Our vision is to be earth's most customer-centric company; to build a place where people can come to find and discover anything they might want to buy online.

Do you find it *clear? Compelling? Complete? Concise?* For the most part, it is. What does it mean to be "customer-centric?" As an Amazon customer, you may have the sense that customer-centric means that your online shopping experience is customized to you; another person, with different interests and purchasing history, will see a different version of Amazon.

Amazon's mission is "to be Earth's most customer-centric company for three primary customer sets: consumer customers, seller customers, and developer customers." (At least for now; wait until they start streaming content to the moon!) The description of what Amazon does is implicit; they will sell anything to anyone who is a customer, and they will make it easy for customers to buy. While there is some overlap in the mission and vision statements, you can see that the vision statement is clearly future oriented and aspirational.

According to another company's[1] website, "Our vision is to be the world leader in transportation products and related services. In order to achieve this vision, we recognize that many issues must be addressed and many goals attained. It is imperative that economic, environmental and social objectives be integrated into our daily business objectives and future planning activities

---

[1] General Motors website, www.gm.com.

so that we can become a more sustainable company." Clear? The term "related services" is vague. In general, the word choice is not very concrete. Compelling? Becoming a "world leader" is certainly aspirational, but there is also reference to "many issues that must be addressed." Concise? Because the statement is so vague, it is hard to say. Complete? It is too broad to be helpful in guiding the company, which has struggled in recent years. How would you improve this statement?

AVOIDING VISIONING PITFALLS

There are plenty of bad vision statements around. What makes them bad? The primary reason is that they don't matter to their organizations. Another is that the words do not compel. The statements may be trite, vague, poorly written, overly wordy, flowery, uninspiring, or even over-whelming. Baldoni (2006, p. 3) suggests that, "to craft a meaningful vision, leaders must strike a careful balance between ambition and actionability, grandeur and simplicity."

Collins and Portas (1991, p. 51) caution against the myth that "building a visionary organization requires the presence of a charismatic leader who is somehow blessed with super-human mystical visionary skills … the leader is to catalyze a clear and shared vision of the organization and to secure commitment to and vigorous pursuit of that vision." Visionary organizations are able to create a preferred future, rather than be simply reactive to future events.

While editing "by committee" can be a painful experience, it is a good idea to involve other people in the visioning process. Multiple perspectives can enhance clarity and provide a reality check on aspirations. Having a critical mass of people who understand and support the vision will also help communicate the vision and broaden the support required for the future state of the vision to be reached.

It is also important to revisit the vision and mission statements periodically. While you may not expect them to change, it is certainly possible that the organization's focus may have soft-ened or shifted altogether. Crotts et al. (2005) suggest an audit process to ensure organizational processes support mission and vision. This audit can be part of the strategic management process on an ongoing basis.

APPLICATION AND REFLECTION

- Continuing with the example of You, Inc., develop a vision statement for your life/career plan.

- Pick an organization where you work or volunteer. Do you know what the mission and vision for the organization are? Can you find the information easily? Evaluate the statements in terms of the criteria for a meaningful vision: clear, compelling, concise, and complete.

- Select two companies competing in the same industry. Contrast and compare their vision statements, mission statements, and business performance.

- Try to think of your own examples for each one of the potential visioning pitfalls.

CLOSING CASE

To reinforce the concepts you need to understand the organization in context, consider the fate of the Eastman Kodak company. After reading the following article, answer these questions:

1. What were the vision and mission statements for the company? Did they limit its strategic options?
2. What happened to the economic logic underlying its business model?
3. How might following the strategic management process have changed Kodak's outcomes?

Eastman Kodak, an integral part of American culture, is no more. Once the centerpiece of every holiday, this film giant was a free enterprise success story. The major market, the baby boomers, grew up with "Kodak moments" capturing life's significant events. Once the icon of Rochester New York, this company is facing bankruptcy and is covering its obligations by selling its patents to cover its pension obligations to employees. Founded in 1880 by George Eastman, Kodak created and owned the market for camera film for decades.

So what went so wrong at Kodak? Well, first, it was not a swift failure, but a long and insidious series of actions—or rather reactions—that led to this corporation's demise. Once trading at $93.00 a share, this company is worth pennies on the dollar.

The collapse at Kodak was due to the environment, both internal and external. The primary internal issue was culture. A company steeped in film production and chemicals was led by those who identified so closely with the original expertise in film, second to none in the world, and who were blind to changes in technology. Although they were involved in the original development of digital photography and even had patents instrumental to the new way to take pictures, they never fully embraced it or even believed it would replace the dependence upon film in picture taking. They hung their hat on film and all things related, such as the early commercial successes with the Brownie camera.

Based on "Eastman Kodak Files for Bankruptcy." *New York Times* (January 12, 2012). Available online: http://www.reuters.com/article/2012/01/19/us-kodak-idUSTRE80I08G20120119

The external environmental issues were multiple. First was global competition and new competitors with pricing that drove down profits; specifically, Fujifilm. Second, technical capabilities not central to the core competency usurped the company's advantage. As late as 2003, the company still believed film to be the single thread in photography, when by this time digital photography had emerged. 2004 was the last year the company was profitable. Although the company desperately tried to restructure and streamline as well as reposition through products such as inkjet printers, all the attempts failed to live up to market expectations and to generate the profits necessary to offset the revenue tailspin. They were simply too late in the shift to digital photography at the same time that digital was replacing other technologies in industries such as communications. But this was not unexpected. As early as 1994, they spun off their chemical business, Eastman Chemical, to generate the cash to underpin the declining camera business.

Kodak got involved in medical imaging in an attempt to diversify its portfolio in a related business line. Ultimately they came to understand that health care was significantly different from their core business and spun off this acquisition.

At the same time that the company divested its assets and spun off subsidiaries to generate cash, it was embroiled in legal battles with Apple, Research in Motion, and HTC of Taiwan. Kodak claimed that these companies owed Kodak "substantial royalties" for the use of its patents in their smartphones. The attempt was fee generation through licensing agreements such as with Motorola and LG.

So what strategic mistakes did Kodak make? First, it simply did not scan the environment to insure that it was always aware and attuned to shifts in the markets. Second, due to the culture, the company could not change the mindset to embrace the environment, not ignore it, and adapt to the change necessary for the evolution in photography as well as the market. But finally, and most tragic, this icon believed it was infallible, and it was not.

Interviews with the most successful CEOs generally reveal confidence peppered with paranoia.

Paranoia was absent at Kodak.

SECTION II
UNDERSTANDING THE ORGANIZATION IN CONTEXT

You cannot compete in a vacuum. A strategy might work in one context, but not another. In this section, we examine the facts that contribute to an organization's context, looking for the "weather" ahead.

CHAPTER 3
ADDRESSING THE GOVERNANCE AND SOCIAL RESPONSIBILITIES OF THE ORGANIZATION

There is one and only one social responsibility of business—to use its resources and engage in activities designed to increase its profits so long as it stays within the rules of the game, which is to say, engages in open and free competition without deception or fraud.[1]

—*Milton Friedman*

OPENING VIGNETTE

What is the value of a company's mission, or more importantly, what is the significance of a company's value system? What is a company creed? Just ask Johnson & Johnson about the importance of their *Credo* to corporate success and in directing company strategy.

The J&J Credo (http://www.jnj.com/connect/about-jnj/jnj-credo/) was written by Robert Wood Johnson, former Chairman (1932–63) and a member of the company's founding family. The Credo, its development, and its influence on the company's value system occurred long before "corporate social responsibility" came into vogue.

The Credo is a recipe for business success. The fact that J&J is one of only a handful of companies that have flourished for more than a century of change is proof. The Credo drives every dimension of company performance, from research and development (R&D) decisions to responses to customers. It provides a clear roadmap to direction and decision-making. There are

---

[1] Milton Friedman quoted in Chemtech (February 1974): 72, and found in Patrick & Charnov, Management, 2/e. Barron's Educational Series.

Based on P. Jones and L. Kahaner. *Say It and Live It: The 50 Corporate Mission Statements That Hit the Mark.* New York, NY: Doubleday, 1995. Accessed online at http://www.kahaner.com/johnson_johnson.shtml

no shades of gray. Consider when J&J pulled the thousands of Tylenol® bottles from shelves. There was no question; the Credo was the answer.

After defining the corporate vision, the next question is how to achieve the vision. In later chapters we will examine a variety of different strategies that companies follow as paths to the vision. In this chapter we will examine the question of *how* the organization will interact with its various stakeholders. Specifically, this chapter explains corporate social responsibility and the importance of governance in strategic planning. With greater demands for accountability by stakeholders, companies must be intentional and specific about their corporate policies, values, and consideration for their stakeholders. Upon successful completion of this chapter you should be able to:

- define corporate governance and social responsibility (CSR)
- identify ways to protect the interests of shareholders
- identify the drivers that are raising the importance of companies' CSR policies
- explain governance and its role in company strategic planning

In addition, companies that decide to become "strategically responsible" may drive competitors to include sustainability concerns in their strategic plans as they compete for financial resources from the investment community as well as field questions from stakeholders, including customers and suppliers.

INTRODUCTION

Corporate governance is the area of study that addresses who makes decisions, how they are made, and why. Topics include: policies, controls, regulations, stakeholder relationships, corporate responsibility, ownership structure, and incentive systems. As you might imagine, these topics have a profound impact on the results an organization achieves.

Corporate governance is a fairly recent concern. In early civilizations, authority was generally quite clear; he who owned the resources made the decisions. Military hierarchies followed a command and control model. Owners ran their own business enterprises, sometimes referred to as "cottage industries."

During the Industrial Revolution, organizations became larger, joint-stock ownership became possible, and a managerial class (i.e., educated, but not wealthy) emerged. As a result, stockholding owners did not necessarily manage the day-to-day operations of the companies in which they were invested. However, as investors, they wanted assurance of getting a return on their investments. The difficulty was that because of self-interest, owners' and managers' interests did not always coincide.

Therefore, corporate governance policies and procedures were established to protect the investors' interests. In those days, the only social responsibility of the firm was to make money for its stockholders, without violating the law. Economic thinking was that the markets would correct for anti-social behavior; employees would leave for better working conditions, and customers would buy from suppliers they liked and respected. The stock price, as a predictor of future earnings, would therefore implicitly incorporate these types of concerns. The challenge, then, was to align owners' and managers' (also called "agents") interests so that decision-making served the stockholders' interests.

PROTECTING THE INTERESTS OF STOCKHOLDERS

Governance protects the stockholders' interests through controls, oversight, and incentives. These methods have evolved, and the expectation of corporate accountability has grown commensurately.

Controls can be implemented with procedural methods. For example, think about how a large company orders its materials for manufacturing. Based on sales forecasts and production schedules, a purchasing agent with an "authority to approve" will place an order for a shipment of materials. When that shipment arrives, the receiving clerk verifies that the bill of lading accurately represents what is in the shipment. The purchasing agent will also inspect the bill of lading to ensure that it matches what was ordered. The next control in the process is comparison of the invoice to the order and the delivery. If all is in order, then payment is remitted. Depending on the amount to be paid, multiple signatures may be required. These procedures are intended to prevent fraud.

Computerized controls can also deter fraud and prevent mistakes. Data "masks" (i.e., specifications of allowable content and format of data entry) can ensure that data are entered fully and correctly. Reconciliation reports can compare general ledger accounts with transactions recorded each day. Database systems can provide different levels of access (e.g., view, alter) to different areas of data (e.g., payroll, order entry), based on the needs of the business.

Oversight in governance comes in many forms: internal and external auditors, boards of directors, and government agencies. Internal auditors check that the controls in place are followed and adequate. External auditors are concerned that the accounting statements accurately and fully reflect the state of the business in the company's report to stockholders. The key is to have truly independent auditors. An example of this lack of independence was Arthur Andersen's culpability in Enron's misrepresentations due to its role as both auditor and consultant to the firm.

As representatives of the shareholders, a committed and involved Board of Directors can also provide oversight, generally at a more strategic level. Typically a board, comprised of inside (employee) and outside (independent) directors, works on matters such as Chief Executive Officer (CEO) selection, executive compensation, review of strategic plans and financial performance, and provision of counsel and advice to management.

However, board members tend to be busy people running their own organizations, so the need to be committed, involved, and informed may be a higher standard than can realistically be met. Also, there have been issues with board interlock, i.e., when members of various boards overlap. The integrity of the oversight is comprised. For example, Sandy is CEO of company A and on the Board's compensation committee for company Z, while Teddy is the CEO of Z and on the Board's compensation committee for A.

The last type, and arguably the last defense, of governance oversight comes from regulatory bodies, such as the Securities and Exchange Commission (SEC) in the United States. Reporting requirements, accounting conventions, and fiduciary laws all shape corporate governance. Unfortunately, though, regulations tend to be lagging indicators of issues in governance; they are the proverbial "barn doors" that shut after the horses have been stolen. Toffler (2003, p. 36) laments, "the sad fact is that all the oversight in the world is not going to change what happens behind company doors."

Perhaps the most effective or at least the most proactive tool of corporate governance is incentive systems that are intended to guarantee that the goals of the agents and the shareholders are aligned. That is, executives are rewarded for good performance in both the short- and long-term. Variable compensation, bonuses, and stock options are ways to increase the stake that the managers have in the shareholders/owners' business. Unfortunately, it may also encourage managers to engage in market manipulation, as we have seen in the reported financial malfeasance of companies such as Tyco, Enron, Global Crossing, and HealthSouth. Failures in corporate governance are not unusual, nor are they a solely an American problem. Nor are they likely to be solved until cost and benefit imbalances are righted.

DRIVERS OF INCREASED CORPORATE SOCIAL RESPONSIBILITY

While governance has been a concern since the industrial revolution and the advent of joint stock ownership, the emphasis on corporate social responsibility (CSR) is a more recent development. With the availability of 24/7 news cycles, the ability of social media to "go viral," and the increasing concern about depleting the planet's resources, the forces driving corporations toward CSR are inexorable. You have unprecedented access to information about corporate performance. You have new channels of communication to build a coalition around issues. You have heightened awareness of your dependence on fossil fuels, your usage of non-renewable resources, and your access to alternative approaches.

Moving from the Industrial Age into the Information Age, the expectations of corporations and their roles in society are changing. Globalization and technology have provided a greater awareness of what companies are doing and what impact those actions have. With increased transparency comes increased accountability. Markets are more responsive to social and environmental considerations. Employment practices, environmental impact, community engagement, and fiscal governance are under examination by shareholder activists and other stakeholders. As shown in Figure 3-1, stakeholders are people who have a stake (personal, financial, and/or altruistic) in the actions of a firm. Corporate Social Responsibility (CSR) is the extent to which an organization holds itself accountable to stakeholders, in addition to shareholders.

Illustration

Accountability may be a defensive measure in response to stakeholder scrutiny. And scrutiny it is—most of us can envision the underwater video of gushing crude during the British Petroleum (BP) oil spill in the Gulf of Mexico in 2010. Since then, the accountability demanded of BP has been fierce. The United States government imposed fines, with a restoration fund mandated. The CEO was fired because of shareholder and board

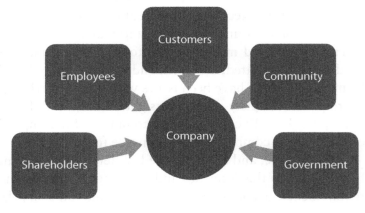

Figure 3-1. Stakeholder Model

dissatisfaction with his handling of the situation. Suppliers were impacted because there was an injunction against deep-sea drilling. Customers, the gas stations' owners, had to advertise to explain to consumers that the gas stations were independent entities of BP, and boycotting BP gas was hurting the local owners, not BP corporate. In this case, you can clearly see the stake that a community has in a corporation's activities. Health hazards, environmental damage, and livelihoods lost were serious and widespread concerns in this case.

INTENTIONAL APPROACHES TO CSR

It has been often said in sports that the best defense is a good offense. The same may be said of corporate social responsibility and strategic management. Being intentional about the corporation's relationships with its stakeholders will go a long way to handling difficult situations—and the situations are only going to become more difficult.

The web of accountability is increasing in complexity. You are not only responsible for how and what you produce, but also how it is used and discarded. In this world of global supply chains, that is a lot of responsibility.

In addition, the stakes are growing higher. Mistakes can have catastrophic consequences. Consider the consequences experienced by the astronauts on the Challenger shuttle who relied on rubber "O-rings" that had not been tested at low launch temperatures. Or, think about the employees of Enron who no longer have retirement savings and have lost their homes. In both cases, those affected were relying on the social responsibility of the agents making the decisions.

It seems clear that with the stakes so high, a company has no choice but to be intentional about its commitment to CSR. There is a range of possible choices, starting with the social obligation approach (i.e., maximize shareholder's ROI and do not violate the law). Many organizations now engage in philanthropy, donating funds and resources to social causes. While admirable, philanthropy can be viewed as public relations.

Enlightened self-interest is a level of CSR that provides a social or environmental benefit that also is strategic for the company involved. For example, the Internet service provider (ISP) America Online (AOL) sponsored a project to extend Internet access to rural and other underserved areas. The communities benefited from crossing the digital divide (the education disparity between served and underserved areas) and AOL benefited from a new set of loyal customers (Brennan and Johnson 2003).

Social responsiveness is similar to enlightened self-interest, but has a broader impact. For example, several years ago, Starbucks was excoriated for buying coffee beans from plantations with horrible working conditions and sub-standard wages. The company has since led the vanguard for ethical sourcing, with a goal to ensure 100% of their coffee is from ethical sources by 2015:

> We define ethical sources as coffee that is third-party verified or certified, either through C.A.F.E. Practices, Fairtrade, or another externally audited system … 84% of our coffee was sourced under C.A.F.E. Practices in 2010, up from 81% in 2009. (Starbucks 2010)

The most emphatic commitment to corporate social responsibility comes from social entrepreneurs: people who start a business to address a social cause with a self-sustaining business model. Social causes range from public health, safety, literacy, and empowerment to economic or infrastructure development.

One of the earliest examples of this business model was in the area of micro-finance, i.e., lending money in small amounts to empower poor people. With the earnings they are able to achieve, they pay back the money with interest.

> The origin of Grameen Bank can be traced back to 1976 when Professor Muhammad Yunus, Head of the rural Economics Program at the University of Chittaagong, launched an action research project to examine the possibility of designing a credit delivery system to provide banking services targeted at the rural poor. The Grameen Bank Project (Grameen means "rural" or "village" in Bangla language) came into operation with the following objectives: extend banking facilities to poor men and women; eliminate the exploitation of the poor by money lenders; create opportunities for self-employment for the vast multitude of unemployed people in rural Bangladesh; bring the disadvantaged, mostly the women from the poorest households, within the fold of an organizational format which they can understand and manage by themselves; and reverse the age-old vicious circle of "low income, low saving & low investment", into (sic) virtuous circle of "low income, injection of credit, investment, more income, more savings, more investment, more income. (Grameen Bank 2011)

Professor Yunnus was named a Nobel Laureate in 2006.

APPLICATION AND REFLECTION

- How can You, Inc. include in your vision statement your commitment to social responsibility?

- Look at the 10K statements of two publicly held companies. Examine the structure of the board of directors, committees, and compensation. Go to the Securities and Exchange Commission website http://www.sec.gov/search/search.htm to find the statements.

- In the following reading, we see examples of companies who have made social responsibility a strategic choice. What other examples can you identify? Can you identify an opportunity that another company might make to be more strategically responsible?

TECHNOLOGY MANAGEMENT
FOR CORPORATE SOCIAL RESPONSIBILITY

Linda L. Brennan and Victoria E. Johnson

Expectations of corporations are higher than ever. Investors and other stakeholders consider companies in terms of the "triple bottom line," reflecting financial performance, environmental practices, and corporate social responsibility. Given the role of top managers in setting the ethical tone and strategic agenda of their corporations—and the role of technology in strategy—can technology management achieve both competitive performance and social responsibility, i.e., "strategic responsibility"? This potential integration is considered in the technology management of eight Internet-oriented companies, specifically for practices integrating the fulfillment of corporate social responsibilities with technology-driven strategies for keeping products competitive, providing the basis for new products, and changing operational conventions.

TECHNOLOGY AND STRATEGY

Technology management is a key element in an organization's strategic planning. As Goodman and Lawless [9] note, technology plays an important role in strategy for several reasons, not the least of which is that technology directly affects competitive position. This role is manifested in three key ways [27]:

Keeping Products Competitive. Technology may be exploited as the products mature, to add features, or to reduce processing or distribution costs. Alternatively, technology substitution may be undertaken, supplanting an older technology with a new one.
Providing the Basis for New Products and Services. This is the essence of innovation. Advances in technology—or in its application—enable corporations to offer new products and services.

Changing Operational Conventions. This is a matter of changing institutional beliefs about what is possible, such as integrating the supply chain, improving customer relationship management, and emphasizing enterprise resource planning.

The Internet has made technology even more central to the question of sustainable competitive advantage. The advent of the Internet as a mainstream business medium has made technology management a key concern for even low-technology companies, for which a Web presence simply provides comparative parity for existing products. The Internet has provided the basis for new services, particularly in the areas of financial services and electronic commerce. New companies, called "infomediaries," have been created to broker the vast amounts of information that are available. Perhaps the most profound impact of the Internet has been the changes to operational conventions, with virtual organization forms, electronic marketing, and self-service businesses. Ultimately, the technology is enabling new income sources, bigger revenue streams, and larger cost reductions, having a direct impact on the financial "bottom line."

At the same time, technology is driving societal expectations of corporations by creating a world of transparency, immediacy, and scrutiny [15]. Certainly, information technology has become a significant managerial asset for promoting, measuring, monitoring, and communicating organizational goals, both financial and social. Beyond providing financial statements and investor information, some companies use the Internet to promote and inform constituencies of their dedication to social issues, safer products, and environmentally sound methods of production and disposal. While beneficial, these efforts are largely decoupled from the competitive strategies of the corporations. It would seem that the extent to which top managers can integrate CSR performance with more strategic initiatives would magnify the achievement of both competitive performance and social responsibility. Given the role of top managers in setting the ethical tone and strategic agenda of their corporations—and the roles of technology in strategy—how can technology management achieve both competitive performance and social responsibility, i.e., strategic responsibility?

To develop a descriptive, positive model [19] of integration, this study examines eight Internet-oriented companies for specific practices integrating the fulfillment of corporate social responsibilities with strategies for keeping products competitive, providing the basis for new products, and changing operational conventions. A general profile of the companies in the study is presented in Table I, noting the age of the company, revenues from the 2000 fiscal year, industry sector, inclusion in the Domini Index fund, and rankings from *Fortune* and *Business Ethics* publications. While certainly not a scientific or random sample, there was some effort to consider both old and new (i.e., "born-on-the-Web") companies as well as firms with and without socially responsible endorsements (e.g., by Domini and *Business Ethics*).

Highlights of the practices and strategies for each of the eight companies are summarized in Table II. Note that not all strategies are included, but rather ones that may be considered as socially responsible. Conversely, not all socially responsible practices are highlighted, but only ones that may be considered to be strategic. The intent is to highlight strategically responsible initiatives.

AMERICA ONLINE

The largest corporation in the e-company sub-sector, America Online (AOL) is the world's largest Internet service provider (ISP), providing access to millions of people. The AOL mission statement is "to build a global medium as central to people's lives as the telephone or television

Table I. General Profile of Sample

Company (Ticker)	Founded	Sub sector (SIC)	Revenues (as of last fiscal year)	Fortune Rankings (2000)	Domini 400 Index (2000)	Business Ethics 100 (2000)
America Online (AOL)	1985	E-company (7370)	$4777M	#337; 100 Best Places to Work; Most Admired Industry Rank #1; Social Responsibility #287	Yes	No
Amazon.com (AMZN)	1994	E-company (5961)	$1015M	N/A	No	No
Microsoft (MSFT)	1975	Net software (7372)	$19747M	#84; Most Admired Industry Rank #1; Social Responsibility, #12	Yes	Yes #23
Oracle (ORCL)	1977	Net software (7372)	$9063M	#195; Most Admired Industry Rank #3; Social Responsibility #199	No	No
International Business Machines (IBM)	1911	Net hardware (3570)	$87448M	#6; Most Admired Industry Rank #3; Social Responsibility #74	No	Yes #1
Lucent Technologies (LU)	1995	Net hardware (4813)	$38303M	#22; Most Admired Industry Rank #2; Social Responsibility #30; 50 Best Companies for Minorities #25	Yes	Yes #68
AT&T (AWE)	1875	Net communications (4813)	$56968M	#8; Most Admired Industry Rank #5; Social Responsibility #90	Yes	Yes #56
MCI WorldCom (WCOM)	1983	Net communications (4813)	$30720M	#25; Most Admired Industry Rank #2; Social Responsibility #406	No	No

… and even more valuable" [40]. The corporate vision alludes to social responsibility in terms of societal benefit, describing "an interactive medium that improves the lives of people and benefits society as no other medium before it" [40].

Table II. Specific strategies in sample
CORPORATE SOCIALLY RESPONSIBLE BEST PRACTICES [25]

COMPANIES	SOCIALLY RESPONSIBLE PRACTICES
Employees	Empowerment, Egalitarianism, and Sharing the Wealth: Job Security; Pay; Benefits: Support for Working Parents; Work Style; Diversity; Promotion from Within; Fun; Training, Education, and Personal Growth; Support for Retirees; Health Care; Safety; Evaluation
Customers & Suppliers	Exceptional Customer Service; Responsible Marketing to Diverse Populations; Social Criteria Purchasing; Social Mission Purchasing; Overseas Suppliers
Community & Society-At-Large	Cash Philanthropy; In-Kind Philanthropy; Volunteerism and Other Community Involvement; Social Entrepreneurship and Community Development; Advertising and Marketing; Social Leadership; Socially Appropriate Product/Service; Activism
Planet	Energy Efficiency; Packaging; Transportation; International Standards; Sustainable Development; Facility Design; Landscaping

Of all the companies considered, it may be easiest for AOL to integrate its financial and social priorities. Improving access to technology directly increases its installed base. Targeting different social causes provides the basis for new products. And providing access to the Internet, almost by definition, changes operational conventions. The company's greatest emphasis is on the "effort to bridge the Digital Divide. ... Through the work of the AOL Foundation, the company works to ensure that the four critical factors necessary to achieve meaningful access to information technology are available to everyone: structural, training/skills, content, and community awareness" [41]. Without these elements, there is substantial evidence that access to technology and its life-improving benefits is inequitably dictated by economic and social factors [34].

Amazon.com

This virtual storefront may be the most widely recognized "born-on-the-Web" e-commerce company, partially because of its unprofitability (a loss of $291 million on $1.015 billion in revenues). It is easy to see where the company might integrate a longer-term financial and social agenda, e.g., by promoting literacy. The only competitive thrust that might be considered as socially responsible stems from the company's efforts to influence public policy regarding protections for proprietary technology and business processes [42]. Instead, the company might be considered as less than socially responsible, with its recent reduction in force [23] and its dynamic pricing trial of testing for consumer price sensitivity [6].

Microsoft

Like AOL, Microsoft is able to integrate social and financial responsibilities by growing its installed base of users under the auspices of its corporate belief: "Give people the resources they need, and they can accomplish great things." Other than its donations to match employees' gifts, the company's contributions of cash and software are largely targeted toward U.S. and international community development by promoting access to technology and enriching education (1999 Giving Annual Report).

The company's technology investments are also changing the operational conventions in the non-profit sector. Microsoft's Technology Leadership grants provide "large, national nonprofit organizations with substantial software donations to enhance communications and organizational efficiency, use of the Internet, and the delivery of service to constituents" [44]. One interesting illustration is the relief support provided to Kosovo refugees to enable them to reconnect with their families and to help with access to food and medicine [45].

Microsoft places a particular emphasis on enabling people with disabilities [46] in its employment practices, donations, and product development. This was recently recognized by *WE* magazine, a lifestyle publication for people with disabilities. "Microsoft received this year's top honor not only for its workplace policies and accommodation strategies, but also for the company's efforts in creating accessible technologies and as a founding member of the Able to Work Consortium" (Microsoft company press release, Feb. 7, 2000). In addition to its efforts to convince the U.S. Justice Department that the company competes fairly, Microsoft is an advocate against software piracy (Microsoft company press release, Mar. 16, 1999) and electronic mail "spamming" (Microsoft company press release, Sept. 22, 1999), and for protections for online privacy (Microsoft company press release, Jan. 4, 1999).

Oracle

Recently named by *Global Finance* as the best global company in the computer software sector, Oracle has a strong reputation. However, "selection criteria include rate of business growth during the last year, profitability, rise in market capitalization, technological or product breakthroughs, success with mergers or acquisitions, percentage of business and employees outside the home country, skill in defusing crises, and aggressiveness in building market share" (Oracle company press release, Sept. 29, 2000).

Social criteria are noticeably absent from the list. Social actions for the company are centered on educational investments. The Oracle Academic Initiative is a commitment from Oracle to provide software, technical support, faculty education, certification, and recruiting resources to post-secondary institutions [47]. The company also sponsors the Oracle Internet Academy to enable secondary schools to "provide students with an introduction to the Internet and web application development" [48].

Oracle's website, Think.com, offers an educational environment for primary students around the world. These philanthropic efforts are considered to be long-term investments in improving the general employment base. One particular initiative, in collaboration with Help Us Help and the New Internet Computer Company, is more focused on crossing the Digital Divide (Oracle company press release, Sept. 29, 2000). The data gathered yield no evidence of Oracle deliberately leveraging its product capabilities for the social good. Special product components could be added to promote customers' corporate social responsibility, e.g., preset fields and queries regarding minority purchasing. As popular as Oracle is in the private sector, it seems that its powerful database and systems integration capabilities could be very beneficial to non-profit organizations. One example on the Oracle website showcases how a government organization used an Oracle tool to warehouse data and consolidate reporting for better environmental management—but this does not seem representative of a specific corporate strategy, and is instead a general illustration.

International Business Machines

Although a significant portion of its business is derived from software and services, IBM is also a manufacturer and the largest company in the sample. As such, it demonstrates more concern about environmental issues and sustainability than the other cases considered. IBM has been widely recognized for its environmental practices. According to IBM's 1998 Environmental Report:

> IBM's Environmentally Conscious Products program was established in 1992. Unique to the industry in its technical breadth, the program has pioneered the industry's best practices in design for the environment, product recycling technologies and product environmental metrics. This program has established five environmental design objectives for IBM products:

- Develop products with consideration for their upgradability to extend product life.
- Develop products with consideration for their reuse and recyclability at the end of the product life.
- Develop products that can safely be disposed of at the end of product life.
- Develop and manufacture products that use recycled materials where they are technically and economically justifiable.
- Develop products that will provide improvements in energy efficiency and/or reduced consumption of energy.

These product stewardship objectives enable IBM to be socially responsible and at the same time make its products more competitive. For example, an innovative power consumption algorithm for disk drives lowers their operating costs for customers. IBM's environmental practices have changed the company's operational conventions and reduced costs with foamless packaging, recycled paper purchasing, semiconductor processing, and cooling water recycling.

IBM's philanthropy also changes the operational conventions of charitable organizations. In the corporate view, technology is offered as a tool for non-profits to increase productivity and service delivery. In other areas of corporate citizenship, the company strategically showcases applications of product capabilities to support arts and culture. Examples include the Bach Digital archive, the TryScience! online science and technology center, and the Michelangelo Pieta digitization.

In terms of community development, like most of the other companies in this study, IBM invests heavily in education and computer skills development. The company recently received the Ron Brown Award for Corporate Leadership for its Reinventing Education program around the world" (IBM company press release, May 18, 2000). Another effort with the Welfare to Work Partnership resulted in the Solutions Network, a website that "connects welfare recipients with gainful employment and links businesses with welfare to work resources in their communities" [49]. IBM and AOL were jointly recognized for their efforts to promote minority advancement at the 1st Annual E-wards Bridging the Digital Gap Conference (AOL company press release, Mar. 14, 2000).

Lucent Technologies

Lucent Technologies affirms a strong sense of social responsibility ... focusing on education, community outreach and support of ... employees' volunteerism and giving (Lucent 1997 Annual Report). Environmental issues seem to have a less predominant role in this company's social agenda than that of the other manufacturer in the sample, IBM. Lucent's 1998 Annual Report does state that "by 2000 we will ... design for environment criteria to produce competitive, environmentally preferable products and services," but no indication of effort or success toward that goal was evident on the company's website. Evidence was strong, however, of Lucent's success in diversity programs and minority purchasing practices. Cited by *Fortune* as one of the "50 Best Companies for Minorities," Lucent has established a Minority & Women Business Enterprises (MWBE) Leadership Council. The intent of the Council is to place emphasis on corporate purchasing practices to "enhance profitability and competitive strategy through MWBE utilization and integrate it into Business Units and the Corporate Center business planning processes" [50]. As a telecommunications system provider, Lucent can promote its competitive agenda by supporting and promoting social uses for telecommunications. For example, the company sponsors Lucent Links grants to celebrate differences by identifying new and innovative multicultural program models. Investments in schools can increase long-term demand for network services, as well as improve the employment base. Company press releases showcase social applications for new products and services, although it is unclear as to whether these are philanthropic efforts or paid projects. Beyond minority purchasing and educational support, Lucent supports philanthropic initiatives that address the needs of communities where employees live and work, and encourage employee volunteerism and giving [51]. Interestingly, the company awards grants of $500 for every 100 hours of service by an employee. It provides further support to volunteerism by sponsoring the Annual Lucent Global Days of Caring, giving more than 15,000 employees worldwide a day off to volunteer.

AT&T

During the study period, AT&T was in the process of dividing again, this time into four publicly held units: AT&T Consumer, AT&T Wireless, AT&T Broadband, and AT&T Business. The data gathered, though, reflect the consolidated organization. The company acknowledges its social responsibilities and goes so far as to suggest that companies must perform to a "triple bottom line ... [that] takes into account social and environmental responsibilities along with financial ones" (AT&T Environmental Health & Safety 1999 Annual Report). There is a corporate emphasis on making environmental enhancements to products and services. In addition, AT&T has initiated "take back programs" for purchased items such as batteries and carpets. Like its progeny, Lucent, AT&T can integrate the fulfillment of its responsibilities by encouraging social uses of telecommunications. Also like the Lucent Foundation, the AT&T Cares program provides cash grants to non-profit organizations in which AT&T employees volunteer their time. Employees are also granted one paid day a year away from their jobs to volunteer [54]. Interestingly, the AT&T Cares program was established in 1994, after Lucent was divested.

MCI WorldCom

MCI WorldCom, the other telecommunication company in the sample, also shares a similarity with AT&T. Like AT&T, MCI WorldCom is splitting into smaller businesses, one focused on consumer telephony (MCIT) and the other cast as a global provider of communications services to businesses (WCOM).

MCI WorldCom sponsors the Marco Polo program, providing free, standards-based Internet content for the K–12 teacher, with lesson plans, classroom activities, and supplemental resources [55]. This program has been extended and supplemented by scholarships, internships, and

Table III. Meta-matrix of strategic responsibility initiatives

CSR Practices	Keeping Products Competitive	Providing the Basis for New Products	Changing Operational Conventions
Employment and Purchasing Practices	AOL	MSFT	IBM LU
Environmental Impact	IBM AT&T	IBM LU	AOL IBM
Corporate Citizenship	AMZN IBM MSFT AT&T	AOL LU AT&T	AOL MSFT IBM AT&T
Community Development	AOL MSFT IBM LU AT&T	AOL MSFT LU	AOL MSFT ORCL IBM LU AT&T WCOM

industry education partnership programs with a $10 million commitment to promote minority representation in the high technology workforce.

Tracking Corporate Responsibility

The cross tabulation of technology-based strategies and corporate social responsibility practices is summarized in Table III. The ticker symbol of a company in the grid indicates the appearance of a socially responsible practice that may be considered as also creating or sustaining a competitive advantage. If an organization is supporting multiple initiatives in a particular grid section, its ticker symbol is noted in bold.

Note that a growth strategy (i.e., one targeted at increasing the installed base of a product or service) is considered to be "keeping products competitive." Long-term investments in raising the employment base for an organization were captured as changing operational conventions for community development.

On the social responsibility side of the grid, efforts at promoting diversity and work–family balance are reflected in "employment and purchasing" practices. Initiatives toward sustainability are shown as "environmental impact." "Community development" efforts tend to be localized and/or targeted toward improving the socio-economic base of a community (e.g., aimed at crossing the Digital Divide), while "corporate citizenship" practices tend to be broader philanthropic, cultural, or policy-shaping initiatives. Table IV highlights specific examples found in the study.

One common thrust is an investment in education, ostensibly raising the skills of the employment base and thereby enhancing competitiveness, increasing future demand, and encouraging company loyalty. Table III shows this emphasis with the number of initiatives targeted toward community development. Another recurring theme is the use of information technology as a vehicle to advance the social good by making the technology more accessible, thus creating a larger demand for products and services. Encouraging nonprofit organizations to use technology to improve their operational conventions is also a common strategy.

Another interesting pattern emerges when the companies that *are* endorsed as socially responsible (AOL, MFST, IBM, LU, AT&T) are compared with the companies that are not (AMZN, ORCL, WCOM). Companies recognized as socially responsible tended to have a more coherent strategy for social responsibility in and of itself. That is, although the socially responsible companies in the sample used a variety of social practices and donated to a variety of charitable

Table IV. Examples of Strategically Responsible Practices

CSR Practices	Keeping Products Competitive	Providing the Basis for New Products	Changing Operational Conventions
Employment and Purchasing Practices	AOL providing free access to employees, arguably helping the work–family balance	MSFT creating accessible technologies and as a founding member of the Able to Work Consortium	IBM enforcing its corporate policy on employee well-being and product safety LU emphasizing minority purchasing practices at a strategic level
Environmental Impact	IBM inventing a power consumption algorithm for disks AT&T making environmental enhancements to products and services	IBM establishing product stewardship design principles LU calling for design for environment criteria to produce competitive, environmentally preferable products and services	AOL promoting online shopping with its 100% Total Satisfaction Guarantee, reducing traffic congestion and fossil fuel consumption IBM making process adjustments to reduce energy consumption and byproduct emissions
Corporate Citizenship	AMZN advocating protections for proprietary technology IBM showcasing products and services in philanthropic efforts (e.g., restoration of the Pieta) MSFT fighting against piracy AT&T offering free anti-spamming service	AOL launching the "My Government" content area, ostensibly fostering "a higher level of civic discourse" [38] LU providing "Lucent Links" grants to celebrate differences with innovative multicultural program models using telecomm AT&T producing HIV/AIDS awareness cable network programming and other technology-based programs promoting culture, such as "Jazz in America", Internet-based curricula and the National Digital Library [52]	AOL addressing digital rights management, partnering with InterTrust [18] MSFT providing computer facilities for disaster relief and contributing to the School of Peace in Brazil IBM providing technology as a tool to non-profits to increase productivity and services delivery AT&T donating wireless phones for the AT&T Safe Schools program and telecommunications services for natural disaster relief

Table IV. Examples of Strategically Responsible Practices

CSR Practices	Keeping Products Competitive	Providing the Basis for New Products	Changing Operational Conventions
Community Development	AOL sponsoring the Rural Telecommunications Leadership awards, promoting access to the Internet in underserved areas and Offering free access to schools in Empowerment Zones, giving disadvantaged children an opportunity to build computer skills MSFT collaborating with advocacy groups, sponsoring a variety of access-to-technology projects at selected institutions, including supporting Working Connections at community colleges providing information technology training to underserved populations IBM earning the Ron Brown award for corporate leadership for reinventing education partnership around the world LU providing advanced network services for a community college LU installing a wireless network for a large public school and videoconferencing for school systems AT&T sponsoring Senior-to-senior Internet training and offering discounts to Hispanics for Hispanic Heritage Month	AOL facilitating e-mentoring, partnering with mentoring.org and Digital Heroes; enabling philanthropy and volunteerism, providing an Internet portal Helping.org; and creating the Civilrights.org portal, highlighting the issue of digital access in the civil rights community MSFT funding research at selected universities, targeting improvements in access LU offering digital cellular service for the hearing impaired	AOL offering free personalized websites for every school, enhancing communications among parents, teachers, and administrators MSFT teaming with community organizations to develop technology centers ORCL sponsoring the Oracle Academic Initiative and the Oracle Internet Academy with other donations to educational institutions IBM sponsoring the Solutions Network for Welfare to Work LU investing in schools to raise skills of employment base, e.g., the "Newark Renaissance" project AT&T creating the Education Alliance to increase curricula for information technology and networking skills and the AT&T Learning Network to link to tools needed to improve teaching and learning [53] WCOM establishing the Marco Polo website to support using the Internet in elementary education

Table V. Positive model of strategic responsibility (preliminary)

CSR Practices	Keeping Products Competitive	Providing the Basis for New Products	Changing Operational Conventions
Employment and Purchasing Practices	Extension of products and services to employees to enhance home life	Products for individuals with disabilities	Proactive purchasing programs to promote diversity
Environmental Impact	Product improvements for energy savings	Product and service innovations for reduced environmental impact	Process improvements for waste reduction
Corporate Citizenship	Advocacy in public policy to also protect proprietary interests	Extension of products and services to support charitable causes	Application of products and services to philanthropies
Community Development	Extension of products and services to cross the Digital Divide	Creation of products and services that "do good"	Application of products and services to schools

causes, most of them have a theme or overarching goal for their philanthropy. America Online is bridging the Digital Divide. Microsoft is addressing accessibility. IBM is leading product stewardship. Lucent is promoting minorities' and women's business interests.

Table V synthesizes these examples into a preliminary positive model of integration. For example, extending products and services to employees to enhance their home life (not extend their work days) might be considered a positive employment practice that also keeps products competitive through increased usage. Using technology to change operational conventions and make process improvements for waste reduction could have a positive environmental impact as well as create operational efficiencies. Creating products and services that "do good" not only grow a company's product portfolio (i.e., provide the basis for new products), they also contribute to community development. In this way, Table V is offered as an illustration, a suggestion, for corporations that are interested in pursuing strategic responsibility.

While some companies seem to be leveraging strategic initiatives to fulfill corporate social responsibilities, it is not necessarily clear how deliberate this integration is—at least across the sample. As noted on IBM's website:

> IBM's contributions target a few key areas and leverage our expertise in technology. In our efforts, we strive to underscore the role of technology as a tool to address societal issues, demonstrate IBM's reputation as a solutions provider, and focus IBM's philanthropic programs to enhance relationships with customers and suppliers. [56]

Interviews of top managers would clarify the strategic intent of the other companies, and the extent to which the apparent integration is intentional. Interviews might also be helpful to gauge the success of these strategies.

It is also important to note that the insights gained from the cross-case analysis are offered as illustrative rather than generalizable. The extent to which companies providing non-electronic services could apply these approaches is unknown. Certainly guidelines such as IBM's Product Stewardship objectives would be meaningful. Also, Lucent's MWBE purchasing policy would benefit other corporations. Showcasing new product applications or services could be appropriate for health-related technologies or other consumer goods. Investment in education is likely to be a strategic initiative for many other organizations as the demand for skilled and knowledgeable workers grows. Further studies could apply this methodology to examine how extensively such practices are used in other industries.

REFERENCES

[1] Baldridge Awards, Malcom Baldridge National Quality Award. National Institutes of Standards and Technology, Gaithersburg, MD, 1996.

[2] A. B. Carroll. "A three-dimensional conceptual model of corporate performance." *Academy of Management J.* 4 (1979): 497–505.

[3] A. B. Carroll. "Stakeholder thinking in three models of management morality: A perspective with strategic implications." In *Understanding Stakeholder Thinking,* J. Nasi, Ed. Helsinki, Finland: LSR, 1995.

[4] S. Cohen and D. Grace. "Engineers and social responsibility: An obligation to do good." *IEEE Technology & Society Mag.* 13, no. 3 (Fall 1994): 12–19.

[5] S. Curkovic, S. A. Melnyk, R. B. Handfield, and R. Calantone. "Investigating the linkage between Total Quality Management and Environmentally Responsible Manufacturing." *IEEE Trans. Engineering Management* 47, no. 4 (2000): 444–464.

[6] K. Dawson. "Amazon says 'Oops' to keep the press at bay." *The Industry Standard.* (September 28, 2000). Available online at http://www.thestandard.com; accessed October 5, 2000.

[7] Domini. "DSEF—The social criteria." Available online at http://www.domini.com/SocCriteria.html; accessed Oct. 9, 2000.

[8] A. Farrell. "Sustainability and the design of knowledge tools." *IEEE Technology & Society Mag.* 14, no. 4 (Winter 1996/1997): 11–20.

[9] R. A. Goodman and M. W. Lawless. *Technology and Strategy: Conceptual Models and Diagnostics.* New York, NY: Oxford Univ. Press, 1994.

[10] K. Hallinan, M. Daniels, and S. Safferman. "Balancing technical and social issues: a new first-year design course." *IEEE Technology & Society Mag.* 20, no. 1 (2001): 4–11.

[11] R. B. Handfield, S. A. Melnyk, R. J. Calantone, and S. Curkovic. "Integrating environmental concerns into the design process: The gap between theory and practice." *IEEE Trans. Engineering Management* 48, no. 2 (2001): 189–206.

[12] C. E. Harris, Jr. "Explaining disasters: The case for preventative ethics." *IEEE Technology & Society Mag.* 14, no. 2 (1995): 22–27.

[13] J. R. Herkert, Ed. *Social, Ethical, and Policy Implications of Engineering: Selected Readings.* New York, NY: IEEE, 2000.

[14] IEEE. "IEEE code of ethics, 1990." In *Social, Ethical, and Policy Implications of Engineering: Selected Readings*, J. R. Herkert, Ed. New York, NY: IEEE, 2000.

[15] V. E. Johnson and L. L. Brennan. "Examining the impact of technology on social responsibility practices." In *Proc. Seventh Ann. Int. Conf. Promoting Business Ethics* (September 21–23, 2000): 447–457.

[16] T. Klusmann. "The 100 best corporate citizens." *Business Ethics* 14, no. 1–5 (2000).

[17] J. V. Koch and R. J. Cebula. "In search of excellent management." *J. Management Studies* 31, no. 5 (1994): 681–99.

[18] M. Learmonth. "AOL and InterTrust: "A legal Napster." *The Industry Standard* (July 3, 2000). Available online at http://www.thestandard.com; accessed Oct. 5, 2000.

[19] T. W. Loe, L. Ferrell, and P. Mansfield. "A review of empirical studies assessing ethical decision making in business." *J. Business Ethics* 25 (2000): 185–204.

[20] J. M. Lozano. "Ethics and management: A controversial issue." *J. Business Ethics* 15 (1996): 227–236.

[21] P. McVeigh. "New Year's feast: Social mutual fund review for 2000." *Bus. Ethics* 14 (2000): 26–30.

[22] M. R. Miles. *Qualitative Data Analysis: An Expanded Sourcebook*, 2nd ed. Thousand Oaks, CA: SAGE, 1994.

[23] K. Ohlson. "Amazon.com cuts 2% of workforce." *Computerworld* (Jan. 31, 2000). Available online at http://www.computerworld.com; accessed Oct. 5, 2000.

[24] J. E. Post, A. T. Lawrence, and J. Weber. *Business and Society: Corporate Strategy, Public Policy, Ethics*. Boston, MA: Irwin/McGraw-Hill, 1999.

[25] A. Reder. *75 Best Business Practices for Socially Responsible Companies*. New York, NY: Putnam, 1995.

[26] D. Rockefeller. *The Corporation in Transition: Redefining its Social Charter*. Washington, DC: Chamber of Commerce of the United States, 1973.

[27] L. W. Steele. *Managing Technology: The Strategic View*. New York, NY: McGraw-Hill, 1989.

[28] P. R. Varadarajan and V. Ramanujam. "The corporate performance conundrum: a synthesis of contemporary views and an extension." *J. Management Studies* 27, no. 5 (1990): 463–83.

[29] S. A. Waddock and S. B. Graves. "Finding the link between stakeholder relations and quality of management." *J. Investing* 6 (1997): 20–24.

[30] S. Waddock and S. B. Graves. "Quality of management and quality of stakeholder relations." *Business and Society* 36 (1997): 250–279.

[31] S. Waddock, S. B. Graves, and M. Kelly. "On the trail of the best corporate citizens." *Business Ethics* (2000): 14–17.

[32] S. Walsh. "Do you, Time Warner, take AOL to be your…" *The Industry Standard* (October 30, 2000): 157–176.

[33] G. R. Weaver, L. K. Trevino, and P. L. Cochran. "Integrated and decoupled corporate social performance." *Management*.

[34] R. Willner and N. Callaghan. "Technology for use by us all." IBM Corporate Community Relations Rep., April 1999.

[35] R. K. Yin. *Case Study Research*. Beverly Hills, CA: SAGE, 1984.

[36] http://www.domini.com

[37] http://www.wri.org/wri/bschools/

[38] http://corp.aol.com/whoweare/who_public.html

[39] http://www.fortune.com/fortune/dex/e50/desc.html

[40] http://www.aol.com

[41] http://corp.aol.com/whoweare/who_public.html

[42] http://corp.aol.com/careers/1/diversity/programs.html

[43] http://www.amazon.com

[44] http://www.microsoft.com/giving/

[45] http://www.microsoft.com/giving/np_tsolu.htm

[46] http://www.microsoft.com/giving/99_story3.htm

[47] http://www.microsoft.com/enable/microsoft/efforts.htm

[48] http://www.oraclespromise.com/pages/oai.html

[49] http://oraclespromise.com/pages/oia.html

[50] http://www.ibm.com/ibm/ibmgives/grant/adult/welfare.html

[51] http://www.lucent.com/news/pubs/mwbe/1996/05.html

[52] http://www.lucent.com/news/about/community

[53] http://www.att.com/foundation/feature.html

[54] http://www.att.com/foundation/programs/education.html

[55] http://www.att.com.foundation/programs/communityl.html

[56] http://www.worldcom.com/marcopolo/

[57] http://www.ibm.com/ibm/ibmgives/about/

Chapter 4
Assuring Corporate and Resource Sustainability

I never had given a thought as to how I was affecting the environment.
—Ray Anderson, CEO, Interface

Opening Vignette

Nau (pronounced "now") is a designer/retailer of "sustainable urban+outdoor apparel." Based in Portland, Oregon, the company was founded by executives of other apparel manufacturers. According to their website (www.nau.com), they wanted to "redesign fashion and to redefine business so that each become a powerful force for change."

To those ends, they have several unique business practices. First, they design their clothing for sustainability, avoiding trendy colors and using long-lasting fabrics that do not require dry cleaning and can be washed in cold water. As they describe it, "We design for lasting beauty—product colors, details, and shapes are minimalist, modern, and timeless."

They also handle logistics differently. Customers visit a Nau store, try on the items, and determine what sizes are needed—and then receive their orders directly from the distribution center. This allows Nau to have smaller store space (they only need one of each product in every size—no other inventory), reduces returns, eliminates cross-shipments, and requires less transportation overall. Nau uses recycled shipping materials, energy efficient transportation modes, and supply chain visibility to minimize the life cycle cost of its goods.

In addition, while fabrics are not strictly speaking, sustainable, Nau makes fabric selections based on what it calls a "Beginning of Life and End of Life (BOL/EOL) model that examines the "energy and resources to create a fabric, and the opportunities and systems to deal with a product at the end of its useful life." It has a restricted substances list to avoid toxins and uses systems to trace the fibers and fabrics for its products.

One other interesting practice: Nau donates 2% of every sale to one of five strategic partners for change. During the checkout process, the customer selects the recipient. Options are Ashoka, an organization that promotes social entrepreneurship; Breakthrough Institute, a think tank devoted to affordable clean energy; Ecotrust, a venture capital firm dedicated to "building resilient economies;" Kiva, a microlending cooperative; and Mercy Corps, a relief organization.

Something that Nau did that is *not* recommended as a good business practice is going out of business. Founded in 2003, it closed its doors and sold off its inventory in 2008. "The irony of Nau's demise is that a company so committed to sustainability was ultimately unsustainable. But not because of its principles."[1] Overexpansion and overspending were its downfall. They were purchased and relaunched in 2009 and are now growing more slowly, even ... organically.

Stockholders and stakeholders are important factors for understanding the context in which an organization operates. In this chapter, we develop the context further by understanding sustainability, from stockholders' *and* stakeholders' perspectives. Will an effective execution of a strategic plan assure that the company will endure in a way that is sustainable? And, is the company's success at the expense of others, the environment, or the community?

The definition of sustainability has evolved dramatically in the past several years, but it means that the actions taken today will enable the company to be an ongoing concern and to continue to deliver the return on investment (ROI) that investors expect. In addition it means that companies will be able to access the necessary resources in the future. In this chapter, we examine both meanings of sustainability. Successful mastery of this material will enable you to:

- understand the history of sustainability and the reasons for its inception
- identify the drivers that are raising questions of sustainability
- recognize organizational sustainability stages and sustainability "maturity"

Although there is a lot of media "buzz" over green, this is not a new idea but one that has re-emerged. But the definition has evolved beyond shortsighted marketing hype to a real concern as to how a company operates and the strategic decisions it makes.

INTRODUCTION

What company does not want to be "sustainable?" It sounds like common sense, right? But in reality, pressures and incentives in the business world as well in the public sector tend to concentrate on short-term rather than long-term considerations. Often, this short-term perspective overlooks the more pragmatic considerations of the long run. There is a tension about time horizon in strategic decision-making, about what is more important: short-term profitability or long-term sustainability.

In recent years, sustainability concerns have expanded from financial viability to resource availability. Much of this concern originated from conversations in the United Nations, some in reaction to disasters directly impacting the environment. These include *Chernobyl*, the *Love Canal* disaster, and the *Exxon Valdez* spill. All of these manmade disasters resulted in significant environmental impact.

---

[1] L. O'Brien. "What Nau? GOOD Business." (November/December 2008): 18–24.

It was the Brundtland Commission in 1987 that first coined the term sustainability, meaning the capacity to endure without harming future generations, specifically, "meeting the needs of the present without compromising the ability of future generations to meet their own needs." Then in 1997, John Elkington developed the concept of the "Triple Bottom Line," also known as the "three-legged stool." The three-legged stool balances people (social), place (environment) and profit (economic) concerns in a company. Again, there is a tension among these priorities that must be addressed strategically. As Carroll (2000, p. 41) warned more than a decade ago, "Companies will be expected to be profitable, abide by the law, engage in ethical behavior, and give back to their communities through philanthropy, though the tensions between and among these responsibilities will become more challenging as information technology continues to push all enterprises toward a global-level frame of reference and functioning."

The Past, Present, and Future of Sustainability

Famed economist Joseph Schumpeter (1883–1950) coined the term, "the creative disruption of capitalism." "Believing that capitalist economic success, because it is incomplete and interrupted, breeds its own backlash" (Samuelson 1992, p. 61), the economist was arguing that the turmoil of capitalism was what made corporate sustainability unlikely. Innovations from outside the companies would unseat them.

In the 1970s, the renowned "Chicago School" of economic thinking, led by Nobel Laureate Milton Friedman, advocated for the benefits of free markets and innovation as the true source of wealth. For a corporation to be sustainable, executives must conduct their businesses so as to maximize profitability. This line of thinking assumes market corrections for anti-societal behaviors or a lack of innovation.

This thinking continued through the 80s and 90s, led by then Federal Reserve Chairman Alan Greenspan and supported by several presidential administrations. Things began to change, however, when large companies began to fail, the housing market crashed under a consumptive culture,[2] and environmental disasters became recurrent.

These days, we see an increasing emphasis on corporate social responsibility, even as businesses are trying to recover from a widespread economic recession. "Sustainability" is a double entendre, with companies showcasing their efforts to improve profits as well as minimize their environmental impact.

---

[2] See J. DeGraf, D. Wann, and T. H. Naylor. "Affluenza: The All-Consuming Epidemic." San Francisco, CA: Berrett-Koehler Publishers, Inc., 2001:

> In each of the past four years more Americans declared personal bankruptcy than graduated from college (p. 4) ... 70% of us visit malls each week, more than attend houses of worship (p. 13). ... Americans spend six hours per week shopping and only forty minutes playing with our kids (p. 14). ... Average house sizes ("starter castles") in the US (p. 24): 50's, 950 sq. ft.; 70's, 1350 sq. ft.; 90's, 2300 sq. ft. ... We drive twice as much per capita as we did 50 years ago, and fly ... 25 times as much (p. 28). ... "Possession Overload" results when you find your life is being taken up by maintaining and caring for things instead of people (p. 39). ... Everything we watch ... is always promoting dissatisfaction. The whole idea of using a thing and then throwing it away is affecting us all (p. 47). ... A recent study showed that while the average American can identify fewer than ten types of plants, he or she recognizes hundreds of corporate logos (p. 150).

The Coca-Cola Company is working with the World Wildlife Federation, an unlikely pairing, to advance technologies and practices for wastewater reclamation (http://www.thecoca-colacompany.com/citizenship/), as a result of issues raised by an Indian community when its water table was being depleted by a bottling plant's operations. Wal-Mart Stores has several environmental initiatives that are cost saving as well as environmentally conscious. They are installing solar panels on the roofs of their stores to move toward renewable energy. Wal-Mart is also collaborating with its suppliers to reduce packaging waste (http://walmartstores.com/Sustainability/9125.aspx). One of those suppliers is Proctor & Gamble, which is following a strategy of "compaction," selling smaller packages of more concentrated products: less material cost, less transportation cost, and less waste (http://www.pg.com/innovatingsustainability/innovating/).

As we look to the future, we see an emerging management practice called "life cycle assessment" (LCA). LCA tracks a product's ecological negatives, quantifying its environmental and public health downsides at each link in its supply chain (e.g., natural resources depleted, pollutants emitted into air, toxins dumped into water, or contaminants buried in landfills) (Goleman 2009).

It may be astounding to know, for example, that producing a hamburger takes 4,000–18,000 gallons of water. "Estimates vary a lot due to different conditions of raising cows and to the extent of the production chain of water that is used. It takes a lot of water to grow grain, forage, and roughage to feed a cow, as well as water to drink and to service the cow" (http://www.worldwater.org/data.html. And that's just getting the raw material, not processing the meat, transporting it, packaging it, selling it, preparing it (hopefully, with hands that have been washed), and disposing of waste.

LCA can be very detailed, even for simple products. Figure 4-1 shows the general considerations that comprise a full analysis. Companies are working now to establish "transparent supply chains," not only for shipment tracking but for LCA, using advanced technologies such as wireless computing and radio frequency identification tags (RFIDs). "RFID tags, well established for inventory management and other purposes, are becoming smaller, cheaper, and more flexible. New generations of tags ... can even be embedded in paper and plastic, making the product's provenance data part of the material itself" (New, 2010, p. 78).

Daniel Goleman (2009), known for his work in managerial, emotional, and social intelligence is now concerned with the development of ecological intelligence and ways to understand how the products we buy, use, and discard affect the environment.

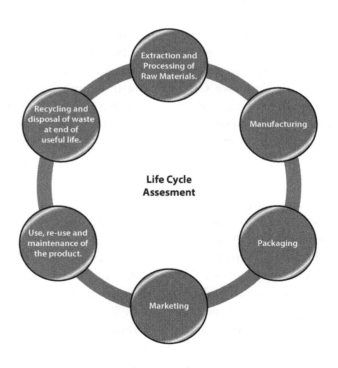

Figure 4-1. Life Cycle Assessment

Illustration

Social media, Internet-based applications with user-created content, also provide transparency. For example, www.goodguide.com has a mission to "help consumers make purchasing decisions that reflect their preferences and values. We believe that better information can transform the marketplace: as more consumers buy better products, retailers and manufacturers face compelling incentives to make products that are safe, environmentally sustainable and produced using ethical sourcing of raw materials and labor." Currently, they have over 120,000 consumer goods (toys, personal care, and household products) scientifically analyzed.

In the future, we can expect more of the same information to inform decisions. Scan a barcode on your smartphone and find out if it is "good" or not, according to your values. For now, the options are limited—and the claims of "goodness" may be marketing. "Green-washing" is the selective display of one or two virtuous aspects of a product; for example, a label on a t-shirt might read "100% organic cotton: it makes a world of difference." That claim is both right and wrong (Goleman, pp. 22–24). The cotton may have been grown organically (and cotton is one of the most water-intensive crops), but the manufacturing process may have included colorful dyes, many of which are toxic.

DRIVERS OF SUSTAINABILITY

When and what drives a company to consider sustainability in its strategic decision-making? Much of this can be determined from where the company finds itself on the sustainability "journey" or its maturity in understanding the value of sustainability on its strategy. In fact, many companies are forced into considering sustainability reactively, due to a violation of pollution laws. An example of this is Exxon following the oil spill in Alaska that required the company to "clean up its act." Another driver is when companies are forced into a compliance with a regulation or requirement, governmental or organizational, such as building "Leadership in Engineering and Environmental Design," LEED-only buildings ,or restricting CO2 emissions by automobiles, thus driving companies to produce more fuel efficient cars.

Some companies think that "going green" will be a good marketing ploy and attract a segment of the market that is concerned with environmental issues. In these cases it may simply be "green washing," a ploy to convince buyers of a company's environmental consciousness (www.stopgreenwash.org). But some companies have moved beyond the reactive and short sighted view of sustainability into a more integrated strategic approach in which there is a direct payback on the investment in more sustainable decisions, such as enhanced productivity, efficiency, resource or asset maximization, and, as a result, more profit!

The Open Compliance and Ethics Group (OCEG) has been a leader in assisting companies to understand the value of sustainability. More and more companies are working to reposition themselves, including Wal-Mart, PricewaterhouseCoopers, and IBM. Why? Because these strategic initiatives get results. Not only are companies reducing their environmental impact, they are often experiencing significant cost savings. An example is 3M, where they eliminated more than three billion pounds of pollution and saved nearly 1.4 billion USD through their Pollution Prevention Program (http://solutions.3m.com/wps/portal/3M/en_US/3M-Sustainability/Global/Environment/3P/).

Other drivers of sustainability include not only customers, but also investors. As a result, many companies are providing annual reports on their social responsibility and sustainability efforts. For example, Johnson & Johnson began adding sustainability and responsibility reports to their company publications in 2009 (http://www.jnj.com/connect/about-jnj/publications/). The Dow Jones Sustainability Indexes (DJSI) have become a major "barometer" for investors as they evaluate potential investment in companies for their sustainability practices as well as their social and environmental responsibility. Socially responsible investing is a trend that attracts investors interested in sustainable and responsible business practices.

 ## APPLICATION AND REFLECTION

- •   How can You, Inc. include in your vision statement a commitment to economic, social, and environmental sustainability?

- •   Look at the web pages of the following companies. Discuss their approaches to sustainability and corporate social, economic, and environmental responsibility and how it is included in their strategy as defined on their websites.
    - Kimberly-Clark: http://www.kimberly-clark.com/sustainability.aspx
    - Toyota: http://www.toyota.com/about/environment/
    - Johnson & Johnson: http://www.jnj.com/responsibility/
    - Walmart: http://walmartstores.com/

- •   The following article, "Sustainability and Competetive Advantage," provides additional insights as to why companies embark on sustainability as part of their way of doing business. Reflect on the examples you evaluated, and determine which might apply.

SUSTAINABILITY AND
COMPETITIVE ADVANTAGE

Maurice Berns, Andrew Townend, Zayna Khayat, Balu Balagopal, Martin Reeves, and Nina Kruschwitz

Forget how business is affecting sustainability ... how is sustainability affecting business? The first annual Business of Sustainability Survey and interview project has answers.

FROM THE EDITOR

Even as attention is increasingly paid to "going green" and to the role business can play to help solve sustainability problems, the flip side of the business and sustainability relationship has gone underexamined. Forget how management can affect sustainability. How will sustainability change management?

The difference between the questions isn't as subtle as it might sound. The first question—how can management affect sustainability?—can be ignored. (Maybe a company still thinks addressing sustainability isn't in its strategic interest, or believes it can't afford it.) The second question, on the other hand, will come find you—whether you want to be found or not. During the research for this *MIT Sloan Management Review* special report, we heard repeatedly of the varied ways that sustainability-related issues were imposing themselves on organizations. Even a partial list of the mentioned impositions is long: volatility of resource availability and price; impending regulation; customer demands; investor pressure; emergence of new markets and evaporation of old ones; effects on attracting and retaining talent; changes in financial operations; necessity for collaboration across boundaries that used to be inviolable; pressure from communities and interest groups; growing economic uncertainty; the need to cultivate resilience; and the general hunt for strategies that could hope to succeed over the longer term instead of just tomorrow. The list goes on.

This special section of the *Review* is the result of a year-long exploration of those sustainability-driven changes to the competitive landscape. (See a much expanded special report online at sloanreview.mit.edu/busofsustainability.)

How should executives think about those changes? What effects can businesses expect to encounter? What should businesses do to exploit emerging opportunities or defend against new threats? How will organizations need to change in order to thrive under the coming competitive conditions? That's what we set out to learn.

In collaboration with knowledge partner The Boston Consulting Group, we explored the management implications of sustainability in three steps.

First, we interviewed leading MIT scholars and thinkers in a wide range of subject areas, including urban studies, energy science, and management. (In this phase, we also interviewed BCG field experts.)

Second, we conducted in-depth interviews with more than 50 sustainability thought leaders and corporate CEOs around the world. Interviewees included executives whose companies are at the cutting edge of sustainability (including General Electric, Unilever, Nike, Royal Dutch Shell, Interface, and BP).

Third, we created a questionnaire shaped by the findings from those interviews and launched the first annual Business of Sustainability Global Survey of more than 1,500 corporate executives and managers about their perspectives on the intersection of sustainability and business strategy.

The insights of both the survey respondents and the thought leader group yielded a picture of sustainability's current position on the corporate agenda—and how that position is likely to shift in the future.

—Michael S. Hopkins
Editor in Chief

The Business of Sustainability: What It Means to Managers Now

Sustainability is garnering ever-greater public attention and debate. The subject ranks high on the legislative agendas of most governments; media coverage of the topic has proliferated; and sustainability issues are of increasing concern to humankind.

However, the business implications of sustainability merit greater scrutiny—and scrutiny of a different kind than the green-oriented focus that's most common. Will sustainability change the competitive landscape and reshape the opportunities and threats that companies face? If so, how? How worried are executives and other stakeholders about the impact of sustainability efforts on the corporate bottom line? What—if anything—are companies doing now to capitalize on sustainability-driven changes? And what strategies are they pursuing to position themselves competitively for the future?

To begin answering those questions, we conducted a year-long inquiry that involved in-depth interviews with more than 50 global thought leaders, followed by the Business of Sustainability Survey of more than 1,500 worldwide executives and managers about their perspectives on the intersection of sustainability and business strategy, including their assessments of how their own companies are acting on sustainability threats or opportunities right now.[1] The survey will be conducted annually in order to track changes in how companies are thinking and acting. (For more about the project, see "From the Editor: Sustainability and Competitive Advantage," p. 19.)

This article can contain only the high-level findings and highlights from the interviews and survey. For a complete look at the survey results, as well as more extensive reporting and analysis, go online to the *MIT Sloan Management Review's* Web-based guide to all the articles, results, and data reports yielded by the project (sloanreview.mit.edu/busofsustainability).

There, as here, you will find not only answers but, equally interestingly, questions that are coming to the fore as sustainability concerns of all kinds reshape management practices and strategy. Why is the business case for sustainability-related investments hard to build, even when opportunities seem apparent? What particular capabilities and characteristics must organizations cultivate in order to compete most effectively in the new, sustainability-altered landscape? How will the relationships among companies, communities, individuals, and governments be changed by sustainability issues, and what opportunities does that present?

First, though, the immediate questions: What are executives thinking and doing about sustainability-driven concerns right now? What's impeding their attempts to both capitalize on opportunities and defend against threats?

Here's what our thought leader interviews and corporate executive survey revealed.

Survey and Interview Findings: What Executives Are Thinking and Doing

When managers and executives refer to "sustainability," what do they mean—and how important do they think it is? The survey revealed that there is no single established definition for sustainability. Companies define it in myriad ways—some focusing solely on environmental impact, others incorporating the numerous economic, societal, and personal implications. Yet while companies may differ in how they define sustainability, our research indicates that they are virtually united in the view that sustainability, however defined, is and will be a major force to be reckoned with—and one that will have a determining impact on the way their businesses think, act, manage, and compete. Over 92% of respondents told us that their company was already addressing sustainability in some way.

Nor does sustainability appear to be an ephemeral strategy concern, if we can judge by how little the view of it has been affected by the pressure of the economic downturn. Fewer than one fourth of survey respondents told us that their companies have pulled back on their commitment to sustainability during the downturn (see "Sustainability Surviving the Downturn," p. 25).

Indeed, a number of thought leaders shared their belief that the downturn has accelerated a shift toward a greater corporate focus on sustainability—particularly toward sustainability-related actions that have an immediate impact on the bottom

KEY FINDINGS

REVISED AGENDA
The survey revealed a strong consensus that sustainability is having — and will continue to have — a material impact on how companies think and act.

- More than 92% of survey respondents said that their company was addressing sustainability.

DOWNTURN?
Sustainability is surviving the downturn.

- Fewer than 25% of survey respondents said that their company had decreased its commitment to sustainability during the downturn.

BUT ACTION LAGS
Although almost all the executives in the survey thought that sustainability would have an impact on their business and were trying to address this topic, the majority also said that their companies were not acting decisively to fully exploit the opportunities and mitigate the risks that sustainability presents.

- The majority of sustainability actions undertaken to date appear to be limited to those necessary to meet regulatory requirements.

- Almost 70% of survey respondents said that their company has not developed a clear business case for sustainability.

AGGRESSIVE ACTION YIELDING REWARDS
A small number of companies, however, are acting aggressively on sustainability — and reaping substantial rewards.

- Examples of leading companies offer some helpful ideas on how to proceed.

- Once companies begin to act aggressively, they tend to discover more opportunity, not less, than they expected to find.

line. At the same time, several survey respondents lamented having to meet higher than normal criteria for sustainability investments.

Opinions diverge on some aspects of sustainability. Although the points above reflect a strong convergence of views on the overarching question of sustainability's impact on business, significant divergence in opinion arose regarding particular aspects of sustainability. We highlight some of the most noteworthy differences below.

Self-identified sustainability experts viewed the topic differently than those who considered themselves novices in the area. We asked survey respondents to rate their experience with sustainability by classifying themselves as either a sustainability expert, an individual with some experience, or a novice. In a number of cases, the perspectives held by these three groups were at odds.

- Experts defined sustainability more comprehensively than novices did. While a plurality (40%) of novices defined sustainability simply as "maintaining business viability," 64% of experts used one of two widely accepted definitions: the so-called Brundtland Commission definition or the triple bottom line definition, both of which incorporate economic, environmental, and social considerations.
- Whereas 50% of the experts we surveyed said that their company had a compelling business case for sustainability, only 10% of the novices we surveyed did.
- Experts believed more strongly in the importance of engaging suppliers across the value chain. Sixty-two percent of the experts surveyed considered it necessary to hold suppliers to specific sustainability criteria; only 25% of surveyed novices felt the same.

It is noteworthy that experts' views on the points above were largely consistent with those of the thought leaders we interviewed, with experience being the common denominator between the groups. Simply put, the more people know about sustainability, the more thoughtfully they evaluate it and the more opportunity they see in it—and the more they think it matters to how companies position themselves and operate.

As an overall group, survey respondents held different opinions from those of the thought leaders we interviewed. On average, the thought leaders had more experience with sustainability than the survey respondents, so it was not surprising that their views diverged on several aspects of sustainability—particularly on the topic's drivers and benefits. The major points of contention included the following:

- **Government Legislation.** Overall, survey respondents deemed government legislation the sustainability-related issue with the greatest impact on their business. Sixty-seven percent of respondents said that this issue had a significant impact on how their organization was approaching sustainability. By contrast, thought leaders placed far less emphasis on government legislation as a driving force in sustainability. Further, many of the thought leaders we interviewed cited instances in which companies had played a role in shaping the regulatory framework rather than simply reacting to it.
- **Consumer Concerns.** Fifty-eight percent of survey respondents cited consumer concerns as having a significant impact on their companies. By contrast, although thought leaders acknowledged that consumer awareness is a reality that businesses must confront, our interviewees cited other drivers—such as climate change and other ecological forces—as more pressing.

- **Employee Interest.** Rounding out the top three drivers was employee interest in sustainability; 56% of survey respondents selected it as an issue having a significant impact on their company. Yet among thought leaders, employee interest was deemed a far less significant issue. Thought leaders, however, consistently cited enhanced recruitment, retention, and engagement—and other employee-related issues—as major benefits of addressing sustainability.

By a wide margin, survey respondents identified the impact on a company's image and brand as the principal *benefit* of addressing sustainability. (See "What Are the Benefits of Action?") But thought leaders rarely cited this factor (or when they did, they described it as a second-order benefit), emphasizing instead a broad continuum of rewards that were grounded more in value creation—particularly sustainability's potential to deliver new sources of competitive advantage. Several thought leaders offered other provocative ideas about the potential benefits of addressing sustainability. For example, some thought leaders suggested that leadership in sustainability might be viewed as a proxy for management quality.

Some companies are acting decisively and winning—but most are not. While the vast majority of companies have yet to commit aggressively to sustainability, our survey and interviews confirmed that there are noteworthy exceptions. The group of so-called first-class companies in sustainability, as identified by survey respondents, is populated by the usual suspects often highlighted in business articles, reports, books, and sustainability indexes. The top five cited most often by survey respondents were GE, Toyota, IBM, Shell, and Wal-Mart. But some lesser-known names also surfaced, such as Rio Tinto, Better Place, and International Watch Co. In aggregate, these companies are demonstrating that a sustainability strategy can yield real results.

That said, we found a material gap between intent and action at most of the companies we examined. Our survey and interviews demonstrated that there is a large degree of consensus regarding the potential business impact of sustainability. And our research further confirmed that there are stirrings of activity throughout the business realm. But most companies are either not acting decisively or are falling short on execution. On the one hand, more than 60% of respondents said that their company was building awareness of its sustainability agenda. On the other hand, most companies appeared to lack an overall plan for attacking sustainability and delivering results. Many of their actions seemed defensive and tactical in nature, consisting of a variety of disconnected initiatives focused on products, facilities, employees, and the greater community. While these efforts might be impressive on some levels, they largely represented only incremental changes to the business.

Clearly, companies can do more to connect their stated intent in sustainability with business impact—and they can do it in a way that maintains explicit links to the bottom line over both the short term and long term. But why aren't they, given that they believe sustainability will materially affect their business?

Why Decisive—and Effective—Corporate Action is Lacking

Many thought leaders and survey respondents viewed sustainability as a unique business issue, both strategically and economically. They embraced the following principles:

- Sustainability has the potential to affect all aspects of a company's operations, from development and manufacturing to sales and support functions.
- Sustainability also has the potential to affect every value-creation lever over both the short term and longer term. Rarely has a business issue been viewed as having such a broad scope of impact.
- There is mounting pressure from stakeholders—employees, customers, consumers, supply chain partners, competitors, investors, lenders, insurers, nongovernmental organizations, media, the government, and society overall—to act.
- The solutions to the challenges of sustainability are interdisciplinary, making effective collaboration with stakeholders particularly critical.
- Decisions regarding sustainability have to be made against a backdrop of high uncertainty. Myriad factors muddy the waters because of their unknown timing and magnitude of impact. Such factors include government legislation, demands by customers and employees, and geopolitical events.

These principles make sustainability a uniquely challenging issue for business leaders to manage and address effectively.

Three major barriers impede decisive corporate action. There are many reasons why companies are struggling to tackle sustainability more decisively. But our research points to three root causes. First, companies often lack the right information upon which to base decisions. Second, companies struggle to define the business case for value creation. Third, when companies do act, their execution is often flawed.

Some companies don't understand what sustainability is—and what it really means to the enterprise. Our survey revealed a pervasive lack of understanding among business leaders of what sustainability really means to a company. This shortcoming results from several underlying information gaps.

- Managers lack a common fact base about the full suite of drivers and issues that are relevant to their companies and industries. More than half of those surveyed stated a need for better frameworks for understanding sustainability.

WHAT ARE THE BENEFITS OF ACTION?
Survey respondents cite the impact on a company's image and brand as the paramount benefit of addressing sustainability. But thought leaders differed — emphasizing instead a broad continuum of rewards grounded in value creation.

What are the greatest benefits to your organization in addressing sustainability issues?

Improved company or brand image
Cost savings
Competitive advantage
Employee satisfaction, morale or retention
Product, service or market innovation
Business model or process innovation
New sources of revenue or cash flow
Effective risk management
Enhanced stakeholder relations
Other

0   10%   20%   30%
Percentage of respondents

- As mentioned earlier, companies do not share a common definition or language for discussing sustainability—some define it very narrowly, some more broadly, others lack any corporate definition.
- The goal or "prize" of concerted action is often defined too loosely and not collectively understood within the organization. And there's often no understanding of how to measure progress once actions are undertaken.

All of these issues point to a critical need for a thorough and structured gathering and sharing of basic facts about sustainability as a first step toward helping managers to be more decisive in the choices they face.

Some companies have difficulty modeling the business case—or even finding a compelling case—for sustainability. Most survey respondents who considered themselves experts in sustainability, as well as most thought leaders, said that their company had found a compelling business case—one that reflected multiple tangible and intangible costs and benefits—for sustainability. (See "How Sustainability Affects Value Creation" for a summary of sustainability's potential impact when viewed through the lens of shareholder value creation.)

The majority of survey respondents, however, disagreed: Almost 70% of overall respondents said that their company did not have a strong business case for sustainability. Of these, 22% claimed that the lack of a business case presented their company with its primary barrier to pursuing sustainability initiatives.

Why do companies struggle in their efforts to develop the business case for sustainability? Our survey uncovered three main challenges that trip up companies. The first challenge is *forecasting and planning beyond the one-to-five-year time horizon typical of most investment frameworks.* It is easy to assert that sustainability is about taking a long-term view. But in practice, calculating the costs and benefits of sustainability investments over time frames that sometimes span generations can be difficult with traditional economic approaches. This is further exacerbated by the short-term performance expectations of investors and analysts. See the Business of Sustainability report on sloanreview.mit.edu/busofsustainability for a framework to provide a starting point for assessing the potential of short- and long-term moves in sustainability to create value.

HOW SUSTAINABILITY AFFECTS VALUE CREATION
Most survey respondents who considered themselves experts in sustainability, as well as most thought leaders, say their companies have found a compelling business case for sustainability-related investments — one reflecting multiple tangible and intangible costs and benefits.

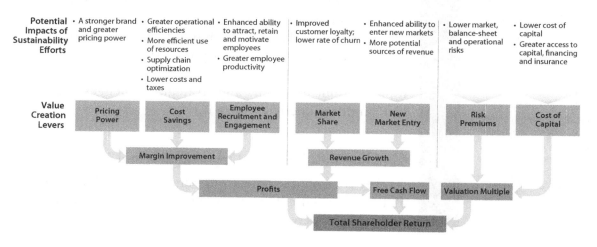

KEY DRIVERS

According to survey respondents, the biggest drivers of corporate sustainability investments — that is, the forces that are having the greatest impact on companies — are government legislation, consumer concerns and employee interest in sustainability.

- Government legislation was cited as the principal driver by nearly all the industries — except agriculture, mining and water companies, which cited environmental pollution as the issue having the greatest impact on their companies, and companies in the media and entertainment and the technology and telecommunications industries, which cited global political security.

- Consumer concerns were viewed as more critical among companies based outside of the United States and Europe.

NEED FOR NEW CAPABILITIES

Interviewees expect sustainability to become increasingly important to business strategy and management over time, and argue the risks of failing to act are growing.

- Companies will need to develop new capabilities and characteristics, including: the ability to operate on a systemwide basis and collaborate across conventional internal and external boundaries; a culture that rewards and encourages long-term thinking; capabilities in the areas of activity measurement, process redesign and financial modeling and reporting; and skills in engaging and communicating with external stakeholders.

The second challenge is *gauging the system-wide effects of sustainability investments.* Companies find it difficult enough to identify, measure, and control all of the tangible facets of their business systems. So they often do not even attempt to model intangibles or externalities such as the environmental and societal costs and benefits of their current business activities and potential moves in sustainability. This hinders their ability to get a true sense of the value of investments in sustainability.

The third major challenge is *planning amid high uncertainty.* Factors contributing to uncertainty include potential changes in regulation and customer preferences. Strategic planning, as traditionally practiced, is deductive—companies draw on a series of standard gauges to predict where the market is heading and then design and execute strategies on the basis of those calculations. But sustainability drivers are anything but predictable, potentially requiring companies to adopt entirely new concepts and frameworks.

Many thought leaders and survey respondents with experience in sustainability believe that clarifying the business case for sustainability may be the single most effective way to accelerate decisive corporate action, since it gets to the heart of how companies decide where they will—and will not—allocate their resources and efforts.

Execution is often flawed. Even if companies surmount the first two hurdles impeding action, they often stumble over the third hurdle: execution. While it is still early days in terms of judging the effectiveness of execution in sustainability, our interviews and survey highlighted three main obstacles in executing sustainability initiatives. The first is overcoming skepticism in organizations. Indeed, survey respondents overall cited outdated mental models and perspectives as the top internal roadblock to addressing sustainability issues.

The second obstacle in execution is figuring out how to institutionalize the sustainability agenda throughout the corporation.

The third major obstacle cited is measuring, tracking, and reporting sustainability efforts.

Some of these barriers, it should be noted, will accompany any major change effort in corporate strategy and operations. But they are intensified in the case of sustainability, given the topic's unique economic and strategic challenges and companies' limited experience with it.

Looking Ahead: Seizing Opportunities and Mitigating Risks

As they confront the barriers to pursuing and achieving sustainability, many—if not most—business managers are struggling to understand where their companies are, where they need to go, and how to get there. They do, however, share a consensus view that sustainability will have an increasingly large impact on the business landscape going forward. Thought leaders and executives who self-identify as experienced with sustainability issues point out the following emerging realities:

SUSTAINABILITY SURVIVING THE DOWNTURN
Fewer than one-fourth of those surveyed say their companies have cut sustainability commitments during the downturn. Thought leaders say focus on it has intensified.

- Prices for food, water, energy, and other resources are growing increasingly volatile. Companies that have optimized their sustainability profile and practices will be less exposed to these swings—and more resilient.
- Stakeholders—including consumers, customers, shareholders, and the government—are paying more attention to sustainability and putting pressure on companies to act.
- Governments' agendas increasingly advocate for sustainability. Companies that are proactively pursuing this goal will be less vulnerable to regulatory changes.
- Capital markets are paying more attention to sustainability and are using it as a gauge to evaluate companies and make investment decisions.
- First movers are likely to gain a commanding lead; it may be increasingly difficult for competitors to catch up.

The experiences of executives already wrestling with sustainability-driven business issues suggest that companies need not make large, immediate investments in new programs. The findings reveal instead that what is essential is that companies start to think more broadly and proactively about sustainability's potential impact on their business and industry—and begin to plan and act.

About the Authors

Maurice Berns is a partner and managing director in the London office of The Boston Consulting Group. **Andrew Townend** is a principal in the firm's Dallas office. **Zayna Khayat** is a principal in BCG's Toronto office. **Balu Balagopal** is a senior partner and managing director in the firm's Houston office. **Martin Reeves** is a senior partner and managing director in BCG's New York office. **Michael S. Hopkins** is the editor in chief of *MIT Sloan Management Review*. **Nina Kruschwitz** is the sustainability editor. Comment on this article or contact the authors at smrfeedback@mit.edu.

References

1. The Sustainability Initiative research project, and the articles and reports that it yields, is a collaboration between the *MIT Sloan Management Review* and its knowledge partner, The Boston Consulting Group, Inc., with additional support from initiative sponsor SAS Institute, Inc. For a complete guide to the project, go to its dedicated *MIT Sloan Management Review* Web page: sloanreview.mit.edu/busofsustainability.

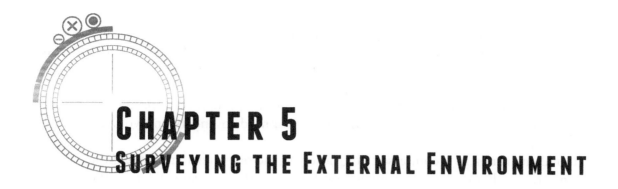

Chapter 5
Surveying the External Environment

Good anticipation is the result of good strategic exploration.[1]

—*Joel Barker*

Opening Vignette

According to *The Wall Street Journal*, it's a "miracle" that US airlines are still in business. Domestic airfares have fallen 21% (in inflation-adjusted dollars) since 1995. The industry is subject to a wide range of external forces, i.e., factors beyond its control that have an impact on its ability to operate. The commercial carrier industry is very competitive, giving customers the power to switch. It is also a labor-intensive industry, so employees are also a strong factor. New entrants, termed "ultra low cost" airlines, such as Spirit Airlines, Inc., sell tickets for almost nothing, basing their business model on fees for seat assignments and baggage. Substitutes such as driving or taking high-speed rail are also competition in certain markets.

Airlines are subject to "external shocks, including terrorism, oil-price spikes, waning consumer confidence and high taxes." Buying more fuel-efficient planes is one strategy some are pursuing; others are cutting costs, reducing seat availability to charge higher fares for remaining seats, and charging extra fees for services such as baggage checking and meals. Not only should airlines survey their external environment, they must continually make adjustments to their business model and strategies in order to remain viable and attract investors.

---

[1] Barker, op. cit.

Based on an article by Susan Carey, reported on October 5, 2011, in *The Wall Street Journal*. Accessed November 4, 2011, at http:online.wsj.com.

Stockholders and stakeholders are important factors in the context of an organization. It is important to be intentional in how the organization holds itself accountable to them. However, it is also vitally important to understand the environmental factors that are largely beyond the organization's control. A ship's captain wants to understand the currents and conditions under which he is sailing; a pilot needs to know the topography and meteorological conditions into which she is flying. In the same way, you need to understand your company's external environment.

The external environment is comprised of a variety of factors—most are beyond the control of the organization—that can have an impact on how well the company achieves the desired results, its vision. *Scanning* the environment is crucial to identify the factors that will impact success. As we scan the external environment, you will see that successful mastery of this material will enable you to:

- understand paradigms and how to leverage them
- employ a variety of paradigms to examine the external environment
- identify those environmental factors that have the most impact on an organization's strategy
- analyze trends to identify potential opportunities and threats

INTRODUCTION

The general environment really represents society at large. What is going on in the world around you that could affect your organization's ability to execute its strategy and achieve the desired results? Do you see opportunities, or do you see threats?

To begin your *scanning* of the environment, it is helpful to understand the power of paradigms. A paradigm is a mental model. Very often, a paradigm is a lens through which we interpret what our senses perceive. We also have to be careful not to be limited by our paradigms.

On a personal level, our paradigms often determine what we should or should not do. For example, he should avoid processed sugars and carbohydrates (paradigm: "white" foods cause obesity). She should avoid credit card debt (paradigm: financial security comes from living within one's means).

Paradigms can change over time. The change may arise from political, legal, technological, economic, or social trends. An example is the role women "should" play in the workforce. The paradigm shift may also occur as new knowledge debunks the previous paradigm, such as when smoking cigarettes was deemed sexy until it was determined that smoking causes cancer.

Paradigms also vary across cultures. The norms of behavior can be very different, as any international traveler can see. The way you dress for a business meeting in Texas is likely to be very different than how you would dress for a business meeting in Milan. The difference between when a meeting is scheduled and when it starts is important in Germany but insignificant in Spain.

Being aware of paradigms is advantageous in environmental scanning. Being able to shift paradigms and use multiple lenses to understand the environment is even more so. These practices alert one to critical conditions that may mean you need to change course.

Doing so also reminds one that there can be more than one way to interpret a situation, e.g., an opportunity or a threat. Think of shifting paradigms like changing a pair of glasses; if you wore the glasses of your competitor, what would you see? Your customer? Your supplier?

Illustration

For centuries, since the development of the printing press, most written information has been conveyed through paper books. With the merging of technologies, books are now available electronically in a 24/7 world, with instantaneous access not limited by time or place. Those book publishers and sellers who saw this immediately included in their offerings the ability for customers to purchase books electronically and then to read them on a device that overcomes the limitations of the computer screen but offers the benefits of accessibility. Examples of these *e-readers* include Amazon's Kindle and Barnes and Noble's

Figure 5-1. Example of several e-readers

Nook. Other companies, such as Borders, have suffered dire consequences for their inability to "shift" their paradigm.

LEVERAGING PARADIGMS

Paradigms are most useful when you are trying to anticipate the future. In particular, being able to identify paradigm shifts can identify profound market opportunities. Note that a paradigm shift is not a trend per se, but represents an entirely different trajectory into the future.

For example, the aging of the population in the United States is a trend. People are living longer, with better healthcare, safer working conditions, and more comfortable lifestyles. This trend has been anticipated since the arrival of the "baby boom." We have seen the development of senior communities, progressive care retirement homes, and a wide array of dietary supplements targeted for the older adult market (which is no longer considered "elderly").

The paradigm shift comes when you think about the careers of this generation, and the ones to follow. Mandatory retirement is generally no longer mandatory. The Internal Revenue Service (IRS 2011) allows for individuals to withdraw from their retirement accounts at 59 and a half years old, and requires that they do so at 70 and a half. The typical age of eligibility for Medicare health insurance is 65, according to the Social Security Administration (SSA 2011). This seems to imply that people will retire in their 60s. Yet they are living another 20 years or more. Whether it is out of boredom, from a desire to maintain mental acuity, or an economic need due to diminished retirement savings, people are going back to work. These "twilight" careers represent a paradigm shift.

How might you leverage this shift? You might restructure your workforce to include the availability of part-time, educated, highly skilled workers. You could start an employment agency that caters to and places these workers in short term assignments. You may even develop a product or financial service that targets this segment of the population. These are just a few examples.

Futurist Joel Barker (1996, pp. 21–23) asserts, "We have been living in a time when fundamental rules, the basic ways we do things, have been altered dramatically. That is what was right and appropriate in the early 1960s is now, in many cases, *wrong*." He continues with a long list of such paradigm shifts, such as the vast amount of data exchanged via computers worldwide, deregulation, terrorism, cellular phones, "safe" sex, and the number of people getting regular aerobic exercise every day.

Illustration

Part urban legend and part truth, one of the top executives of Sony Corporation was credited with the idea for a personal music player after visiting the United States and seeing people carry around large sound systems, referred to as "ghetto blasters." According to www.who-invented-it.net, the first Walkman® was created for the personal use of the company's co-chairman, a portable music player that he could use to listen to classical songs during his trips. Because of the efficiency and high quality performance of the product, Sony decided to introduce the music player to the public. The first batch of Sony Walkmans was released in Japan in 1979.

EMPLOYING PARADIGMS

In strategic management, paradigms are helpful frameworks by which to scan the external environment of the organization. There are many, but for our purposes here we will go into detail on two frameworks: one that focuses on key factors in the general environment and one that focuses specifically on industry-based factors.

General Economic Factors

The PESTEL framework can help you to systematically examine the general environment. PESTEL stands for Political, Economic, Social, Technological, Ecological, and Legal factors. The framework is an extension of earlier versions of the PEST, or STEP, model, which did not cover the ecological or legal factors, the last two factors. Let's examine each factor individually.

Political. The political environment represents the government structure, stability, and foreign policies that pertain to the organization. If operating in multiple countries, the political system

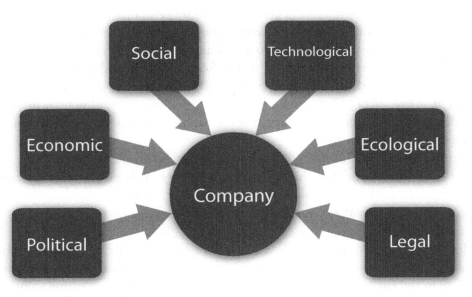

Figure 5-2. PESTEL framework

of each country should be considered. Social unrest, political strife, opposing groups, and the government's policy toward foreign firm investment can also be considerations. For example, with the 2011 "Arab Spring" and ensuing unrest in the Middle East, the price of crude oil has increased dramatically based on speculation of an interruption in the supply. Not only has this raised the price of fuel for consumers, it has raised transportation costs for companies and direct material costs for petroleum-based products (such as nylon rope and insect repellant).[2] Another example is the rush to purchase handguns in the time period before President Obama was inaugurated, with the expectation of stronger gun control under a Democratic administration (Johnson 2008).

Economic. Exchange rates, monetary policy, and taxation systems can have a significant impact on how an organization can operate. For example, Fallows (2010) asserts that:

> the Chinese government's insistence on holding the RMB's value steady against the dollar—rather than letting it rise, as it naturally would because of China's huge trade surpluses—has become pernicious and destructive for the world economy. … During a worldwide economic slowdown like the one of the past two years, the immediate problem is a failure of demand. There is too much productive capacity, relative to private and public purchases. Thus factories—and, more important, workers—stand idle. The point is elementary, and is the reason governments around the world, from China to Britain to the US, have been pumping new "stimulus" (demand) into their economies. But it also means that anything one government does to depress demand—or to shift some other nation's demand to its own factories—has a beggar-thy-neighbor effect and slows down recovery world wide.

Another significant macro-economic factor is the increasing number of regional trade agreements. They are particularly relevant to location and outsourcing decisions. For example, *maquiladoras* (manufacturing plants in Mexico that typically import US inputs, process them, and ship them back to the United States) have increased significantly, arguably as a result of the North American Free Trade Agreement (NAFTA) (Gruben and Kiser 2001).

On a micro-economic level, per capita income, unemployment rates, and wage, salary, and compensation levels also affect firms' demand levels, cost structure, and employment decisions. Sales of consumer goods and restaurant meals decrease as per capita income decreases and/or unemployment increases.

Social. Demographic trends, cultural considerations, literacy levels, social infrastructure, consumer confidence, and religious beliefs are external factors that are beyond the firm's control, but can fundamentally affect its operation. As we will discuss in a later chapter, the effect of this aspect of the environment is even more profound when crossing international borders. Domestically, in the United States, our traditional melting pot of immigrants is increasingly Hispanic. El Nasser (2003) reported that Hispanics are the largest minority group, and the fastest growing part of the population. The ripple effect of this demographic shift is still being felt, whether it is how to reach the Hispanic demographic in a marketing plan, where to find bilingual employees, or if an English-only workplace rule is appropriate.

---

[2] See http://www.ranken-energy.com/Products%20from%20Petroleum.htm for a partial—but extensive—list of petroleum-based products.

Technological. Entire books have been written about the impact of technology on governments, businesses, and individuals. The amount of business transacted electronically is staggering. The pace of technological change is accelerating, as is the volume of information available. Social media, i.e., Internet sites with user-created content, have exacerbated the acceleration. They have also provided new opportunities for businesses to recruit employees, identify prospects, engage customers, share information, and solve problems (Shih 2009). The expansion of e-commerce illustrates the impact on business.

Ecological. Climate and weather may be an important consideration, especially for companies with supply chains that start with agriculture. Flooded fields or a hard freeze could ruin a crop's harvest and disrupt the supply chain. Protected habitats, endangered species, and local regulations may constrain an organization's operation because of wastewater disposal, toxic emissions, or non-renewable extraction. An increasing issue is a company's concern for the environment and ecological sustainability.

Legal. Regulations, property rights, and liability concerns must be an ongoing concern for businesses. Mistakes in the legal environment can be quite costly. Witness the Enron debacle and the implosion of Arthur Andersen, a long-respected accounting and auditing firm. As a result of Enron's poor strategic decisions and short-sightedness, there are now another series of regulations requiring companies to attest to the validity of their financial statements to protect their shareholders and which require considerations as companies decide how to comply with these regulatory requirements.

Industry Factors

Another paradigm that is useful for examining the environment is the industry in which a firm or organization operates. This directly determines the firm's immediate competitive environment. An approach to scanning industry factors for the firm is known as the Five Forces model, developed by Harvard Professor Michael Porter and illustrated in Figure 5-3. This model looks at the immediate competitors, potential new entrants, and substitutes, as well as the powers of the suppliers and customers, in examining a company's immediate environment. The powers of these forces are then evaluated as to their strength and the concern with inclusion into the strategic plan. The more powerful a force, the more the strategic plan must accommodate or shift the strategy to overcome or mitigate the force.

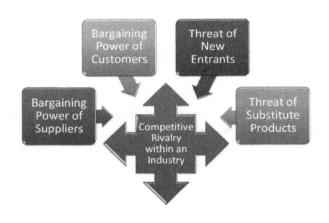

Figure 5-3. Porter's Five Forces Model

ANALYZING TRENDS

Of course it is necessary to understand the *current* external environment. The *future* environment is perhaps more important to a company's ability to achieve its desired results and achieve its vision. Therefore, your understanding of external factors should lead to analysis of future trends and possible scenarios.

In some cases, it is enough to use mathematical models such as regression analysis to predict a trend's progression. To consider alternate futures, you might use a decision tree with branches to different expected values. While decision trees are helpful in decisions such as, "should I expand capacity," and evaluating the probability of demand increases, the future environment is generally more complex. When the data is not available, more subjective techniques may be required, such as Delphi studies, where experts and other professionals offer their perspectives based on their professional expertise.

APPLICATION AND REFLECTION

- Continuing with the example of You, Inc., analyze the competitive job market.

- Select three companies or organizations and identify environmental forces that have required them to change their strategy.

- In your own life, discuss three external events that have required you to rethink your assumptions and change your decisions.

CLOSING CASE

To reinforce the concepts you need to understand the organization in context, consider the challenges a local library faces. After reading the following article, respond to the following:

1. What governance does a community library need?
2. Who are its stakeholders?
3. What social responsibilities does it have?
4. Will being "rebooted" assure its sustainability? Why or why not?
5. Evaluate the environmental impact of a community library.
6. Using Porter's Five Forces, evaluate the competitive environment for the community library.
7. Using the PESTEL model, evaluate the general environment for the community library.

Given your analysis above, which of the seven imperatives suggested are most important? Are there other actions you would recommend?

THE LIBRARY REBOOTED

Scott Corwin, Elisabeth Hartley, and Harry Hawkes

Up until a decade ago, the community library was the go-to place for the sixth grader writing a report on a political election or the parent helping her child investigate college options. There was no better source for that information. Research libraries served a similar function for scholars needing access to rare documents, authors looking into remote corners of history, and lawyers seeking precedent. Again, no place was like the library.

The Internet has supplanted that core function of the library's purpose by giving users access to much of the world's information in roughly the time it takes them to start their computers and make a cup of coffee. In the era of the instantaneous Google search, information research and retrieval are irrevocably changed. And Google itself has, to all appearances, stepped into the library business directly with a massive project in which it intends to digitize all of the world's books.

How to stay relevant? That question has been gnawing at library administrators and boards for years, as more and more information makes its way to the Web. And the question has become especially pressing amid a global economic downturn that is reducing libraries' funding at the very moment when they would like to experiment and stake out new ground in the digital future. In this respect, library administrators are a lot like executives at newspaper companies, magazine publishers, movie studios, and major music labels—indeed, any business that markets something that can be delivered digitally. They must break out and offer something new and different at the same time that their investment capital is shrinking.

And yet even as the Internet encroaches on their turf, one seldom sees signs of lifelessness or decline at libraries. To be sure, some research libraries that have done little to stay current have lost visitors and are fading. But all over the world, from the East End of London to malls in Singapore to just about every part of New York City, libraries are serving hundreds of thousands of visitors each year, bustling with activity, and increasing the number of items they loan out. Their vitality is unmistakable. Libraries, it's clear, retain at least some control over their future—and the changes they are making may be instructive to information organizations throughout the private and public sectors. Those changes include overhauling operating models that in some cases are decades old, and launching new digital initiatives to meet users' needs.

THE COMMUNITY LIBRARY'S RELEVANCE

Like many for-profit industries, the library business isn't monolithic. Libraries exist in two fundamental forms. There are the public, or community, libraries, usually funded by local city and state taxes and charged with a civic mission. They provide a place for young children to learn, for students to socialize and study, for job applicants to gather information, for immigrants to learn their adopted country's language, for seniors to read the newspaper, and for any cardholder to borrow books, music, or videos. The good ones are run by entrepreneurial librarians who understand the needs of the community and actively seek to meet them. Second, there are the research libraries, like the U.S. Library of Congress, the British Library, and university libraries that serve as repositories for unique or important documents that never leave the building, and that are used primarily by scholars, authors, and graduate students with serious academic and research needs.

Not surprisingly, it is the community library that is finding it easier to demonstrate its relevance in the age of the Internet. To see why, one need look no further than the Bronx Library Center, a three-year-old branch of the New York Public Library (NYPL).

Near the entrance are shelves holding DVDs and CDs. Shopping baskets—the kind you'd pick up at the entrance of a supermarket—are stacked on the floor, inviting visitors to carry multiple items. A back wall displays the library's collection of illustrated novels—the full-length adult comic books that have recently become popular with younger readers. A sign with scrolling red type above the checkout desk advises patrons of the live performances that will be taking place over the next few weeks in the downstairs auditorium; today it features a show by the Thunderbird American Indian Dancers, a cultural preservation group. Inside the auditorium, powwow drums thump out their rhythms; most of the 150 seats are filled.

On the library's four main floors, the stacks of books have been placed at each end, leaving ample space in the middle for tables that have computers on them, many with broadband access to the Internet. The people using the computers are young and aren't necessarily using them for academic purposes—there is one doing a Google search on Hannah Montana pictures, there is one updating his Facebook page, and over there a few children are playing video games, including The Fight for Glorton. Librarians answer questions and organize online gaming tournaments, and none of them are shushing anyone. The place is packed with people, most of them under the age of 18. They have been drawn by an environment that seems more reminiscent of a community center, Internet cafe, or bookstore than a library. An observer might quarrel with the library's de-emphasis of books, but he or she would be wrong to assume no learning is going on here. Kids are reading, exploring, and acquiring knowledge. They're just not doing it the old-fashioned way.

Clearly, what this branch of the New York Public Library is doing is redefining the business it is in. The Bronx Library Center is no longer just in the book-lending business; rather, it is in the gaming business or the entertainment business or maybe the information connectivity business. And yet, these "loss leaders" (the language of retailing seems appropriate) allow the library to also offer services that are consistent with its civic mission. The high school junior can find SAT and ACT test books. At the career and education center, visitors can learn to write a resume or cover letter, find out about scholarships, or get help applying to college. And the library's overwhelmingly young audience *does* take out books, as well as CDs and DVDs—four times the number of these items borrowed at the average NYPL branch.

The NYPL isn't alone in following this approach to maintaining relevance in its branches. Library systems in Los Angeles, Singapore, and Alexandria, Egypt, among others, have likewise added youth centers to drive foot traffic. The Toronto Public Library encourages teens to drop in for online games and music videos on Friday afternoons. The Stanford University library has created an online identity in Second Life, the online virtual world, allowing users to explore the library in this popular new medium. The Idea Stores, which the London borough of Tower Hamlets is building in some of its most densely populated neighborhoods, provide Internet access in a country where only about 42% of the population has Internet access at home.

Community libraries might offer a similar benefit in nations such as Italy, Greece, and Turkey, where adult literacy rates are high (99, 98, and 88%, respectively) but the vast majority of homes do not have Internet access. In all countries, Internet-connected computers at community libraries offer a bridge across the digital divide to immigrants and those on the lower rungs of the economic ladder. In a more abstract sense, community libraries also embody a civic virtue, since they remind us of what it means to live in a society that is enlightened and progressive and that values the intellectual enrichment of its citizens. This is good for the users of the libraries, good for the libraries' communities, and—ultimately—good for the taxpayers who fund the libraries.

THE RESEARCH LIBRARY'S DIGITAL CHALLENGE

It is at the research library that we run smack up against the power and ubiquity of the Internet, and where the question of future relevance becomes harder to answer. Why would you go to a research library if you can find what you need faster and more efficiently online? The answer is you wouldn't, and this explains why, globally, visits to research libraries have been declining dramatically. The decline may become even more precipitous as Google gets deeper into its Google Books Library Project; for this multiyear effort, the search giant has been scanning tens of millions of books and has already secured the cooperation of about two dozen richly endowed library systems, including Harvard's, Princeton's, and Columbia's.

By turning over substantial parts of their collections to Google, aren't libraries contributing to their own obsolescence? That risk is always there, but the libraries' hands are tied. Most of them barely have the funds to preserve and expand their physical collections—and a comprehensive digitization initiative, at a cost of roughly $15 to $25 a book (in USD), would cost some of these institutions $1 billion or more. There's no getting around the fact that in working with Google, the libraries are taking the same kind of chance newspapers have taken in making their content free on the Internet—the risk that fewer and fewer people will feel the need to hold the physical object in their hands.

Research librarians need to accept that people will no longer come to them for certain things now that the information is available online, but they also need to think about the role-expanding possibilities that the Internet affords them. Where research librarians were once primarily in the business of being collectors and curators, and of providing one-on-one research assistance to those seeking it, they now have an opportunity to share their expertise and collections with a much wider audience. Digitizing the best parts of what's in the vault and making a virtual exhibit out of it. Bringing related collections from other research libraries under one digital roof.

Helping to actively build a virtual community of scholars and shaping the research agenda. The research-librarian-cum-blogger. It's time to try new things. The alternative is having no digital strategy to speak of at a time when research is overwhelmingly moving online.

The issue of copyright has already slowed Google's efforts to create a universal online library. Many of the most valuable rare materials that libraries possess, and that researchers would be interested in—early versions of a manuscript that would go on to become a literary classic, for instance, or the correspondence between world leaders during a time of crisis—are protected by U.S. copyright laws, which cover written materials from 1923 onward. A library acting as the guardian of such materials couldn't turn them over to Google even if it wanted to. Complicating matters further, many libraries have rights to use and share physical documents but don't have intellectual property rights to digitize or create a digital representation of them, since agreements to manage many of these collections predate the Internet.

Google is, of course, aware of the copyright issues, which it spent two years negotiating with the Authors Guild and the Association of American Publishers. And it went a long way toward settling the matter in October 2008, when it agreed to pay $125 million to compensate authors and publishers and to set up a registry to guarantee copyright holders payment for the use of their materials. As a result of the settlement, the vast majority of rights holders are likely to let Google post the full content of their books online. That may prompt research libraries to opt to not digitize some of their most valuable collections, to preserve exclusivity through physical possession—a move that may help them in the short run but that could cause disaffection among researchers in the long run.

As they struggle with their shrinking domain in a digital era, the best research libraries aren't standing idly by. The NYPL is re-creating its landmark Fifth Avenue research library by moving much of the storage of its vaunted research collection underground, beneath the adjacent Bryant Park, and devoting the freed-up space to a lending library and areas for children, teens, and seniors. The library is also narrowing its research focus and selectively digitizing some parts of its collections, while looking for ways to get users to interact with those digital collections. Prioritization and selective digitization are going to become important capabilities at all research libraries in the future. Indeed, such libraries may want to consider commercial enterprises' approaches in this regard, even to the point of selling off or exchanging "nonstrategic" parts of their collections in arrangements with other libraries.

But can research libraries really make their treasures (often created with quill pens on parchment) come alive online? The United Kingdom's biggest library provides an exuberant answer to that question. Under Chief Executive Lynne Brindley, the British Library has created digital exhibits of some materials complete with a curator's narration. The project amounts to a guided Web tour of some of the most prized parts of the library's collections, and one could argue it provides a more compelling experience than seeing the physical pieces under glass. An online visitor can use the library's Turning the Pages software to view the original manuscript of Lewis Carroll's *Alice's Adventures in Wonderland,* browse through Leonardo da Vinci's notebooks, or see some of the notations that Mozart made in December 1784 as he worked out parts of a piano concerto. (A link allows the visitor to listen to the passage being played on a piano.) These are examples of repurposing content using an engaging interactive experience, as a television network might do by putting snippets of its shows online or a movie studio might do by posting outtakes or behind-the-scenes features.

These approaches partially address the question of how to maintain relevance. None of them, it must be said, provide a full answer. However, together they offer insights into the steps libraries are taking as they seek to ensure their value at a time when the Internet has reset user expectations.

SEVEN IMPERATIVES FOR LIBRARY LEADERSHIP

The challenge of relevance is leading libraries away from a conventional mind-set toward one that is analytical and pragmatic about opportunities, yet open to transformation and effective at implementing new strategies. In a sense, what library executives need to do is not that different from what their business-world peers are doing in media industries threatened by the Internet, and it is just as important to survival and continued service. Following are seven imperatives that we have identified through our work with leading libraries around the world—including assisting the NYPL in designing its new strategic plan.

1. Rethink the operating model.

Many of the old assumptions about running a library—that the measure of a library's quality is the size of its book collection, that there's value in keeping even infrequently loaned books on the shelves, that library staffing decisions shouldn't be questioned—are outmoded and need to be set aside. This is not to say that libraries will be able to recreate themselves as purely digital, service-oriented organizations; that would be a lot to ask of an institution that got its start some 5,000 years ago, with business records and hymns engraved in clay tablets in ancient cities. But many libraries today, operating in paper and film, haven't changed some of their operating practices since World War II. Their role as the preservers of recorded history means they have to spend a lot of their resources just maintaining the assets they already have.

Still, they can and should try many other things. Libraries may not have the budget to put their entire book collections online—but they should focus on building and enhancing those collections where they have unique strengths that can be leveraged. They should also explore new ways of serving users more conveniently, effectively, and efficiently. Perhaps they can create an online reservation system that patrons can use for a small fee if they want to have a book waiting for them at the front desk when they arrive. Libraries may not have the budget to add a collection of foreign films on DVD, but perhaps they can "find" the money in their budget by eliminating acquisitions of the kinds of books that experience shows have rarely left the shelves. Libraries may be under political pressure to keep all branches open, but they must at least tailor their staffing approaches at these branches to make more efficient use of their resources.

One library we worked with was able to stay open for two hours more per day simply by altering workers' shifts, rethinking services, and changing library layouts. Such analytically enabled improvements are necessary as libraries come under increasing budgetary pressure.

2. Understand and respond to user needs.

Libraries have only the most general information about their users—how many of them there are, what they do when they are at the library, and what they borrow. We don't blame libraries for not wanting to put themselves in the position of having to provide information to government authorities about their users' reading habits and other activities. In the United States, for example, library administrators are right to be concerned about some provisions of legislation enacted after the terrorist attacks of September 11, 2001.

However, the solution most libraries have settled on—namely, to avoid gathering any detailed information about users' needs and activities—is far too timid. Libraries should develop advanced capabilities to build aggregated profiles of users, or what retailers call customer segmentation analysis. Who is visiting the library and how often are they coming? What are they doing once they get there? Which books do they borrow most often? Which books never leave the shelves? Which services get used most often; which least? Merchandisers and retailers have tools to help them answer these kinds of questions. Libraries, too, should adapt or create these and similar tools.

3. Embrace the concept of continuous innovation.

This is not the time for libraries to shy away from new strategies. Library executives need to do more than innovate, however. They need to approach the innovation challenge with an entrepreneurial mind-set: test, measure, refine. And if something does not work, they must go through the process again: test, measure, and refine using new ideas and concepts.

The innovation doesn't have to be of any one type; it can happen across the whole library value chain. For instance, changes might be operational—like the Toronto Library's use of radio frequency identification (RFID) readers to bring a measure of self-service to the checkout function, or the Seattle Public Library's creation of a conveyor-belt book sorter to reduce handling time. Changes might be atmospheric, such as the background music the Seattle Library now pipes into its domed young-adult sections. Finally, there might be changes in format, including the opening of smaller library "outlets" in what is essentially a variation on a theme already being practiced by retailers like Lowe's, Wal-Mart, and Tesco. Libraries should appropriate the many traffic-building enhancements that retailers are making to their stores.

4. Forge a digital identity.

As non-profit institutions, libraries have limited operating funds. In its 2007 fiscal year, for instance (before the crisis hit Wall Street), the NYPL had operating support of about $300 million; the British Library of about $220 million (£111 million). By our estimate, no more than one-fifth—and probably far less—of any library's funds are used to advance its digital initiatives. By contrast, Google, in its 2007 fiscal year, spent more than $2.1 billion on research and development alone.

Clearly, there is no way that libraries could transform themselves into leading-edge Internet organizations even if they wanted to. Nor should they aspire to that. A great many things are in flux, and a library that goes too far with a digitization initiative today runs the risk of creating data structures that will be incompatible with future standards. But some experimentation is in order. Should libraries let people reserve books remotely, from their home or office? Should they adopt a convenient delivery-to-home model, a la Netflix? Should they make their librarians available at all hours to respond to online inquiries? And to the extent that they do these things, should they (as part of rethinking their operating model) charge for some of these services, as the Toronto Library does with a fee-based custom research service? Finally, should libraries pursue these initiatives alone or in concert with one another?

5. Connect with stakeholders in ways pure Internet companies cannot.

What determines who wins in a fight between a bear and an alligator, as one saying goes, is the battleground—where the fight takes place. Libraries can't provide faster online data retrieval than a search engine, and that's not where they should try to compete. What they can do, on the community library side, is take advantage of their local strength, and, on the research library side, share their service-oriented expertise in new ways and through new channels.

In practice, this means that the leaders of community libraries should have an understanding of the institutions in their community so they know how to serve students, seniors, the poor, and those without Internet access. Community library leaders who get out and make connections in the community will successfully transform their institution into a fulcrum for many of the issues and concerns that touch local residents. Their programs, services, and offerings will all be better off as a result of this outreach and connectedness.

Research librarians must move beyond collecting and curating and become more adept at connecting with scholars. They should aspire to help build broader and more connected communities among the primary users of their collections. In this regard, they may want to take a page from newspapers' new playbooks, where staff are increasingly breaking out of standard news-reporting mode to contribute to blogs, produce online video segments, and answer questions in reader forums. This more personalized approach keeps news—which is already available from innumerable online aggregators—from becoming a commodity. Likewise, the research librarian who enters into an online dialogue with users offers something that will never be available directly from a search engine.

6. Expand the metrics.

As they refine their mission, libraries will also have to change how they measure success. Keeping track of the number of monthly and annual physical visitors will still matter, as will monitoring the number of books (and other offerings) in circulation. But online-specific metrics will have to be added, especially as libraries invest more resources in digital initiatives and put bigger parts of their collections online. And it will be important, no matter whether the asset is a physical or a digital one, for the measurements to move beyond the strictly countable (number of books on loan, number of page views, etc.) into attitudinal areas like level of engagement and customer satisfaction.

And at a time when budgets are tight and new operating models are being explored, libraries will have to introduce new metrics to measure staff performance. There may be some resistance to this, especially if the library's staff is conditioned to think of what it does as a government service that isn't in jeopardy, that could never *be* in jeopardy, and that doesn't operate in a changing "marketplace." But in the bigger context of changes, this resistance to measurement should be easy to surmount. Institutions that proactively measure performance, embrace change, and look for ways to serve users will have an easier time getting financial support in an era of reduced public resources and private donations.

7. Be courageous.

It's no wonder that the best library executives are feeling a sense of urgency these days, along with a little uneasiness. Their world has changed—a lot. The library's underlying promise hasn't changed; the library is still a way for us to break beyond the immediate boundaries of our world, to help our children become better educated, to foster literacy and self-improvement, and to make our societies more prosperous. But the environment in which libraries operate has certainly shifted, and the challenge for those running them is to figure out the evolutionary path they should follow. There is no one answer, which may provide an advantage to those with an appetite for intelligent risk taking. After all, nothing nowadays—nothing at all—is written in stone.

Robert Darnton. "The Library in the New Age." *New York Review of Books* (June 12, 2008). www.nybooks.com/articles/21514: Eight reasons libraries are more important than ever.

Anthony Grafton. "Future Reading." *New Yorker* (November 5, 2007). www.newyorker.com/reporting/2007/11/05/071105fa_fact_grafton: What digitization means for reading and the library.

Miguel Helft and Motoko Rich. "Google Settles Suit over Book- Scanning." *New York Times* (October 28, 2008). www.nytimes.com/2008/ 10/29/technology/internet/29google.html: The impact of Google's settlement with authors and publishers.

Robin Pogrebin. "A $100 Million Donation to the N.Y. Public Library." *New York Times* (March 11, 2008). www.nytimes.com/2008/03/11/arts/ design/11expa.html?scp=1&sq=Pogrebin%20schwarzman&st=cse: News story on the charitable gift by financier Stephen Schwarzman.

Jeffrey Toobin. "Google's Moon Shot." *New Yorker* (February 5, 2007). www.newyorker.com/reporting/2007/02/05/070205fa_fact_toobin: Google's ambitious plan to digitize all the world's books.

Google Books Library Project Web site, http://books.google.com/ googlebooks/library.html: Provides an explanation of how its digitized book site works.

For more business thought leadership, sign up for *s+b*'s RSS feeds at www.strategy-business.com/rss.

About the Authors

Scott Corwin (scott.corwin@booz.com) is a partner with Booz & Company based in New York, with extensive experience in developing enterprise transformation strategies for clients in the automotive, media, information, and consumer industries. Elisabeth Hartley (liz.hartley@booz.com) is a senior associate with Booz & Company in New York, with experience supporting clients in media, consumer, and nonprofit sectors to develop growth and organizational strategies. Harry Hawkes (harry.hawkes@booz.com), a partner with Booz & Company based in New York, leads the firm's operations work globally for media and entertainment clients and focuses primarily on performance improvement and business transformation.

Section III
Considering Strategic Options

At this point, you are nearly ready to begin considering your strategic options. Before navigating through the maze of possibilities, you want to make sure you are prepared with the right resources and capabilities.

SECTION III

CONSIDERING STRATEGIC OPTIONS

CHAPTER 6
ASSESSING THE ORGANIZATION'S CAPABILITIES

My goal has been to get Apple healthy enough so that if we do figure out the next big thing, we can seize the moment. … You have to rebuild some organizations, clean up others that don't make sense, and build up new engineering capabilities.[1]

—Steve Jobs, 2000

OPENING VIGNETTE

Ford Motor Company has executed quite a turnaround: a new product portfolio and a 180 degree change in corporate culture. So how does a long-established company reinvent itself, and how has its portfolio contributed to this revival?

The Ford Motor Company, founded by Henry Ford, told customers that "you can have any color of Ford as long as it is black"—so much for product portfolio and choice! It took generations of slow evolution for this company to produce a portfolio of products responsive to customer demands. In recent years, Ford reported substantial losses, but unlike its two Detroit rivals, has not declared bankruptcy nor accepted government funds to bail out the troubled automobile industry. Instead, the company renewed its emphasis on product portfolio development to better meet customer demands and environmental needs.

In addition to the Ford and Lincoln lines of automobiles, Ford now owns a stake in Mazda in Japan and Aston Martin in the United Kingdom. Ford's former Jaguar and Land Rover divisions were sold to Tata Motors of India. In addition, Ford sold Volvo and discontinued production of Mercury automobiles.[2]

Ford further moved to introduce a range of new vehicles, including crossover SUVs, and is developing the hybrid electric power train technologies for its Escape Hybrid SUV. Ford actually licensed Toyota hybrid technologies to avoid patent infringements and is now exploring

---

[1] Interview with Brent Schlender, reported in *Fortune's* January 24, 2000, issue.

[2] From an AOL posting. "Is Ford really going to cut its product lines?" http://autos.aol.com/article/ford-cut-product-line/

plug-in electric hybrids, the very technology it once discontinued to make market space for the traditional carbon based fueled automobiles. The need for these changes was driven by competition, primarily from higher quality, lower cost global competitors. By shedding divisions and redirecting product development, Ford is beginning to resemble Toyota, with the mass-market appeal that made Toyota, a global competitor, successful.

The new CEO of Ford strives to change the culture of Ford, to question the assumptions and the traditions of the past, and to admit mistakes. This has profoundly changed how Ford's capabilities are assessed. Named *Automobile Magazine's* 2010 Man of the Year, Alan Mulally has almost single-handedly saved the automaker.[3]

Before deciding what you *should* do to achieve the vision, you have to understand what you *can* do. Are there resources that you need to develop? Are there distractions holding you back? Can you create and/or sustain your competitive advantage?

When facing a competitor, a coach determines the game plan based on the strengths of the team in light of the playing conditions. A commander facing an armed conflict builds the combat strategy around the people and weapons available to fight in the expected battle conditions. A mayor needs to garner the resources provided by the citizens of the community to react to an emergency. Are you ready for the challenge? The competition?

Upon successful completion of this chapter you should be able to:

- explain why internal assessment is key to strategy development
- apply a portfolio view to a product set
- select among the different approaches to resource and capability assessment
- interpret financial measures with a strategic perspective

Once you have established your vision, including your governance practices and stakeholder relationships, you have surveyed the external environment, and you have conducted an internal assessment, you will be ready to begin your consideration of strategic options.

INTRODUCTION

Internal assessment is more than asking, "How are we doing?" It is a deliberate analytical process that is fundamental to strategic planning. If you do not understand your current state, you are unlikely to select the right strategy to achieve your vision or desired future state. Think about trying to give someone navigational directions:

"Hi! How do I get to the convention center for the exhibition?"
"Hi, mom. Where are you?"
"Well, I don't know. I'm lost—that's why I called you for directions!"

---

[3] 2010 Man of the Year: Alan Mulally, CEO Ford Motor Company. http://www.automobilemag.com/features/awards/1001_2010_man_of_the_year_alan_mulally_ceo_ford_motor_company/viewall.html#ixzz1ibEoR700

Your starting point strongly determines your strategic options. Internal assessment often identifies potential strategies to be considered. It might point to a product capability that could be improved, an underutilized asset that could be leveraged, a particular technology that could be acquired, or a vulnerability that should be mitigated.

There is also internal communication and development that makes this assessment so valuable. Undergoing the assessment exercise as a management team helps to create a shared understanding of the company's current state. Without this common view, it would be extremely difficult to gain consensus on priorities, strategic options, or next steps.

In the following segments, you will read about a variety of approaches to assess corporate capabilities. If you only use one type of assessment, you are likely to overlook important considerations.

PRODUCT PORTFOLIO EVALUATION

A *portfolio* is typically a collection viewed as a whole. Sometimes a portfolio is used to provide a "big picture" from individual components. For example, a commercial artist will bring several different examples of his work for an interview at an advertising agency. Other times, a portfolio concept is used to assess the diversity of its contents, such as when a financial advisor encourages her client to diversify his or her investments to reduce the overall investment risk.

In the same vein, companies should look at their products—goods and services—as a collective. There are several different ways to analyze a product portfolio; we will focus on three. One is based on life cycle, one is based on project risk, and one is based on future potential.

Life Cycle

A life cycle analysis considers where each product is in its product life cycle. Typically, the product life cycle is depicted as an S-curve, as shown in Figure 6-1. The early stages of the product are characterized by slow growth, low customization in production factors, and a propensity to change in response to market feedback. The next stage is the growth stage; a company may choose to invest in customized technology, e.g., manufacturing automation, to respond to the growth in demand. As the growth levels off, a product is considered to be in its maturity phase; the focus is on extending this phase for as long as possible. This might be accomplished by entering new markets, e.g., international ventures, or by developing minor modifications to the existing product to make it "new and improved." Once a product enters a decline phase or a stall, it is extremely difficult to recover (Christensen and Raynor 2003).

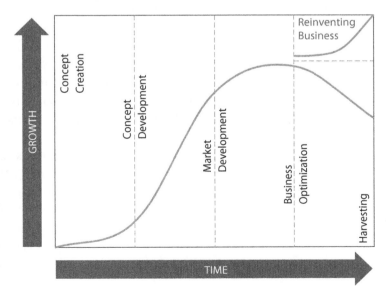

Figure 6-1. Product Life Cycle

Illustration

There are a number of examples of the impact of product life cycle on a company's strategy and market position. One of these is Sears & Roebuck. For over 50 years, Sears was the household word for catalog sales and family appliances. Due to changes in demographics and consumer trends, the company was unable to match the competition or adapt to changes in buying patterns, and it lost market position, especially in its central business, catalog sales. Replaced by emerging retailers using the big box store models, such as Wal-Mart, Costco, and the do-it-yourself home improvement retailers such as Home Depot and Lowe's, Sears lost its position in the emerging competitive landscape. Internally, Sears did not have the resources required to scan the competitive landscape and react quickly enough to fend off its competitors.

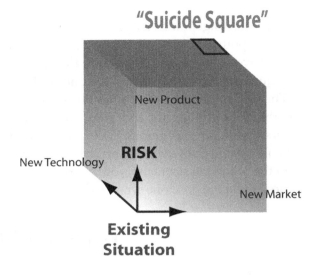

Figure 6-2. Suicide Square

Project Risk

The next type of portfolio development centers on project risk. How much change is being undertaken by the organization, specifically in the area of development projects? Steele (1989) describes a suicide square, where change is introduced in three dimensions: product, technology, and customer. This is illustrated in Figure 6-2. For example, a company might implement a completely new enterprise-wide system, such as customer relationship management (CRM). Perhaps the database technology underlying the application (i.e., product) is one that is new to the company. In addition, perhaps new departments and users (i.e., customers) are expected to use the system. This project is extremely risky and can be considered in the suicide square.[4]

In a similar vein, Wheelwright and Clark (2003) suggested using an aggregate project plan to evaluate risk. Specifically, considering all research and advanced development projects that are—or could be—in process, consider the amount of *process* change and the amount of *product* change being undertaken. Are you doing too many things at once? Are the key people focused on the right priorities? Can projects be sequenced so as to best utilize resources? The authors suggest that managers map the different types of development projects (pp. 2–4):

> *Derivative* projects range from cost-reduced versions of existing projects to enhancements to an existing production process (low change). *Breakthrough* projects establish core products and processes that differ fundamentally from previous generations (high change). *Platform* projects fall somewhere in between the derivative and breakthrough projects, perhaps an addition to a product family, or a significant change to an existing process (medium change). The remaining two types of projects are "research and

---

[4] Since it is a three-dimensional model, it should really be a suicide "cube," but "square" is the given title by the author.

development, which is the precursor to commercial development, and alliances and partnerships which can be either commercial or basic research" (p. 2).

Future Potential

The last type of product portfolio analysis that we will describe was developed by the Boston Consulting Group, and is known as the "BCG Matrix." The two-dimensional matrix, shown in Figure 6-3, categorizes products by their potential for growth and their relative market share. As with all portfolio analyses, balance among the categories is recommended. In addition, the matrix factors in trends and competitive positions (Allan and Hammond 1975, p. 6):

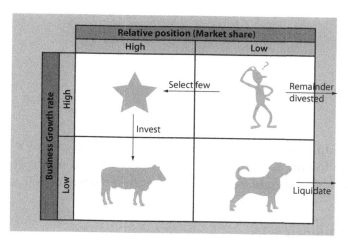

Figure 6-3. BCG Matrix

Cash cows are products that characteristically generate large amounts of cash—far more than they can profitably reinvest—and typically have high market share and low growth. *Dogs* are products with low market and slow growth ... often called "cash traps." *Question Marks* are products with high growth but low share that require large amounts of cash to maintain market share, and still larger amounts to gain share. *Stars* are high-growth, high-share products which ... promise a much larger net cash generation in the future.

The challenge for companies is to maintain the cash cows, fund the stars, and figure out the reason why the question marks are not producing the expected results, while divesting the dogs.

Market analyses should be data-based, using market research and consulting expert industry analysts. Companies need to honestly appraise their position as compared to their competitors on these criteria as well as to weigh their importance. Another insight this type of market analysis can provide is to identify key success factors (KSFs). As companies compare their products with their competitors' products, they can identify the specific product attributes that the market demands, i.e., the KSFs. Knowing their offerings' positions relative to the KSFs, executives can use this knowledge to direct resources for strategic positioning. This is illustrated in Table 6-1 on the following page.

RESOURCES AND CAPABILITIES APPRAISAL

Product portfolio analysis is a good way to "see the forest for the trees." As you appraise resources and capabilities, you will focus more on the individual trees. Which are healthy? Which need more sunlight? Which should be cut down? Which should be propagated?

Table 6-1. KSF Illustration

KSFs	Our Company	Competitor #1	Competitor#2	Competitor #3
Price	10	8	9	7
Quality	6	9	7	4
Customer Service	8	9	5	3
Location	7	8	4	2
Total	31	34	25	16

As with product portfolio analysis, there are many different ways to appraise a company's resources and capabilities. The ones in the following sections have been selected based on their popularity and/or their usefulness. Either way, you should be familiar with these approaches.

Core Competencies

The unique combination of capabilities that are central to a firm's main business operations and which allow it to generate new products and services might be considered core competencies. They tend to be very narrow and hard to identify. Prahalad and Hamel (1990, pp. 83–84) caution, however, that:

> At least three tests can be applied to identify a core competency in a company. First, [it] provides potential access to a wide variety of markets. … Second, [it] should make a significant contribution to the perceived customer benefits of the end product. … Finally, a core competence should be difficult for competitors to imitate.

Illustration

The owner of automated car washes is interested in investing in an ice dispensing operation because he views his core competency as "coin-operated, unattended vending," not as car washing.

The term *core competency* is often misused and tends to be a buzz phrase. There is no established technique for evaluating core competencies, beyond the three tests, although some have been suggested (c.f., Gallon et. al. 1995; Hamel and Prahalad 1996). The bottom line is that using this framework requires a deep understanding of your business and ability for lateral thinking.

Resource Based View

As with the core competency approach, a resource based view (RBV) is an internal assessment of what gives—or can give—a company its competitive advantage. A RBV is perhaps more straightforward and "useful" (Barney 1991), as it starts with an inventory of key tangible and intangible assets and capabilities, i.e., resources. Wal-Mart's locations are tangible resources. Coca-Cola brand recognition is an intangible resource. Warren Buffet's investing savvy is a capability.

Then you determine whether these resources are (V)aluable, (R)are, (IN)imitable, and/or (E)xploitable, using the "VRINE" model.[5] A resource that is valuable and rare may help you to establish a competitive advantage; when that resource is also inimitable and exploitable, it can enable you to sustain that advantage.

For example, consider when Xerox's Palo Alto Research Center (PARC) was working on developing a pointing device for mini and microcomputers in the early 1980s. This was a very valuable technology, as it was different from other human–computer interfaces that were available at the time. It was rare, because these were still the early days of personal computing. It was hard to imitate, because patents protected it. However, PARC was not prepared to organize or exploit it, which is why we usually associate the origin of the mouse with Apple.

The idea of inimitability is at the heart of competitive advantage. How does one achieve inimitability?

A capability may be difficult to imitate because of its path dependency, meaning it was accumulated over time. The "magic" of Disney is hard for others to imitate because of its unusual history, starting with cartoons, moving into feature films, commercializing characters, and building theme parks.

Inimitability may also result because it is unclear to competitors how this capability was created (known as "casual ambiguity"), as in the case of Dell Computer's material handling technology. Or it may be socially complex in a way that is hard to copy, as when key personalities or a distinctive corporate culture are in play—consider Chik-fil-A or Southwest Airlines (Brennan 2010, pp. 7–8).

By conducting an RBV assessment, you can identify opportunities and prioritize investments in strategic resources.

SWOT Analysis

This is a popular but often misused approach that assesses positives and negatives, from an internal and external perspective. Simply listing the internal (S)trengths and (W)eaknesses and the external (O)pportunities and (T)hreats is not very useful. The real value of SWOT is when you consider strengths and how they might be used to take advantage of opportunities and avoid threats. Similarly, you should consider weaknesses and how you need to address them to mitigate threats and possibly pursue opportunities (David 1997). An example of a SWOT matrix is presented in Table 6-2 on the following page.

Illustration

Partners of a management consulting company are working on their strategic plan. They develop a SWOT matrix, which includes the following thoughts, shown in Table 6-2.

Value Chain Analysis

Developed by Michael Porter (1995), the concept of a value chain applies a systemic view to an organization that transcends its boundaries. The key to this conceptual view is to consider the

---

[5] This model is sometimes called the VRIO model, with "O" standing for "organized."

Table 6-2. Sample SWOT Matrix

	STRENGTHS (S)	WEAKNESSES (W)
	Net income is 10% ahead of last year. *Firm has a national reputation for process improvement.* ...	*Partners are over-extended with billable activities and do not have time for business development.* *Affiliates have not been a good source of new business.* ...
OPPORTUNITIES (O) *Concerns about companies' environmental impact are increasing.* *A few clients have expressed interest in "lean consumption," making it easier for customers to do business with them.* ...	SO STRATEGIES *Invest in hiring associates with experience in Life Cycle Analysis (S1,O1)* *Extend process improvement practice to market a lean consumption practice (S1, S2, O2).* ...	WO STRATEGIES *Subcontract some work to part-time (contract) consultants so the partners can cross-sell lean consumption to existing clients (W1, O2).* *Release non-productive affiliates; recruit local ones with environmental expertise (W2, O1).* ...
THREATS (T) *The economy has been stagnant.* *Manufacturing applications for process improvement are declining.* ...	ST STRATEGIES *Increase cash reserves (S1, T1).* *Prospect past manufacturing clients to apply process improvement to other departments (S2, T2).* ...	WT STRATEGIES *Leverage resources such as part-time local consultants to avoid over-extending salary base in firm (W1, T1).* ...

organization as a system (i.e., a "chain" of activities) by which value is added through primary activities that are supported by secondary activities. Value chain analysis can be used to identify opportunities for differentiation as well as sources of waste (i.e., where value is not added). This topic is covered in more detail in the following chapters.

APPLICATION AND REFLECTION

- What tangible and intangible assets can you identify for You, Inc. for your employer—or for your employer's closest competitor?

- Think of illustrations for quadrants of the BCG matrix.

- For tablet computers, what do you think the KSFs are?

- Develop a SWOT matrix for You, Inc. What strategies for your career can you identify?

- Using your own RBV of a firm, evaluate three resources according to the VRIO application.

CHAPTER 7
EVALUATING THE VALUE CHAIN

The value chain disaggregates a firm into its strategically relevant activities in order to understand the behavior of costs and the existing and potential sources of differentiation.[1]

—Michael E. Porter

OPENING VIGNETTE

Starbucks CEO Howard Schultz continues to enrich the "experience" for customers as he continually refines and expands the Starbucks brand. The expansion is not only in the geographic placement of stores around the globe, but also in product line offerings. Taking a page from Pine & Gilmore's book *The Experience Economy* (1999), Schultz understands that "businesses that relegate themselves to the diminishing world of goods and services will be rendered irrelevant. To avoid this fate, you must learn to stage a rich, compelling experience."

Starbucks has been able to leverage the core competency of experience and change the coffee retail shop modeled on Italian coffee bars into a global consumer phenomenon. But in order to guarantee the continuity and richness of this experience, the basic ingredient of his company, the coffee bean, had to be protected.

Shultz realized early on that although he could not "backward integrate" and become a coffee bean producer, he could protect the integrity of the tangible part of the intangible experience, the bean. He did this by investing in and supporting the bean growers: "we work on-the-ground with farmers to help improve coffee quality and invest in loan programs for coffee-growing communities. It's not just the right thing to do; it's the right thing to do for our business."[2]

Not only has Starbucks insured the consistency of the brand and preserved the experience for customers, but it also has leveraged this effort into support for the bean growers' communities

---

[1] M. E. Porter. *Competitive Advantage: Creating and Sustaining Superior Performance.* New York, NY: The Free Press, 1985. The quotation is from p. 33.

[2] http://www.starbucks.com/responsibility/sourcing/farmer-support

and furthered endorsement of social and environmental responsibility, a "win-win-win" for the firm, the customer, and the supplier of the bean.

In this chapter, we examine generic strategies for an organization's value chain—the sequence of activities and functions by which value is added to inputs to create desired results. Here we examine models and strategies that simply provide more specific direction, e.g., how will you become a low-cost provider in a broad market? Successful mastery of this material will enable you to:

- define generic strategies and the forces of competition
- describe the value chain concept
- explain strategies for differentiation in the value chain
- understand waste and lean operations

We close this chapter with a reading that challenges you to think about ways in which to reduce the environmental impact in your supply chain.

INTRODUCTION

When you think of a sports team, it is clear that competitive advantage is what enables the team to win. How does a sports team create a competitive advantage? It could be better, faster, stronger, specialized, for example. It is differentiating itself on quality characteristics. Perhaps the general manager thinks that competitive advantage comes from creating a loyal base of fans and a steady set of ticket subscribers. This may call for a strategy based on cost savings and profitability. You win by being different and/or providing a cost advantage.

GENERIC STRATEGIES

In Michael Porter's (1980) model of generic strategies, he identifies three alternatives: competition on cost, differentiation, or competition in a focused market niche. His model has evolved into the inevitable matrix. Cost leadership and differentiation are the two main ways that a company can compete. He also suggests those two approaches will vary, depending on whether the company is pursuing a narrow market segment or a broad one. For example, consider the different types of shoes a company might produce, as shown in Table 7-1.

Any strategy has risks, but some are more predictable than others. One risk of cost leadership is that there may be too much focus on one or a few activities. Such simplicity exposes the

Table 7-1. Generic Strategies Illustration

	NARROW MARKET	BROAD MARKET
DIFFERENTIATED	Cowboy Boots	Work Boots
LOW COST LEADERSHIP	Trendy Heels	Flip Flops

company to easy imitation. Also, there may be an erosion of the cost advantage when pricing information available to customers increases, as is inevitable. The risks of differentiation are, first, that the differentiation is not valuable to the customer. The perception of the difference might vary, or be unattractive because it creates a price premium. And there is always the risk that differentiation can be imitated.

Porter (1979, 2008) has categorized these risks as forces that require consideration of their impact on any strategic decision. The forces are supplier forces, customer forces, new entrants, substitutes, and rivalry among competing firms, as shown in Figure 7-1. Porter's Five Forces can have a direct effect on the success or failure of the strategic choice. For example, in a differentiation strategy, the supplier force may be very strong if the raw materials required are unique. An example is the coffee beans that directly impact product quality. And in order to mitigate that risk, Starbucks has invested in the coffee bean growers. Customers have a strong force in low cost strategy, as the switching costs are minimal and customers can easily choose competitors when competing on price alone. Customer service may then be a premium differentiator. The strengths of these forces are categorized and tabulated and can be used to determine the likelihood of success of a strategy as well as the favorability of an industry sector.

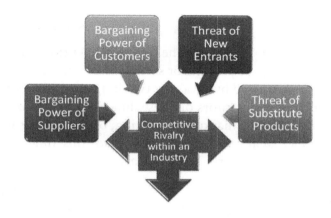

Figure 7-1. Porter's Five Forces Model

Illustration

Panera Bread is a company that differentiates itself from other restaurants through its unique menu, service, and an environment in which customers are comfortable. Using a Five Forces analysis to evaluate the strength of their differentiation, we find that its:

1. Supplier forces are low, with a strong emphasis on Panera's supply chain to its 1,362 locations in 40 U.S. states.
2. Customer forces are high, as there are low switching costs and high price sensitivity.
3. Threat of new entrants is low, because of the capital investment required to open a restaurant and the high rate of failure in the restaurant industry.
4. Possible substitutes are high, such as eating at home, fast food restaurants, and pre-prepared supermarket meals.
5. Direct competition is moderate. Au Bon Pain and Atlanta Bread Company are competitors, but they do not have the atmosphere or menu alternatives that Panera does, albeit at a slightly higher price point.

The analysis indicates that Panera's competitive position is currently very strong, but that they might be vulnerable when customers are price-sensitive.

Strategic Maps

Another way to look at the direct competition is by using a strategic map. It is a graphical positioning of your product or service as compared to your competitors on one or more dimensions. It is constructed by choosing two important dimensions or key success factors and mapping you and your competitors on these dimensions. The size of the circle on the map can be an indicator of market size, market penetration, or some other indicator of relative positioning.

Once again we use Panera Bread, this time to illustrate positioning in the casual dining restaurant industry. The two variables on which we map this company and their competitors are (1) quality of menu offerings and (2) number of locations and location saturation. We see that Panera is highest in quality, and might be watching Starbucks which has perceived equal quality, but is more predominant in the market by sheer "footprint," creating superior market awareness and customer accessibility.

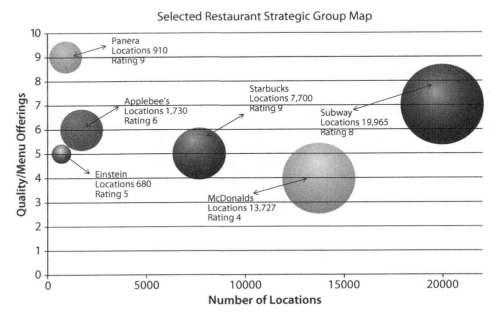

Figure 7-2. Strategic Map for Panera Bread

VALUE CHAIN

The Value Chain, according to Porter (1985), is a model that separates the overall business system into a series of value-generating activities that develop competitive advantage. The value chain distinguishes between primary activities, i.e., inbound/outbound logistics, operations, marketing and sales, and service. The secondary, or support, activities are administration, human resource management, technology development, and procurement, as shown in Figure 7-3. The metaphor of a chain is powerful for two reasons. The first is that it emphasizes the interdependency of the activities. The second is that it transcends organizational boundaries. For example, third party logistics providers (3PL) serve

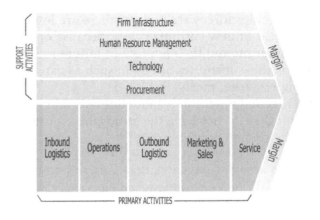

Figure 7-3. Porter's Value Chain Model

as inbound and outbound logistics providers for other companies—sometimes they will even provide the assembly operation.

DIFFERENTIATION IN THE VALUE CHAIN

Each link in the value chain can provide opportunities for differentiation as a basis for competitive advantage. Wal-Mart has differentiated itself based upon its inbound logistics and its operational optimization. Toyota, renowned for its lean logistics and operations across its value chain, has also achieved differentiation based upon services used in its Lexus vehicle line to guarantee satisfaction, so much so that it has been copied by other luxury vehicles such as BMW and Cadillac. Ryder Systems has renamed itself as a logistics company, understanding the importance of efficiency and economies of scale in moving freight from warehouses or holding centers to transportation such as on-road trucking and rail. Chik-fil-A's marketing and sales, from its infamous cows encouraging us to "Eat Mor Chikin'" to its fast drive-through and well-trained associates who respond to a "thank you" with "my pleasure" has differentiated it from other fast food chains. By focusing on the "value" delivered in its operational or primary chain of activities, a company can differentiate its quality of product or service.

The firm may also gain competitive advantage by driving primary and secondary activities to create a cost advantage. Information technology application, considered a secondary activity, can offer automation and other efficiencies that reduce costs in the value chain. Caremark, the prescription-by-mail fulfillment company, makes extensive use of technology to receive and process the prescriptions, remind a patient of refills, notify a patient of order status, and receive payments.

Table 7-2. Examples of Low Cost Differentiation

Economies of scale	Wal-Mart's purchasing power
Learning	Apple's product upgrades
Capacity utilization	Seasonal Concepts's switch in product lines from holiday décor to patio furniture
Linkages among activities	UPS package tracking and delivery
Interrelationships among business units	Cross-marketing across Proctor & Gamble brands
Degree of vertical integration	Niagara Water's manufacturing its own bottles
Timing of market entry	Toyota's introduction of its compact cars to the US during the 70's oil embargo
Firm's policy of cost or differentiation	Southwest Airlines's decision to not serve meals in-flight
Geographic location	Denver redeveloping the reclaimed land when Stapleton Airport closed to create a series of communities with green spaces and sidewalks
Institutional factors (regulation, union activity, taxes, etc.)	Ford renegotiating with the United Auto Workers union to avoid bankruptcy

Porter (1985) identified 10 cost drivers related to value chain activities. Table 7-2 gives examples of each and is followed by an illustration.

Illustration

Georgia Pacific once not only manufactured paper products but also at one time owned the pine forests that were the source of the pulp, the lumber and transport capabilities that cut and transported the trees, and the manufacturing that transformed the raw material into paper. They now also market the containers to dispense their paper products in customer locations through motion sensor devices, such as the one shown in Figure 7-4.

Figure 7-4. Automated towel dispenser

LEAN OPERATIONS AND WASTE REDUCTION

Just as the value chain helps managers focus on activities that add value, it is important to understand that most activities that do not add value are waste. Sometimes, an activity is neither value adding or wasteful, as when a patient signs a Health Insurance Portability and Accountability Act (HIPAA) notification; it is necessary because of regulations intended to protect the patient, but the patient does not necessarily perceive its value.

A central component to the operations/manufacturing of a company and an important component in the low cost alternative is the elimination of waste and the decrease in variability. The Toyota Production System (TPS) is acknowledged as a model for decreasing waste and variance in processes to enhance efficiency in operations, while at the same time producing consistency in products and services (Likert and Meier 2005). TPS includes many concepts, including lean manufacturing, which focuses on reducing or eliminating waste.

The seven sources of waste are: overproduction, waiting, unnecessary transport, unnecessary processing, excess inventory, unnecessary movements, and defects. Not only can these types of waste be manifest in manufacturing and service operations, you can apply them to information processing and overload (Brennan 2012) and the customer's experience, also known as "lean consumption" (Womack and Jones 2005).

APPLICATION AND REFLECTION

- Consider the competitive environment for You, Inc. What are the five forces that you should consider?

- For each quadrant of the generic strategy matrix, find a product or service example in a particular industry.

- Select a process of which you are a customer. Identify the sources of waste and how you could have a better experience with lean consumption.

- We can extend our view of waste by reflecting on the topic of sustainability and corporate social responsibility. The following article, "'Greening' Transportation in the Supply Chain," integrates these two strategic considerations with research about what corporations are actually doing. What are the steps for reducing the supply chain footprint? What best practices are highlighted?

"GREENING"
TRANSPORTATION IN THE SUPPLY CHAIN

Susan L. Golicic, Courtney N. Boerstler, and Lisa M. Ellram

Even corporations with clear environmental aims fail to go the distance when it comes to their supply chains. But lessons from a small group of Fortune 500 companies can give them the direction they need.

Not long ago, it would have been considered unnatural for corporations to set their priorities and goals with an eye toward improving their environmental performance. But a steady flow of high-profile corporate initiatives and studies of customer behavior have revealed a change in the business climate. Companies that integrate sustainability practices throughout their supply chains are experiencing a clear benefit. Increasingly, key stakeholders—from investors to customers to prospective employees—are monitoring sustainability efforts for themselves and making their decisions accordingly.

But more than just the threat of negative publicity is pushing corporations into the green zone. With domestic policy makers debating the merits of cap-and-trade legislation and world leaders struggling to agree on a climate change treaty, it's only a matter of time before environmentally unaware companies will face steep fines for their failure to keep pace. At the same time, the slow-growing U.S. economy is forcing companies to focus on improving their efficiency to offset tepid demand and counterbalance the price volatility of commodities such as water and energy.

For corporations, the commitment to reducing their carbon footprint is the first of many daunting steps. Executives must organize both interior and exterior expeditions. By turning their organizations inside out, they can pinpoint how and where energy is consumed. They need to monitor innovations from the outside world in fields like genetic engineering and improvements in battery performance for electric vehicles. With what they learn, they need to take a fresh look at every aspect of their business: packaging, cleaning—each link in each supply chain. If that sounds utterly overwhelming, it is.

S. Golicic, C. Boerstler, and L. M. Ellram. "Greening the Transportation in Your Supply Chain." *MIT Sloan Management Review* 51, no. 2 (2010): 47–55. Copyright © 2010 by MIT Sloan Management Review. Reprinted with permission.

Or, rather, it must be. That would help to explain why many eco-conscious companies overlook one of their supply chain's costliest and most environmentally damaging components: transportation.

Until very recently, freight transportation was a negligible consideration in company strategy with regard to environmental responsibility. However, current business practices such as international sourcing and quick turnaround times challenge this by extending transportation distances and minimizing lead times in the supply chain. Standard modes of transportation consume fossil fuels, generate noise and emit toxic compounds. In 2007, transportation accounted for 28.4% of U.S. energy consumption and 33.6% of carbon dioxide emissions.[1]

THE ROAD TAKEN: THE COLLISION OF LOGISTICS AND THE ENVIRONMENT

International sourcing has grown steadily over the past few decades, and the economic theory of trade suggests that increased specialization by country and region will prevail—meaning that trade will continue to grow. Corporations buy from foreign suppliers for many reasons, including to establish a presence in foreign markets, to increase their ranks of suppliers, and to react to competitors by lowering prices. Sourcing materials from other countries, however, naturally increases transportation distance and the associated environmental consequences.

The need to boost supply chain responsiveness has had a major impact. Increasingly demanding customers, outsourcing, globalization, and advances in technology have forced companies to develop agile supply chain processes.[2] To minimize financial risk in the face of uncertain demand, companies keep less inventory, which requires them to make smaller but more frequent shipments—possibly using faster transportation modes to support reduced lead times. While these activities may minimize manufacturing waste, these *lean* practices rarely consider the greenhouse gas impact associated with more frequent transportation, which also can emit higher levels of greenhouse gases. Offshore manufacturing compounds the problem because it extends the supply chain, causing companies to work even harder to reduce these longer lead times.

Supply chain management has largely overlooked the greenhouse gas impact of transportation decisions. This lack of attention is surprising, especially given growing global dependence on freight transportation; in the next 20 years, the amount of cargo shipped is expected to triple.[3] To support supply chain agility, many companies are accelerating their spending on faster kinds of transportation, that is, motor (trucks and other vehicles) and air, the same modes that have the most unfavorable environmental impact per ton mile. Motor transportation is four times less fuel-efficient per ton mile than rail,[4] and emissions from airfreight are 600 times higher than those from rail or ocean shipping and nearly 90 times higher than those from motor transportation in the United States.[5]

Given the high greenhouse gas impact of such transportation, it is vital to alert top executives to the importance of including transportation impacts in any environmental analysis of their supply chains. We explored the strategies and practices of more than three dozen Fortune 500 companies to determine the extent to which they acted beyond merely acknowledging the emission impact of their transportation. It's a long way between heightened awareness and effective action.

We examined 44 Fortune 500 companies that addressed 11 transportation practices, ranging from creating specific goals to implementing explicit changes to transportation in the supply chain. (See "How Fortune 500 Companies Address Environmental Impacts of Transportation," p. 50, and "Key to Transportation Practices," p. 51.) The 11 practices were grouped into three levels based on the apparent amount of environmental sustainability demonstrated in the supply chain. The first, the foundation level, includes initial steps that acknowledge the company's transportation emissions impact. These themes establish a foundation or basis for the company to begin to address transportation emissions, rather than being specific activities to reduce the impact. All but one of the 44 companies provided evidence of this level of engagement. A subset of 28 companies went beyond this to internal company practices, taking initial actions to educate personnel and build a culture that encourages the reduction of greenhouse gas emissions from transportation. Finally, 22 companies reported implementing supply chain practices, tactics that begin to reduce the greenhouse gas emissions resulting from freight transportation in their supply chain.

Establishing a Foundation

Activities at the foundation level include developing goals for limiting transportation's impact, using metrics to measure that impact, building partnerships with other organizations to help the focal companies accomplish their goals, and acknowledging that additional benefits are possible.

Twenty-five corporations have explicit goals for decreasing the impact of transportation. Of these, 23 describe general plans to reduce energy or fuel usage. For example, E.I. du Pont de Nemours and Co. intends to "introduce fleet vehicles with leading technology for fuel efficiency and fossil fuel alternatives," according to the sustainability page on its Web site. Some objectives are more specific: In its "2008 Global Citizenship Report," FedEx Corp., which has one of the largest commercial hybrid fleets in North America, set a goal to improve its overall fuel efficiency 20% by 2020. Five companies share the goal of optimizing their supply chain network. The Home Depot, Inc., for example, plans to begin using an environmental clause in its transportation-related contracts.

Any entity serious about change must include measurement as a fundamental starting point. Nine companies report measures of the current emissions impact of their transportation of products or employees. Seventeen companies offer metrics that report improvements over the past year. For example, Dell, Inc. measures its greenhouse gas emission reductions, and Office Depot, Inc. and FedEx track fuel usage and its associated greenhouse gas impact.

Twenty-one companies mention partnerships—with specific government organizations (15), nongovernment organizations (5), and/or supplier and customer companies (7)—in order to help them tackle their environmental impact. The most frequently mentioned partnership (11 companies) was with the U.S. Environmental Protection Agency's SmartWay program, which is targeted at helping shippers and carriers reduce emissions.

Although one argument against implementing sustainable practices is the cost of doing so, some proponents of sustainability argue that it is not only free but can actually improve company performance. Eight companies specifically acknowledge that reducing energy and emissions saves money for the company and its employees. Bristol-Myers Squibb Co. recognizes that it experiences increased productivity due to its commuting practices. Dell acknowledges that its practices reduce product delivery times, thus recognizing the positive impact on customers.

ABOUT THE RESEARCH

This study, conducted in 2008, explored the strategies and practices of more than three dozen Fortune 500 companies to determine the extent to which they acted to improve supply chain and transportation sustainability. To obtain a sample of companies with environmental business strategies, we first researched three environmental supply chain initiatives: EPA's Climate Leaders, EPA's SmartWay Transportation Partnership and the Global Environmental Management Initiative. They consider greenhouse gas emissions across industries and provide a way to target companies that have a particular interest in supply chain sustainability. The companies participating in the three initiatives were cross-referenced with Fortune 500 and Roberts Environmental Center listed companies, yielding a total of 294 businesses demonstrating environmental strategies (58.8% of the Fortune 500), with 76 (15.2%) participating in at least two of the three initiatives. Eight companies that participated only in SmartWay were added to the list of 76.

We examined public information provided on the Web sites of the 84 total sample companies. The annual report, corporate responsibility report if it existed, and the Web site itself were reviewed to categorize the businesses according to how they addressed environmental concerns. In order to specifically determine which companies addressed transportation emissions, we independently categorized the information as to whether it was relevant to transportation. This yielded a total sample of 44 companies that addressed transportation emissions in some fashion.

Each entry discussing environmental transportation from these 44 companies was copied verbatim from the reports and/or Web site into text documents. Although self-reported, these data are reports of the companies' strategies and tactics used to address transportation emission impacts and thus are appropriate for our study. Content analysis was used to extract themes related to environmental transportation practices from the data, facilitated by a software package. We developed some content themes in advance based on the literature and knowledge of the industries; others emerged from reviews of the data for a total of 11 themes: mode, fuel, technology, volume, commute, training, fleet, metrics, goals, partner, and benefits. Each document was analyzed independently by two researchers, yielding a coding reliability of 71.3%, acceptable for this type of analysis. A third researcher reviewed the codes and resolved any discrepancies. The 11 themes were then analyzed further to determine relationships among them so they could be grouped based on the extent to which they addressed transportation practices.

Changing Internal Company Practices

Twenty-eight companies had moved to the second level, making changes to internal company practices aimed at reducing transportation emissions. These include managing the company's fleet of vehicles to reduce its environmental impact and creating training programs to teach employees how to make positive changes. Establishing employee commute programs that target personal travel to and from the workplace is included as well. While practices focused on employee transit are outside the domain of freight transportation, they do contribute to educating employees on greenhouse gas emissions and reinforce a corporate culture of environmental awareness. Twenty-one companies reported the use of fleet management to improve energy

HOW FORTUNE 500 COMPANIES ADDRESS ENVIRONMENTAL IMPACTS OF TRANSPORTATION

Among Fortune 500 companies, 44 have publicly addressed the environmental effects of transportation in their supply chains — some just acknowledging them ("Foundation"), some altering practice ("Internal"), and some achieving reductions ("Impact"). See "Key," p. 51.

COMPANY (FORTUNE 500 RANKING, 2008)	INDUSTRY	FOUNDATION NODES	INTERNAL COMPANY PRACTICE NODES	SUPPLY CHAIN IMPACT NODES
Raytheon (97)	Aerospace		Commute; fleet	
DuPont (73)	Chemical	Goals		Fuel
Air Products and Chemicals (282)	Chemical	Metrics		Volume
Owens Corning (341)	Chemical	Partner	Fleet	Fuel; mode; technology; volume
Ecolab (459)	Chemical	Goals		Fuel
HP (11)	Computer	Benefits; goals; metrics; partner	Commute; fleet; training	Mode; volume
Dell (25)	Computer	Benefits; goals; metrics	Commute	Mode; technology; volume
Xerox (142)	Computer	Benefits; metrics	Fleet	
Sun Microsystems (211)	Computer	Benefits	Commute; training	
General Electric (7)	Diversified	Goals	Fleet	
AMD (367)	Electronics	Partner	Commute; training	
Rockwell Automation (427)	Electronics	Goals; partner		
Whirlpool (152)	Electronics	Goals; partner		
Tyson Foods (80)	Food and beverage	Goals; partner		Fuel; technology
Coca-Cola (89)	Food and beverage	Goals; partner	Fleet	Fuel; technology
Smithfield Foods (205)	Food and beverage	Metrics		
UPS (44)	Freight/shipping	Goals; metrics; partner	Fleet; training	Fuel; technology; volume
FedEx (70)	Freight/shipping	Goals; metrics; partner	Fleet	Fuel; mode; technology; volume
CSX (266)	Freight/shipping	Goals; metrics; partner	Fleet	Fuel; technology
Wal-Mart (2)	General merchandiser	Benefits; goals; partner		Fuel; technology
Walgreen (45)	General merchandiser	Metrics	Fleet	Fuel
Nike (163)	Household/personal	Benefits; goals; partner		
Limited Brands (246)	Household/personal	Metrics; partner		Mode; volume
Estée Lauder (340)	Household/personal	Metrics; partner	Commute	Mode; volume
Cisco Systems (83)	Information technology	Goals; partner	Commute; training	
Oracle (196)	Information technology	Goals	Commute	
Baxter International (240)	Medical products	Goals; partner		Mode; volume
Pfizer (31)	Pharmaceuticals	Goals; metrics; partner	Fleet	
Johnson & Johnson (32)	Pharmaceuticals	Goals; metrics; partner	Fleet	Fuel; mode; volume
Abbott Laboratories (93)	Pharmaceuticals	Metrics; partner	Commute; fleet; training	
Merck (95)	Pharmaceuticals	Metrics		
Bristol-Myers Squibb (110)	Pharmaceuticals	Benefits; goals; metrics; partner	Commute	
Wyeth (119)	Pharmaceuticals		Commute; fleet	
Schering-Plough (250)	Pharmaceuticals	Metrics	Commute; fleet	
Home Depot (14)	Retail	Goals; partner		
Lowe's (42)	Retail	Metrics; partner		Mode; volume
Best Buy (76)	Retail	Goals		
Staples (137)	Retail	Metrics	Fleet	
TJX (138)	Retail			Mode; volume
Office Depot (154)	Retail	Benefits; goals; metrics	Fleet	Mode; technology; volume
Agilent Technologies (319)	Scientific/photo	Metrics	Commute; fleet; training	
Qualcomm (381)	Telecommunication		Commute; fleet	
American Electric Power (185)	Utilities	Goals	Fleet	Fuel
FPL Group (195)	Utilities	Goals; metrics	Fleet	Fuel

efficiency and reduce emissions from transportation. Eighteen companies provided specific methods of reducing carbon emissions, most opting for more energy-efficient vehicles. Johnson & Johnson had the largest corporate fleet of hybrid vehicles in the United States as of March 2008, with 978 hybrids in operation and 508 more ordered. Office Depot replaced oversized diesel delivery trucks with lighter Dodge Sprinter cargo vans that have twice the fuel efficiency of their predecessors. Freight carrier CSX Corp. has invested more than $1 billion since 2000 to upgrade its fleet with more efficient clean air locomotives; it plans to reduce fuel consumption by another 10 million gallons by upgrading 1,200 additional locomotives.

Fourteen companies mentioned employee commute programs as part of their efforts to reduce their transport-related carbon footprint. Thirteen companies encourage the use of alternative transportation options, including shuttle buses, carpools, bicycles, and public transportation. Five companies have installed and use videoconferencing and other communication technologies, thus reducing transportation emissions from employee travel.

Impacting Supply Chain Practices

Only a very small percentage of Fortune 500 companies have tried to significantly reduce greenhouse gas emissions from freight transportation in the supply chain through technological or operational tactics. These 22 companies are aggressively decreasing fuel use, switching loads to more environmentally friendly modes (i.e., forms of transportation such as rail), adopting technology to increase shipment efficiency and effectiveness, and reducing shipment volume.

Among the 13 companies implementing tactics to conserve fuel and/or substitute alternative fuels, six have shifted to less polluting fuels, including biodiesel. In its 2006 sustainability report, utility giant FPL Group, Inc. noted the recognition it received from the Council for Sustainable Florida for its use of 2 million gallons of soybean diesel in 2005. Seven companies are either using auxiliary power units or changing delivery practices to reduce truck idle time, a large contributor to fuel waste. FedEx, Johnson & Johnson, and Wal-Mart report using wider tires on their trucks, and Tyson Foods uses aluminum wheels on its tractors, theoretically reducing road friction and thus increasing fuel efficiency and reducing emissions. Besides implementing tactics to reduce fuel emissions, FedEx is advocating that the U.S. Senate Energy and Natural Resources Committee establish vehicle efficiency standards that would ultimately impact all road shipments.

Eleven companies are decreasing the impact of their mode of transportation by switching to a more environmentally friendly mode or improving the existing method's capacity utilization. HP, Baxter, Lowe's, and Johnson & Johnson are all shifting portions of road transport to rail, and HP, Dell, Limited Brands, and Estee Lauder are converting air shipments to ground or ocean transport. Eight companies are reconfiguring pallets and packaging to increase trailers' volume efficiency. Baxter International, Inc. collaborates with supply chain partners to decrease the number of loads and eliminate empty miles.

Companies are deploying new technologies to increase mode and shipment efficiency. United Parcel Service, Inc. has multiple IT programs that optimize ground and air routes for its fleet as well as surface taxiing for its aircraft. Office Depot uses Roadnet Transportation software to arrange smarter delivery routes, eliminating 30% to 50% of local shipments by enabling more first-time deliveries. Tyson Foods, Inc. uses software to remotely monitor engine diagnostic information to help reduce truck engine idle time. Seven other companies utilize various devices

KEY TO TRANSPORTATION PRACTICES
Analysis of the transportation-related sustainability practices of Fortune 500 companies (see p. 50) revealed 11 distinct practices or tactical areas.

NODE	MEANING
Commute	Efforts targeted at personal travel to/from work
Mode	Modal decisions to decrease impact for shipments of goods (this includes switching modes or reducing idle or wait time)
Fuel	Use of alternative fuels for shipments of goods
Technology	Use of technology to decrease impact for shipments of goods
Volume	Decrease in volume of goods shipped or number of shipments (includes anything done regarding the efficiency of shipments)
Metric	Measurement/tracking of transportation (goods or personnel) impact on environment
Training	Actions taken to inform employees of impact of transportation or ways to decrease impact
Fleet	Mention of actions taken regarding fleet of vehicles used, whether for goods or personnel transport (e.g., sales personnel)
Partner	Any other organizations involved with helping the company reduce transportation impact
Goals	General statements about improving environmental impact from transportation
Benefits	Additional benefits achieved when implementing something to decrease environmental impact

that affect modal efficiency. For example, CSX has installed automatic shutdown systems on its locomotives to reduce fuel usage.

Many of these mode changes and technologies are targeted at reducing total shipment volume or weight, the ultimate means of reducing emissions from transportation. Reports from 10 companies describe reducing the number of shipments through better vehicle utilization or efficient routing.

In 2006, Owens Corning received a SmartWay Excellence Award from the EPA, as have Lowe's and Limited Brands. Four companies, including Dell and Air Products and Chemicals, Inc., have gone beyond routing and describe decisions made with respect to positioning local offices and distribution centers to decrease the physical distance between themselves and supply chain partners.

Given the state of the economy, it's hardly surprising that all kinds of customers—from consumers to industrial buyers—scrutinize prices. When procuring or manufacturing a product overseas is substantially cheaper than doing so in the United States, it is difficult to justify buying locally in order to reduce transportation greenhouse gases. Since many of the goods produced in developing countries are consumed in more industrialized nations, shipping goods long distances from point of manufacture to consumption creates a much greater transportation burden than do local manufacturing and consumption.[6] Companies shouldn't have to make a trade-off between being profitable and reducing transportation emissions.

It's possible that the companies studied haven't gotten as far along—or as much out of—their transportation-related environmental projects as their public pronouncements indicate. The difference between a planned project and one that is actually implemented is often hard to detect from the outside. And corporations frequently hesitate to share detailed results with the outside world, which includes their competitors. For example, on the sustainability page of its Web site, Owens Corning reports implementing several fuel efficiency practices, such as considering intermodal transportation and increasing truck utilization, but does not specify the fuel consumption or emission results of these practices. And although FedEx's Web site describes the usage of in-gate aircraft auxiliary power units that reportedly reduced fuel consumption by an estimated 5.5 million gallons, this savings is not put in the context of FedEx's total annual consumption.

FUEL FOR THOUGHT: BEST PRACTICES ON THE ROUTE TO CHANGE

For any company to reach the highest level of accomplishment in the emissions-reducing realm, it would have to work closely with its supply chain partners throughout its global logistics network. None of the companies in our study had achieved this. But from their experiences so far, here are some best practices that are emerging as companies make strategic progress toward achieving sustainable supply chain transportation.

As with any major change initiative, it is best to begin with the "low-hanging fruit," or those projects that are relatively easy to implement, have a high probability of measurable success, and are readily visible to key stakeholders. It would be ideal if these initiatives also saved money or were at least cost neutral, such as reducing the volume of transportation moves through more efficient loading.

During the initial stage of developing environmentally sustainable transportation practices, what we call "establishing a foundation," a company identifies what it wants to accomplish, how the results will be measured and reported, what benefits the company may receive, and with whom to engage in its sustainable transportation initiatives. This may include memberships in environmentally oriented organizations, partnerships with suppliers and transportation providers, and even alliances within the company. For example, if metrics will be created to measure the impact of emission-reducing efforts, the people who will have input into implementing the efforts should be involved in advance. This stage is important for fact finding and bridge building. UPS established a fuel conservation committee to examine the way it uses fuel for its ground fleet in order to establish reduction goals. Such success stories play an important role in institutionalizing sustainable transportation practices.

Once research has been conducted and some baseline goals and measurements have been established, implementation of the next level, improved internal company practices, can begin. The organization may focus on approaches that simultaneously save money or improve service while training employees and building a culture receptive to reducing transportation-related greenhouse gases. Examples of such projects include Hewlett-Packard Co.'s and Bristol-Myers Squibb Co.'s use of videoconferencing. It is important for employees to understand the customer service effects and for executives to get buy-in prior to implementing any changes, so that all of the outcomes and associated visibility of the projects are as positive as possible. It is also critical that management measure the costs and the results, so that the project's impact is clear and uncontested. For example, Abbott Laboratories and Schering-Plough Corp. both report specific fuel economy improvements—which can be translated into dollars saved—from their fleet initiatives.

Impacting supply chain practices with respect to transportation emissions involves decreasing fuel use through adjusting the volume, distance, and mode of shipping and using technology to increase shipments' efficiency and effectiveness. Meaningful measurements are essential here to continue the visibility and growth of environmental transportation tactics. Fourteen companies reported measures of efficiency such as saving money, reducing weight, or reducing inventory levels. Routing changes enabled Office Depot to increase the number of packages on a truck from about 130 to about 190. Twelve companies provided measures of effectiveness such as reducing greenhouse gases and other forms of pollution and improving service. By working with customers to schedule preferred delivery times, Dell increased first-time deliveries to customers by 80%, reducing their overall transportation needs.

These first three levels of environmentally sustainable transportation are really a progression of programs that do not require uncomfortable or difficult choices and yield solid environmental and financial results. Once a certain level of success has been achieved, an organization may be ready to move to the ultimate goal of strategic sustainable supply chain transportation. This entails working more closely with supply chain partners on an overall strategy for actively minimizing the supply chain's transportation greenhouse gas emissions. At this point, the trade-offs—societal impact versus business performance—become difficult. Executives must learn to manage mountains of data to get a decent view of the consequences that will be set off by any changes they make.

EMISSION ACCOMPLISHED: MAKING THE ENVIRONMENT A SUSTAINABLE PRIORITY

Companies that are serious about developing strategic sustainable supply chain transportation need to elevate environmental considerations when selecting transportation modes and particular carriers. Environmental considerations also must be factored into supplier selection and location of distribution and manufacturing sites. While environmental transportation may not be a direct driver of these decisions, it should be an explicit consideration. To facilitate the consideration of transportation and other environmental impacts in the supply chain, corporate executives should consider the following actions:

- Structuring their supply chain with suppliers and customers that have similar cultures with respect to sustainable practices and that are proactively focused on initiatives that minimize the impact of their transportation greenhouse gas emissions (such as partnering with SmartWay carriers for transport of goods throughout the supply chain);
- Utilizing transportation technology that reduces fuel and therefore emissions (for example, when purchasing new trucking equipment, purchasing only equipment that improves aerodynamics, such as low-resistance tires);
- Optimizing their supply chain's logistical network such that transportation distances are minimized (sourcing locally when feasible, moving operations closer to suppliers or customers, and eliminating unnecessary moves such as those between distribution centers);
- Developing detailed metrics that monitor actual as well as relative results from all implemented initiatives to determine which strategies have the biggest emission and cost impacts on the supply chain (measuring emission reductions and tracking the associated cost savings; for example, X tons of carbon dioxide in the past month, which amounts to X% of total carbon dioxide emissions, saving $X in fuel costs or X% of total fuel costs); and
- Utilizing knowledgeable personnel with skills in logistics and environmental sustainability to develop and implement company and supply chain transportation strategies.

This final level is an area that few companies have reached, but one in which the greatest potential improvements can be made with regard to freight transportation emissions. However, it is an area with potential for savings but also potential for initial higher costs. For example, companies such as HP, Dell, and Estee Lauder probably reduced their overall supply chain costs in converting air shipments to ground or ocean transport. On the other hand, FedEx's extensive introduction of alternative fuel technology may not have an immediate positive financial payback. But the company is willing to use the savings from some of its other environmental projects to fund further improvement in the hopes of eventually seeing a positive return on this technology. There is a limit to the improvements that companies can make in the supply chain by focusing solely on cutting waste and reconfiguring products and purchasing policies. Investing in environmentally friendly transportation technologies is the only way to encourage implementation of strategic initiatives that will ultimately lead to improvements in and reduction of the price of such technologies. The money that is saved through early efficiency improvements could be used in this way.

Few companies do this now, but that may change—although more out of necessity than environmental enlightenment. Since the end of 2006, diesel prices have risen 63.2%, peaking in summer 2008, decreasing through March 2009, and now slowly climbing again. The price of a barrel of oil during this period has been as high as $136.32 and as low as $31.84.[7] Regional shortages have occurred due to natural disasters such as Hurricane Ike and turmoil within the U.S. economy. This volatility is a lens into the future of oil and gas prices and supply. One way for companies to take some control over this fluctuation of pricing and availability is to lessen their dependence on these energy sources, which may also help the environment and reduce greenhouse gases from transportation.

Will corporations do it? They could, in fact, be on their way already. Since this study began, the economy has undergone seismic changes. Some companies may well have begun implementing transportation changes as part of cost-cutting plans.

In addition, companies do not always immediately update the information in their public documents. A recent check of the EPA SmartWay partner list shows 40 of the Fortune 500 companies have become partners since this study began in 2008. However, results from a recent McKinsey & Co. survey of 296 top executives regarding their top two supply chain priorities show that reducing costs is most important, with 57% including it among their top priorities. Only 4% indicated greenhouse gases emissions reduction among their top two priorities.[8] While the increased attention companies have given transportation practices during 2008 and 2009 is promising, the current economic downturn and the ongoing emphasis on supply chain cost-cutting may divert companies' funding and attention from nonmandatory spending, such as greenhouse-gas-reducing initiatives. Time will tell if they will progress to strategic sustainable supply chain transportation, although it seems from many accounts that time is running out.

REFERENCES

1. "U.S. Primary Energy Consumption by Source and Sector 2007." Dec. 5, 2008, www.eia.doe.gov; and "Emissions of Greenhouse Gases in the United States 2007." Dec. 5, 2008, ftp://ftp.eia.doe.gov

2. H. Lee. "Aligning Supply Chain Strategies With Product Uncertainties." *California Management Review* 44, no. 3 (2002): 105–119.

3. D. Lovaas. "Moving Freight: Transport Beyond Oil." *In Business* 29, no. 1 (2007): 19–21.

4. C. Facanha and A. Horvath. "Environmental Assessment of Logistics Outsourcing." *Journal of Management in Engineering* 21, no. 1 (2005): 27–37.

5. Calculated from Bureau of Transportation Statistics. "Commodity Flow Survey." (1997). www.bts.gov; and U.S. Environmental Protection Agency. "Inventory of U.S. Greenhouse Gas Emissions and Sinks: 1990–2005." http://epa.gov

6. S. Murphy. "Will Sourcing Come Closer to Home?" *Supply Chain Management Review* 12, no. 6 (2008): 33–37.

7. Energy Information Administration. "Real Petroleum Prices." http://tonto.eia.doe.gov

8. "Supply Chain News: Reducing Supply Chain Costs Is Top Executive Priority—to No One's Surprise." (September 1). www.scdigest.com

About the Authors

Susan L. Golicic is an assistant professor of management at Colorado State University's College of Business. **Courtney N. Boerstler** is a Ph.D. candidate in marketing at the University of Oregon's Lundquist College of Business. **Lisa M. Ellram** is the James Evans Rees Distinguished Professor of Distribution in the Farmer School of Business's marketing department at Miami University in Oxford, Ohio, and currently serves as the coeditor in chief for the *Journal of Supply Chain Management*. Comment on this article or contact the authors at smrfeedback@mit.edu.

CHAPTER 8
IDENTIFYING THE PATHS TO TAKE TOWARD THE VISION

In real life, strategy is actually very straightforward. You pick a general direction and implement like hell.[1]

—*Jack Welch, former Chairman & CEO, General Electric*

OPENING VIGNETTE

Taking the path less traveled can be a strategic move. Begun in the 1940s by Sidney Garfield, the "corporate" doctors rode barges up and down the Colorado River to treat injured lumberjacks working for the industrialist Henry Kaiser. In this "Wild West" territory, the relatively sparse population and the distance between towns prevented access to rapid medical care, essential not only to save lives but also to keep Kaiser Construction Company in business.

This early model of the HMO (Health Maintenance Organization) provided the prototype for the future of what we now call managed care, the norm for contemporary medicine in the United States. Doctors were paid "prospectively" per member per month. Kaiser, from its inception, delivered medicine a different way, essentially delivering the birth of prepaid healthcare.

It was President Richard Nixon who, in the 1970s, promoted the California style Kaiser HMO model in the Health Maintenance Organization Act of 1973 as the initial development of market competition into the health care arena. It was not until the passage of the DRG (diagnostically related groupings) of Medicare Prospective Payment in the 1980s that the HMO model was established as a way to attract corporate America into providing health care benefits to employees. HMOs were billed as a way to limit the expense of providing medical benefits to the workforce.[2]

Today Kaiser Permanente has 8.7 million plan members and revenues of 42.1 billion dollars.[3] This ingenious solution, crafted due to necessity, is the largest non-profit managed care orga-

---

[1] J. Welch, with S. Welch, *Winning.* New York, NY: HarperBusiness, 2005.

[2] S. Jonas and A. Kovner. *Health Care Delivery in the United States*, 10e: 207–210. Springer Publishing, 2011.

[3] "Kaiser Permanente." Wikipedia, http://en.wikipedia.org/wiki/Kaiser_Permanente

nization in the United States. It focuses on standardizing medical care to optimize outcomes; operating under one name, with one set of policies; and creating both economies of scale and enhanced quality of care.

In this chapter, we consider specific strategies that can be used. Think of yourself at a crossroads, trying to decide what path to choose to get you to where you want to go. These paths are like the different strategies from which you can choose.

Organizations may choose to implement these strategies in some combination or in a sequence. Certainly large corporations are following more than one strategy at a time due to the complexity of their products and markets. The strategies you select should be determined based on your starting point, derived from your internal and external environmental assessment, and your destination—your vision and long-term goals.

The generic strategies we discussed in the previous chapter still apply, but these strategies simply provide more specific direction, e.g., how will you become a low-cost provider in a broad market?

Successful mastery of this material will enable you to:

- define a grand strategy
- describe strategies to promote growth internally
- explain strategies to promote growth by leveraging external resources
- identify strategies for retrenchment when a business is in trouble
- apply models for strategy selection

Following this chapter is a deeper look at the strategy of innovation.

INTRODUCTION

The types of strategies covered in this chapter are often referred to as *grand* strategies. The idea of a grand strategy dates back at least to the Roman Empire. Sun Tzu's *The Art of War* is almost certainly the most famous study of strategy ever written and has had an extraordinary influence on the history of warfare; it has been dated back to 512 BCE (Tzu and Sawyer 1994). In the context of business, Hitt et al. (1982) assert that business strategy scholarship began in the 1960s with a variety of terms for corporate strategy at different levels of an organization. They define a grand strategy (p. 262) as "the major plan of action for achieving the sales and earning goals for an industrial firm as a whole" (rather than a product, division, or market segment) and suggest that the "grand strategies pursued by an organization are" (p. 267):

1. Stability
2. Internal growth
3. External acquisitive growth
4. Retrenchment

In the last two decades, scholars and executives have expanded the list, but these categories still apply. In our earlier chapter on sustainability, we addressed an organization's need for stability. In this chapter, our focus is on the last three types of grand strategies.

INTERNAL GROWTH

When a company uses its own capabilities and resources to grow, it has a range of options with different risk/reward ratios. The choice should depend on the results of the internal assessment, e.g., if a product is reaching maturity in its life cycle, you might pursue a concentrated growth or market development strategy. If you find your portfolio of development projects is insufficiently diverse, you might want to devote some additional resources and pursue a product development or innovation strategy.

Concentrated Growth

The simplest and least risky internal growth strategy is for dedicated effort and resources to expand an existing product's market share. This strategy is typically used in mature markets with relatively stable supply sources so that the operation is scalable. One example is when Gillette introduced the Fusion® razor and invested heavily in advertising and promotion, using celebrities such as Roger Federer and Tiger Woods to encourage customers to switch to the more expensive razor.

Market Development

In this strategy, growth comes by introducing an existing product or service into new market segments or channels of distribution. For example, when Microsoft invested in Facebook, it was trying to tap into a younger generation of tech-savvy users. Lumigen®, originally developed to treat glaucoma, is now also marketed as a product to grow eyelashes. Certainly, when a company decides to become international, it is looking to develop new markets.

Product Development

As you would expect, this strategy involves a substantial modification of an existing product, such as the Apple iPhone 4S, and the introduction of Siri. According to Apple's website (http://www.apple.com/iphone/features/siri.html), "Siri on iPhone 4S lets you use your voice to send messages, schedule meetings, place phone calls, and more. Ask Siri to do things just by talking the way you talk. Siri understands what you say, knows what you mean, and even talks back."

Product development can also take the form of creating related products that can be marketed to existing customers. For example, Amazon.com's Kindle® e-reader leveraged its reading customer base and the fact that most content has a digital format.

Innovation

This is the riskiest approach to internally-driven growth, but it also has the potential for high rewards. Pharmaceutical companies pursue many different projects to have only one make it through the gauntlet to become approved for sale. 3M is renowned for its research culture, where

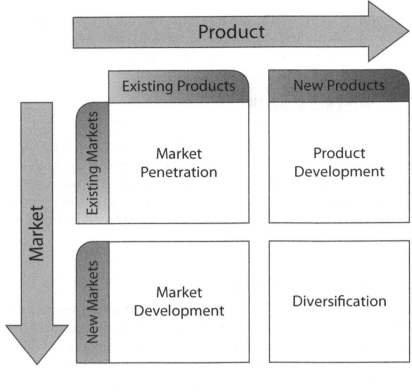

Figure 8-1. Ansoff Matrix

scientists are encouraged to spend 20% of their time on unsponsored research. Innovative capability is so important, we will devote an entire chapter to it. For now, understand that innovation is the most aggressive way to generate growth from within an organization.

These internal growth strategies can be considered in two dimensions: oriented by products and by markets, whether new or existing. The Ansoff (1957) matrix (shown in Figure 8-1) was intended to help companies, especially those that find themselves in the mature stage of the product life-cycle, to ensure growth through one of four approaches: market penetration, market development, product development, and diversification, the most risky of the four alternatives. Ansoff defined the lowest risk as market penetration, increasing the percentage of consumers using a product or increasing the product usage by existing customers.

EXTERNAL ACQUISITIVE GROWTH

Often companies will look outside of their organizations for opportunities to grow by some form of acquisition. The motives for these strategies vary. Rarely is it easy to accomplish acquisitive growth.

Horizontal Integration

When two competitors merge, or one acquires the other, it is considered to be a horizontal integration, growing bigger in the same segment of the value chain. Size matters, so firms will do this to dominate a market, create economies of scale, and leverage negotiating power. XM and Sirius Satellite Radio merged in 2008 to become Sirius XM. They still seem to be separate networks, perhaps because of different radio receivers' capabilities (http://www.siriusxm.com/subscriptions).

Vertical Integration

A merger or acquisition is considered to be *vertical* if it involves companies in different parts of the same value chain. Backward, or upstream, integration is when a company acquires a supplier;

forward or downstream integration happens when a channel of distribution or customer is acquired. Shaw Industries started its path toward vertical integration in 1972 by acquiring a yarn producer (upstream supplier). It created its own trucking subsidiary to exert greater control over the logistics functions in its value chain. Downstream efforts include the establishment of retail operations with Shaw Design Centers and Shaw Flooring Galleries (http://www.shawfloors.com/About-Shaw/Timeline).

Concentric or Related Diversification

This is a strategy pursued by businesses to expand within an industry, generally to counterbalance certain weaknesses. For example, when The Quaker Oats Company (TQOC) purchased Stokely Van Camp (SVC), the two companies were in the same core business: consumer groceries. However, the real impetus behind the acquisition was a then little-known product of SVC called Gatorade®. The intent was to offset the seasonality of the hot cereals division with an offering that would appeal to consumers in the hot weather. With the marketing prowess of TQOC, a new category of beverage was created, and sales initially overwhelmed its distribution capacity.

Conglomerate or Unrelated Diversification

As the onomatopoeic "conglomerate" would indicate, this form of organization combines companies that only fit together as a diversified glob. There is generally no real effort to create synergies among the subsidiaries. A popular approach in the 1980s, it has fallen into disfavor—with one notable exception. Warren Buffet's Berkshire Hathaway has businesses ranging from ice cream and candy to furniture and car insurance. He treats the companies as a stock portfolio and does not get involved in day-to-day operations. In fact Buffet writes in the annual report (2010, p. 7):

> At Berkshire, managers can focus on running their businesses. They are not subjected to meetings at headquarters nor financing worries nor Wall Street harassment. They simply get a letter from me every two years (it's reproduced on pages 104–105) and call me when they wish. And their wishes do differ: There are managers to whom I have not talked in the last year, while there is one with whom I talk almost daily. Our trust is in people rather than process. A "hire well, manage little" code suits both them and me.

In 2010, the net earnings per share of BK-A holders was $7,928.

Joint Ventures

When two (typically) companies agree to create and operate a new entity, it is considered a joint venture (JV). It can take the form of majority/minority JV or be a 50/50 JV. For example, in August 2010, General Electric and Intel Corporation:

> announced the entry into a definitive agreement to form a 50/50 joint venture to create a new healthcare company focused on telehealth and independent living. The new company will be formed by combining assets of GE Healthcare's Home Health

division and Intel's Digital Health Group, and will be owned equally by GE and Intel. (Bruner 2010)

In early 2011, the venture achieved regulatory approval and went operational as "Care Innovations" (IntelPR 2011).

Strategic Alliances

Rather than creating an independent venture, strategic alliances tend to be characterized by legal agreements and expiration dates. The general idea of a strategic alliance is to create a shared result that the participants could not otherwise achieve. TiVo, Inc. and Sony Corporation of America announced a strategic alliance to manufacture Sony personal video recorders that enable the TiVo Personal Television Service. It is a non-exclusive agreement that may lead to the integration of Sony products and original content, including games, music, and movies (PRNewswire 2011).

Consortia

Less structured that a strategic alliance, a consortium represents strong interlocking relationships that are maintained by mutual benefit rather than by legal agreements. Known in Japan as *Keiretsu* and in South Korea as *Chaebois*, these families of companies work together for a common good. For example, the Georgia Research Alliance (www.gra.org) is a consortium of companies, universities, and developers who are working to promote innovation and job creation in the state of Georgia.

Of course, in considering the strategic alternatives that involve collaboration, there is both opportunity and risk. One of the greatest concerns is the amount of control the company has in determining the outcome of the venture; another is the cost that may or may not result in the desired objectives. Just as in a personal relationship, a business relationship depends upon intangibles such as reputation and trust to make the collaboration successful.

RETRENCHMENT

Our last category of grand strategies falls under retrenchment, i.e., what companies do when business is in decline.

Turnaround

A turnaround strategy is used in the case of a long-term decline and is often characterized by corporate restructuring. An example of this was when Anne Mulcahy was selected to be the CEO of Xerox in 2001, under extremely adverse conditions. Her turnaround strategy was to unbind the product matrix structure of the organization, resurrect the innovative culture of Xerox, and communicate. In a 2006 interview at the MIT Sloan School, she said that two thirds of Xerox's revenue came from products developed in the last two years (Mulcahy 2006).

Divestiture

This type of retrenchment is like throwing ballast out of an air balloon to make it lighter. Companies selectively sell off product lines or divisions to strengthen the financial condition of the remaining businesses. Proctor & Gamble is selling its Pringles snack line, as it is under-performing expectations (Ziobro 2011). In the 1980s, The Quaker Oats Company spun off its subsidiary, Fisher Price, because management believed that the stock market was undervaluing the contribution of the toy company in the overall stock price.

Bankruptcy

There are different forms of bankruptcy, but all involve court action. Like liquidation, some bankruptcies involve selling the assets and distributing the proceeds to creditors, usually at a fraction of what is owed. Another type is a "reorganization bankruptcy," which holds creditors back temporarily. Delta Airlines was declared bankrupt in September 2005. It successfully emerged from bankruptcy after establishing a new route structure, cost-cutting aggressively, merging with Northwest Airlines, and getting creditors to cede 15% ownership to employees (Foust 2009).

Liquidation

When the sum of the parts is greater than the whole, i.e., the pieces of a business are worth more than its market valuation, it makes sense to liquidate. Initially, the Borders chain of bookstores filed for Chapter 11 bankruptcy protection, reorganizing by closing more than 400 stores and letting go of more than 10,000 workers. When these measures were not enough, management sought a buy-out, which fell through. They are currently undergoing liquidation (including a guitar signed by former Beatles guitarist George Harrison, found in the company's headquarters) of its corporate property (Cohen 2011).

STRATEGY SELECTION

Why do some strategies seem to work for some companies and not for others? One possibility is a company's *personality* or *typology*. Just as humans are wired to have preferences and seem to excel in certain situations, as sociological entities, companies also have cultures and climates. As shown in Figure 8-2 on the following page, Miles and Snow and their colleagues described in their work the *cultures* of companies as defenders, prospectors, analyzers, and reactors. These types are a combination of product and behavioral dimensions and characterize the competitive environment as well as product position and dominance in their respective markets.

Another model that helps companies to navigate the uncertain waters of strategic alternatives is known as the Strategic Position and Action Evaluation (SPACE) matrix. The SPACE approach integrates environmental analysis with strategic alternatives to select the optimum strategic alternatives based on the company's situation.

The four dimensions of the SPACE model are the external factors of environmental stability (ES) and industry strength (IS), and the internal factors of the company's financial strength (FS) and its competitive advantage (CA). Through a series of questions, companies are scored on each of these dimensions, which ultimately determine in which quadrant the company finds

	Strategy	Environment	Organizational Characteristics
Prospector	Innovate. Find new market opportunities. Grow. Take risks.	Dynamic, growing	Creative, innovative, flexible, decentralized
Defender	Protect turf. Retrench, hold current market.	Stable	Tight control, centralized, production efficiency, low overhead
Analyzer	Maintain current market plus moderate innovation	Moderate change	Tight control and flexibility, efficient production, creativity
Reactor	No clear strategy. React to specific condi9tions. Drift.	Any condition	No clear organizational approach; depends on current needs

Figure 8-2. Miles and Snow's Strategy Typology

itself and which strategic alternatives should be considered: aggressive, competitive, conservative, or defensive, as shown in Figure 8-3.

The steps required to develop a SPACE Matrix follow:

1. Develop a set of questions and variables to define financial strength (FS), competitive advantage (CA), environmental stability (ES), and industry strength (IS).
2. Evaluate the dimension and score with a number ranging from +1 (worst) to +6 (best) to each of the variables that make up the FS and IS dimensions.
3. Assign a numerical value ranging from -1 (best) to -6 (worst) to each of the variables that make the ES and CA dimensions.
4. Compute an average score for FS, CA, IS, and ES by summing the values given to the variables of each dimension and dividing by the number of variables included in the respective dimension.
5. Plot the average scores for FS, IS, ES, and CA on the appropriate axis in the SPACE Matrix.
6. Connect the four coordinates which results in a diamond shape with SPACE that predominately occupies one of the four quadrants.
7. The upper right quadrant is the **Aggressive** quadrant, the upper left quadrant **Conservative**, lower left **Defensive**, and lower right **Competitive**.

- **Aggressive** strategies include: market penetration, market development, product development, backward integration, forward integration, horizontal integration, conglomerate diversification, concentric diversification, and horizontal diversification, or a combination strategy are alternatives due to favorable financial and industry strength.
- **Defensive** strategies include: divesture, liquidation, and retrenchment due to unfavorable positions in all four dimensions.
- **Conservative** strategies include: status quo, unrelated diversification, or harvesting.
- **Competitive** strategies include: market penetration, product enhancement, product development, market development, and status quo. (Radde and Louw 1998)

SPACE MATRIX

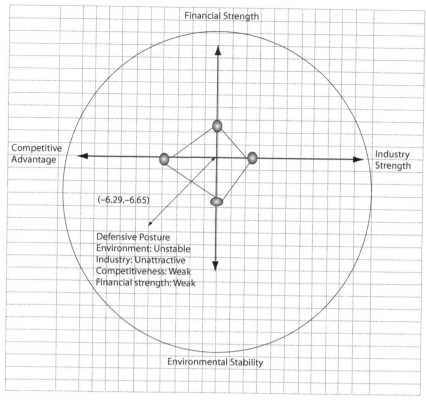

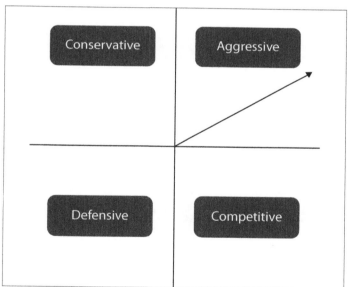

Figures 8-3a and b. Sample SPACE Matrix (a) and Quadrant Labels (b)

APPLICATION AND REFLECTION

- Pick a product category and identify different brands that fit each of the four generic strategy types.

- For the different types of grand strategies described, identify your own example.

- Social media, i.e., Internet content that is user-generated, is transforming personal and professional lives. Shih (2010) describes how businesses are using the "social graph" to recruit employees, identify prospective customers, manage public relations, and solve problems. In the following reading, you will learn more about the power of social media. Challenge yourself to think of the possibilities.

CHAPTER 9
TAKING A DEEPER LOOK AT INNOVATION

As a matter of fact, capitalist economy is not and cannot be stationary. Nor is it merely expanding in a steady manner. It is incessantly being revolutionized from within by new enterprise, i.e., by the intrusion of new commodities or new methods of production or new commercial opportunities into the industrial structure.[1]

—Joseph Schumpeter

OPENING VIGNETTE

Do you think all basic manufacturing has been sent overseas from the United States? Think again. According to *The Wall Street Journal,* many people are surprised to learn that most of the 11 billion paper clips used in the United States are manufactured domestically. ACCO Brands, Inc. self-described as a "global powerhouse of leading office-product brands," is introducing a new paperclip. The Klix clip is made of stainless steel, comes in a variety of colors, and costs sixteen times more than a conventional paper clip.

Import tariffs have protected (non-plastic) domestic clip makers from competition, especially from China. Product innovation has been almost non-existent, although ACCO puts a strong emphasis on process innovation and lean principles. The new Klix represents a rare innovation in what is considered a commodity product.

---

[1] J. Schumpeter. *Capitalism, Socialism, and Democracy.* Part I, Chapter III (1942): 31.

Based on an article by James R. Hagerty, reported on August 29, 2011, in *The Wall Street Journal.* Accessed September 15, 2011 at http:online.wsj.com

Akey characteristic of strategic management is its dynamic nature. The external environment changes, you adapt your strategies. The competition takes an unexpected turn, you adjust accordingly. If something does not turn out as intended, you modify the approach. A strategy itself represents a plan for change.

Abrahamson (2000) suggests that companies can bring about change without the pain, confusion, cynicism, or burnout that seems inevitable by adopting a process of *dynamic stability*. The idea is that organizational members have a sense of security in a culture of flexibility. The process alternates major change efforts with smaller ones, such as *tinkering, kludging,*[2] and *pacing*. While you will not practice tinkering in this chapter, you will understand the need for dynamic stability and an emphasis on innovation. Successful mastery of this material will enable you to:

- articulate the importance of innovation
- identify sources of innovation
- understand disruptive innovation
- explain reverse innovation
- illustrate different ways in which companies innovate

INTRODUCTION

One of our grand strategies for internally-generated growth was innovation, specifically as new product development. In this chapter we are taking a broader view of innovation, and we will end with a reading, "12 Different Ways for Companies to Innovate," to emphasize that perspective. Innovation is the introduction of new things or methods (www.dictionary.com). More specifically, management authority Peter Drucker (1985) defines innovation as an act that endows resources with a new capacity to create wealth.

THE IMPORANCE OF INNOVATION

As our opening quote from the renowned economist suggests, innovation is central to being competitive in a capitalist economy. Maintaining a company's status quo is likely to result in it falling behind as other companies innovate. This is what Schumpeter and others have termed "the creative destruction of capitalism." Competitive forces drive innovation—and a lack of innovation drives destruction.

OK, so you need to innovate. The problem is that it is easier said than done. In fact, in its 2002 issue devoted to "The Innovative Enterprise," the *Harvard Business Review* suggests that one of the toughest challenges an executive faces is inspiring innovation while keeping everyday operations running smoothly, i.e., maintaining dynamic stability.

One key hurdle is a fear of failure. The adage "nothing ventured, nothing gained" is familiar to all of us, yet we hesitate. Our education tends to train our minds to think there is only one right answer, and if you do not select it, you lose credit. If you make a mistake in business, will it be a career-ending move? Organizational cultures that inspire innovation encourage creative exploration ("there is no such thing as a bad idea") and are not punitive when it comes to innovations that disappoint ("it's OK to make a mistake; just don't make the same mistake twice;

---

[2] According to Abrahamson (2000), kludging is tinkering, but with a college education (i.e., it has more complexity).

learn from it). A climate of safety goes a long way in encouraging people to share their ideas. *The Wall Street Journal* reported that companies are rewarding employees' mistakes to spur innovation (Shellenbarger 2011).

Another obstacle to innovation is inflated expectations about what it takes to be creative. Some people think you have to have artistic skills or a radical idea to be innovative; in reality, there are different ways to be creative. For example, Eisner (1966) describes boundary pushing (expanding limits) and boundary breaking (reversing assumptions) as two types of creativity. His view of invention is not limited to the radical idea, but encompasses "useful combinations, congruencies [and] … discovery followed by purposeful activity" (p. 327).

Illustration

Who would have ever thought that a snowboarding kid from Utah would not only create a product, but take a company public? Well, the snowboarding founder of Skullcandy, Rick Alden, did. His company specializes in earphones and headphones that fly off the shelf. When Skullcandy stock went public on NASDAQ with an initial price 15% above the projected IPO ask, Alden was named one of *Spring Capital's* "Top 100 Venture Entrepreneurs." In 2008, the Skullcandy ear bud was named "the world's coolest ear bud" by *Fortune*. The company has quickly jumped to its place as the third most-sold headphone in the U.S. marketplace. Revenues have grown from 9 million in 2006 to 231 million in 2011 (Tillman 2011).

So why did these earphones take off? The combination of focus on the niche market of young athletes listening while participating in action sports with specialized distribution through sports retailers and high tech gear stores, in combination with celebrity sports endorsement, set this company "sailing." Alden, an avid athlete and snowboarder, demonstrated creativity with the combination of musical entertainment and action sports.

This unique combination of needs, followed by purposeful activity such as product development and niche marketing behind a clear vision, drove this entrepreneur to financial and market success. Innovation does not need to be complex, just timely, translatable, and desirable.

In the following section, we discuss ways to overcome these stumbling blocks by being aware of different sources of innovation.

SOURCES OF INNOVATION

Divine inspiration not withstanding, it is possible to be deliberately analytical in an innovative process. Just as strategic management is a process that leads you to a desired result, innovation is also a course of action that can be accomplished in a progression. As part of understanding the company in context and performing environmental scanning, you can be alert to various sources of innovation.

Drucker

Peter Drucker acknowledges that innovations can spring from a flash of genius, but argues that (2002, p. 4):

> Most innovations, however, especially the successful ones, result from a conscious, purposeful search for innovation opportunities, which are found only in a few situations.

Four such areas of opportunity exist within a company or industry: **unexpected occurrences, incongruities, process needs, and industry and market changes.** Three additional sources of opportunity exist outside a company in its social and intellectual environment: **demographic changes, changes in perception and changes in knowledge.** [emphasis added]

According to Drucker (1985, p. 35), "the overwhelming majority of successful innovations *exploit* change. ... There are innovations that in themselves constitute a major change ... but these are exceptions. ... Most successful innovations are far more prosaic. ... Systematic innovation means monitoring *seven* sources for innovative opportunity."

Illustrations

Of the seven sources, we will illustrate three here. *Unexpected occurrences* can be unexpected successes or failures. Pharmaceutical company Pfizer's introduction of Viagra™ might well be considered both. During clinical trials of the medication as a heart medicine, it was found to have an unexpected side effect, increasing blood flow to the penis during sexual stimulation.

Incongruities are disparities between what is and what could be or what should be. Anyone who has carried an infant in a car seat can tell you it *should* be easier. To protect the baby, the car seat is understandably bulky, but this makes it necessary to carry it away from the body. You can take the baby out of the car seat and put it into a stroller, but depending on the child, that process *could* be easier. Graco®, a leading manufacturer of baby strollers, has addressed this incongruity with "travel systems" that allow infant seats to be securely attached to stroller frames, as shown in Figure 9-1.

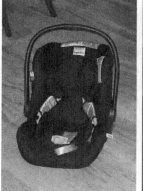

Process need can point to innovations, particularly in services. Berry et al. (2006, p. 59) categorize four different types of market-creating service innovations, according to type of benefit, i.e., whether they offer a new core benefit or new way of delivering a "core" benefit, and type of service, i.e., if the service consumption is separable or inseparable from its production.

Figure 9-1. 3-in-1 stroller

- Flexible solutions—separable service with a new core benefit, e.g., CNN delivering news 24 hours/day.
- Controllable convenience—separable service with new delivery, e.g., Netflix offering movies by mail or via the Internet.
- Comfortable gains—inseparable service with a new core benefit, e.g., Starbucks offering high quality coffee in a relaxing atmosphere at convenient locations.
- Respectful access—inseparable service with a new delivery that respects the customers' time and physical presence, e.g., Southwest Airlines offering affordable, no-frills, short-haul transportation.

Sustainability

In Chapter 4, we introduced the idea of sustainability. Not only is innovation necessary to generally sustain the organization over the long term, the push for environmental sustainability is creating many opportunities for innovation. Nimodumolu et al. (2009, p. 58) assert that sustainability is now the key driver of innovation, and that, "in the future, only companies that make sustainability a goal will achieve competitive advantage. This means rethinking business models as well as products, technologies, and processes." They present a five stage process, identifying sustainability challenges, competencies, and opportunities (p. 60):

1. Viewing compliance as an opportunity
2. Making value chains sustainable
3. Designing sustainability products and services
4. Developing new business models
5. Creating next-practice platforms

It is important for any kind of innovation process to be forward-thinking, and this is especially true with efforts to become sustainable. Current benchmarks for emissions, for example, are likely to be outdated within the time it takes for a company to become compliant.

In their assessment of successes and failures from other emerging technologies, Day and Schoemaker (2011) propose 10 lessons for green technologies, including: "technology substitution is rarely a zero-sum game" (p. 39), acknowledging that green innovations will not only substitute for but also coexist with existing technologies. They emphasize the importance of collaboration, thinking beyond industry boundaries, and sharing knowledge for innovative synergies.

Base of the Pyramid

The base of the pyramid (BOP) refers to the billions of people who live on less than 2,000 USD per year. This market is a source of innovation:

> when [multi-national corporations] MNCs provide basic goods and services that reduce costs to the poor and help improve their standard of living—while generating an acceptable return on investment—the results benefit everyone. … Businesses can gain three important advantages by serving the poor—a new source of revenue growth, greater efficiency, and access to innovation. (Prahalad and Hammond 2002, p. 51)

Building on this insight, Anderson and Markides (2007, p. 84) offer that strategic innovation at the BOP is based on four A's:

- affordability, delivering offerings at a price point that enables consumption by even the poorest consumers;
- acceptability, responding to specific cultural issues and local business practices;
- availability, distributing or delivering products and services to the most isolated communities; and
- awareness, learning to use alternative communication modes and methods for marketing.

In India, the influence of Mahatma Gandhi's emphasis on affordability and sustainability has fueled "Gandhian Innovation" by Indian companies, by either creating or sourcing new capabilities, modifying organizational capabilities, or by disrupting business models (Prahalad and Mashelkar 2010). While the first two practices are familiar as a resource-based view of management, the idea of disruptive models is explained below.

DISRUPTIVE INNOVATION

The term *disruptive innovation* was brought to the forefront of management thinking by Harvard professor Clayton Christensen in his 1997 book, *The Innovator's Dilemma*. In basic terms, market leaders tend to make incremental improvements to extend their products' life cycles. They focus on the needs or expectations of their existing customers[3] and disregard new entrants who typically have an inferior product, which initially garners a small amount of market share. As shown in Figure 9-2, some new entrants become *disruptors*, by displacing the incumbent and becoming dominant in the market.

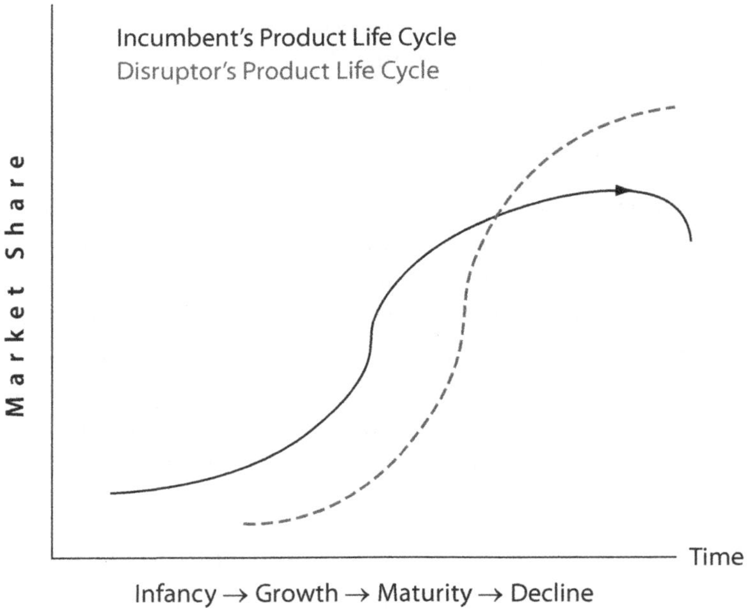

Incumbent's Product Life Cycle
Disruptor's Product Life Cycle

Market Share

Time

Infancy → Growth → Maturity → Decline

Figure 9-2. Disruptive Innovation

Illustration

For those of us who can remember the introduction of mobile phones, they were clearly inferior to landline connections. Although bulky, expensive, and unreliable, they did provide a new functionality: untethered communications. As we have witnessed over the last two decades, cell phones have become so far superior and "smart" that many people forgo having a landline telephone number, or have one only for emergencies.

REVERSE INNOVATION

The idea of *reverse innovation*, a term coined by General Electric (GE), is a combination of disruptive innovation and Gandhian innovation. Innovations typically start in industrialized nations, and as the products mature, they are disseminated to other markets to extend the products' life cycles. Reversing that process and innovating for the people at the base of the pyramid can lead to disruptive opportunities:

---

[3] As Henry Ford is credited with saying, "If I had asked people what they wanted, they would have said faster horses;" customers' demands can be limited by their familiarity with existing capabilities.

Developing countries are ideal target markets for disruptive technologies for at least two reasons. First, business models that are forged in low-income markets travel well; that is, they can be profitably applied in more places than models defined in high income markets. ... In addition to having more adaptable business models, disruptive innovators also compete against nonconsumption in low-income markets. (Hart and Christensen 2002, p. 53)

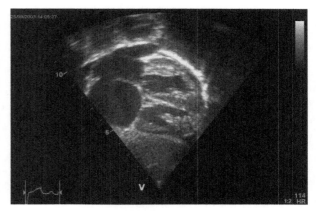

Figure 9-3. Ultrasound Picture of a Heart

What GE is doing is disrupting itself by pursuing reverse innovation—to avoid being displaced by other disruptors. For example, they collaborated with Chinese doctors to develop an inexpensive ultrasound machine. It is inferior to GE's other ultrasound machines in terms of resolution, but available at a fraction of the others' costs. It is affordable and accessible, and provides a service that might not otherwise be available to 90% of China's population (Immelt et. al. 2009). It is also now being sold in the United States.

APPLICATION AND REFLECTION

- Identify an example of a service innovation and categorize it according to the four types of market-creating service innovations.

- Brainstorm ideas of products that would be well-suited to reverse innovation.

- In the following reading selection, we close our deeper look at innovation with an emphasis on types of innovations beyond new product development—other opportunities to provide resources with a new ability to create wealth. For You, Inc., apply the 12 different ways companies innovate to your own professional career.

THE 12 DIFFERENT WAYS
FOR COMPANIES TO INNOVATE

Mohanbir Sawhney, Robert C. Wolcott, and Inigo Arroniz

The 12 Dimensions of Business Innovation

Dimension	Definition	Examples
Offerings	Develop innovative new products or services.	•Gillette Mach3Turbo razor •Apple iPod music player and iTunes music service
Platform	Use common components or building blocks to create derivative offerings.	•General Motors OnStar telematics platform •Disney animated movies
Solutions	Create integrated and customized offerings that solve end-to-end customer problems.	•UPS logistics services Supply Chain Solutions •DuPont Building Innovations for construction
Customers	Discover unmet customer needs or identify underserved customer segments.	•Enterprise Rent-A-Car focus on replacement car renters •Green Mountain Energy focus on "green power"
Customer Experience	Redesign customer interactions across all touch points and all moments of contact.	•Washington Mutual Occasio retail banking concept •Cabela's "store as entertainment experience" concept
Value Capture	Redefine how company gets paid or create innovative new revenue streams.	•Google paid search •Blockbuster revenue-sharing with movie distributors
Processes	Redesign core operating processes to improve efficiency and effectiveness.	•General Electric Design for Six Sigma (DFSS)
Organization	Change form, function or activity scope of the firm.	•Cisco partner-centric networked virtual organization •Procter & Gamble front-back hybrid organization for customer focus
Supply Chain	Think differently about sourcing and fulfillment.	•Moen ProjectNet for collaborative design with suppliers •General Motors Celta use of integrated supply and online sales
Presence	Create new distribution channels or innovative points of presence, including the places where offerings can be bought or used by customers.	•Starbucks music CD sales in coffee stores •Diebold RemoteTeller System for banking
Networking	Create network-centric intelligent and integrated offerings.	•Otis Remote Elevator Monitoring service •Department of Defense Network Centric Warfare
Brand	Leverage a brand into new domains.	•Virgin Group "branded venture capital" •Yahoo! as a lifestyle brand

Mohanbir Sawhney, Robert C. Wolcott, and Inigo Arroniz. "The 12 Different Ways for Companies to Innovate." *MIT Sloan Management Review* 47, no. 3 (2006): 78. Copyright © 2006 by *MIT Sloan Management Review*.

CLOSING CASE

We close the section on considering strategic options with a case study about the Intel Corporation. You may find it helpful to also consult www.intel.com. As you read the case, be prepared to respond to the following:

1. Evaluate Intel's product base using the BCG matrix.
2. What grand strategies have Intel used in the past?
3. Why is management concerned with pursuing an innovation strategy?
4. What types of innovation are being considered?
5. What are the challenges and obstacles that prevent Peter Hake from creating a portfolio of new initiatives within the organization?
6. If you were Hake, what would you do differently?

INTEL CORPORATE VENTURING

Nicholas Dew

Peter Hake, senior vice president of Intel's Growing Green Businesses project, took a moment before entering his weekly strategy meeting. As he quietly collected his thoughts, it occurred to Hake that wherever he went at Intel, he seemed to see people being "chased by bears." Hake chuckled to himself and thought: "If you are being chased by a bear, you really have to run faster than the other guy to ensure that he will be eaten instead of you." The same point had been made by Andy Grove, the former CEO of Intel, whose management philosophy seemed to have served the company so well for many years. Grove had always explicitly stressed, "If the competition is chasing you (and they always are—this is why 'only the paranoid survive'), you only get out of the valley of death by outrunning the people who are after you."[1]

THE COMPANY

Intel was founded in 1968 by Gordon Moore, Robert Noyce, and Andy Grove. The company's original focus was on computer memory chips, and the firm experienced extremely rapid growth after going public in 1971. In 1978, Intel introduced its first microprocessor, the 8086, and the company's microprocessor strategy fed the growth in personal computing throughout the 1980s. Faced with the commoditization of the memory-chip business in the mid-1980s, Intel made a strategic leap of faith and exited that business in 1985, "betting the farm" instead on its technological leadership in microprocessors.

From 1987, the company's visibility accelerated rapidly under the leadership of the people-oriented Andy Grove (president and CEO) and the technically savvy Gordon Moore (chairman). In 1991, it began its Intel Inside marketing program, in which it cooperated with PC makers in a

---

[1] Andy Grove. *Only the Paranoid Survive*. New York: Doubleday, 1996.

major advertising program to build the Intel brand. This marketing strategy proved enormously successful and made the company the largest co-op advertiser in the world.[2] The year 1993 saw the introduction of the now ubiquitous Pentium chip, the fifth-generation microprocessor spawned by Intel technology.

With PC sales continuing to boom and Intel's market segment share standing at around 85%, the leadership of the company passed to Craig Barrett (president and CEO) in 1998. Barrett faced the challenge of an extraordinary legacy: In the 20 years since its founding, Intel's revenues had grown at an average rate of 27% a year.[3] But insiders were confident Barrett was up to the task of continuing Intel's lavish success. "I think of Gordon Moore as the greatest technologist the industry has ever seen, Andy Grove as the greatest strategist, and Craig Barrett as the greatest manager," said Patrick Gelsinger, an Intel vice president.[4]

By 1999, Intel racked up over $29 billion in sales and made profits of $7.3 billion. The company's headcount grew to 70,000 people globally, ranking it as one of the top employers of the New Economy. The company, listed on NASDAQ, saw its market capitalization grow to a staggering $450 billion as of June 2000, making it a Fortune Top 10 firm.[5] Also in June 2000, Intel announced its Intel Pentium 4 processor brand name for its new generation of desktop microprocessors. The new Pentium 4 continued to build upon what had become, in less than 10 years, one of the world's most recognized brand names. Scheduled to be introduced in the second half of 2000, the Pentium 4 processor was based on what Intel press releases described as "revolutionary" technology designed to maximize the performance of Internet applications.

COMPETITIVE ADVANTAGE AT INTEL

Intel witnessed extraordinary growth during its 22-year life by largely concentrating on one product area: microprocessors. The company's competitive advantage rested on the fact that it had been tremendously successful in breaking down and rationalizing the manufacturing process for microprocessors—a product it practically invented—to an incredible level of precision. As Moore pointed out, "If you look at our semiconductors and melt them down for silicon, that's a tiny fraction of cost. The rest is intellect and mistakes."

This rationalization process had been achieved over a 20-year period at the price of keeping the entire organization focused on the scientific principles of getting higher yields from its raw materials and inputs. During its extensive growth period, Intel decentralized into small operating units. The company instituted its McIntel approach to production—named after McDonald's approach to flipping hamburgers. This approach focused on perfecting production in a small unit and then cloning the unit's processes and practices at other Intel production sites.[6]

Intel enjoyed a significant cost advantage in producing microprocessors compared with all its rivals in the world. This fact had resulted in an enviable position for individuals in the company with sophisticated engineering expertise. Intel became a company regarded, by insiders and outsiders, as a showcase in how engineering excellence could drive high-technology firms.

---

[2] Intel Web site, July 2000.

[3] Elizabeth Corcoran. "Reinventing Intel." Forbes, May 3, 1999.

[4] Corcoran.

[5] Intel Web site, July 2000.

[6] J. B. Quinn. Intelligent Enterprise, 1992.

Moreover, the learning-curve effects Intel was able to drive into its production processes also had significant repercussions on the company's competitive pricing strategy. Intel used production learning as a competitive weapon by pricing its most advanced and newest chips high and pricing its less-advanced and older chips low. By 1999, chip prices ranged between $3,693 for a high end Xeon processor and $63 for a modest Celeron processor.[7]

COMPANY CULTURE AT INTEL

Intel was a company noted by insiders and outsiders alike for its distinctive culture. The company took very deliberate measures to inculcate employees with The Intel Culture. One notable aspect of the company's culture was the policy of "constructive confrontation" that Intel deliberately fostered. Intel employees were discouraged from letting social graces get in the way of problem-solving processes, and the policy was thought by many commentators to be a major influencing factor on Intel's success. The company was aware of its own aggressiveness; Barrett once commented to Grove, "There may be an alternative to grabbing someone and slamming them over the head with a sledgehammer."[8]

The company also strove hard to remove the trappings of executive authority from the organization: even Intel cofounders Moore and Noyce worked in office cubicles with no doors and walls. Parking spaces at the company were on a first-come, first-served basis. Project engineers were given authorization to spend up to $250,000 with no prior agreement from their bosses.[9]

Indeed, a bias toward numbers was a general and strongly exhibited part of the company's culture. Performance measurement pervaded everything. Noyce once observed, "We are seeking higher achievers. And high achievers love to be measured, because otherwise they can't prove to themselves that they are achieving. Measuring them says you care about them."[10]

Intel was also notable for how its engineering bias seeped into nonengineering parts of the organization. Engineering dominance even extended to the company's marketing function.

Indeed, up until the time Intel began its Intel Inside brand-building campaign, even the marketing function at the company had been organized around the engineering demands of the product. Intel's engineers worked at customers' premises to understand customer needs in great detail and participated extensively in next-generation product development processes at Intel.[11]

INTEL'S MANAGEMENT PHILOSOPHY

Several important ideas evolved to be deeply rooted in the corporate psyche at Intel. First, the company had paid close attention to Moore's Law. Moore, one of the great engineering brains behind Intel's extraordinary success, suggested Moore's Law as a rule of thumb for the progress of chip technology. Put simply, Moore predicted in 1965 that the number of transistors that the industry would be able to place on a computer chip would double every year. In 1995, he updated his prediction to once every two years. Moore's Law subsequently emerged as a guiding

[7] Corcoran.

[8] Corcoran.

[9] Quinn.

[10] Quinn.

[11] Quinn.

principle for the industry to deliver ever-more-powerful semiconductor chips at proportionate decreases in cost. As Intel's Web site pointed out, "Moore's observation, now known as Moore's Law, described a trend that has continued and is still remarkably accurate. It is the basis for many planners' performance forecasts. In 26 years the number of transistors on a chip has increased more than 3,200 times, from 2,300 on the 4004 in 1971 to 7.5 million on the Pentium II processor."[12]

Second, Grove's "paranoia" became a mantra for strategic management at Intel. Grove's perspective is best known from his 1996 management book, *Only The Paranoid Survive*. Grove's "paranoid" management style motivated the Intel organization to act on Moore's Law and drive technological progress in microprocessors. As Grove commented, "We live in an age in which the pace of technological change is pulsating ever faster, causing waves that spread outward toward all industries. This increased rate of change will have an impact on you, no matter what you do for a living. ... In technology, whatever can be done will be done."[13]

Grove saw early on that the high-tech business would be driven by two factors. The first was horizontalization: "As an industry becomes more competitive, companies are forced to retreat to their strongholds and specialize, in order to become world class in whatever segment they end up occupying." Indeed, the PC industry developed along predominantly horizontal lines, with companies competing either to make processors, build computers, or design software, but very rarely competing in all areas at the same time (i.e., Intel did not dabble in software, Dell did not dabble in processors, Microsoft did not dabble in building computers). Horizontalization was Grove's expression of watch-that-basket theory: As Mark Twain put it, "Put all your eggs in one basket and watch that basket." Grove pointed out that in horizontal industries the company with the highest market share wins because it has the best opportunity to recoup R&D and manufacturing-plant investments. This idea particularly applies to industries where technology is developing rapidly.

Grove's second idea was strategic inflection points (SIPs): "A strategic inflection point occurs where the old strategic picture dissolves and gives way to the new." Grove maintained that every company had a theory of business, and when fashion or technology or something else changed, that theory was undermined to the point where the company had to find a new theory. He believed that SIPs usually left telltale signs around: "The trade shows seem weird"; puzzled managers observed, "Things are different. Something has changed"; and "there is a growing dissonance between what your company thinks it is doing and what is actually happening inside the bowels of the organization." (In Intel's case, middle management had directed resources into microprocessors and away from memory chips long before the Intel senior team decided to get out of the memory business in the crisis of 1985.) Grove pointed out, "Senior managers ... will keep implementing the same strategic and tactical moves that worked for them during the course of their careers. ... I call this phenomenon the inertia of success. It is extremely dangerous."

Grove's idea of the strategic inflection point assumed an even stronger place in Intel's management philosophy with the appearance of Clayton Christensen's Innovator's Dilemma. First published in 1997, Harvard Business Professor Christensen pointed to the inability of most leading companies to adapt their businesses to major technology changes. With the idea of the dilemma, Christensen seemed to be pointing directly at companies like Intel: "The dilemma is that the criteria that managers use to make the decisions that keep their present businesses

---

[12] Intel's Web site, June 2000.

[13] Grove.

healthy make it impossible for them to do the right thing for their future. What's best for your current business could ruin you for the long term."[14]

In Christensen's analysis, the emergence of new technologies threatened to destroy the existing competencies of companies like Intel:

> I describe such radical innovations ... as "disruptive technologies." Although they initially emerge in small markets that seem remote from the mainstream, they are disruptive because they subsequently can become full-blown competitors against established products. Sound market research, skillful planning, and a strong customer focus, followed by diligent execution according to plan, are readily accepted as the classic hallmarks of good management. And it's true—when applied to sustaining an existing business, such practices are invaluable. Ironically, it's the firms with the strongest customer relationships that find it the hardest to convert disruptive technologies into new revenue streams. It's not that pleasing your best customers is itself dangerous, but pleasing them exclusively means that the growth opportunities presented by new markets will go ignored and uncultivated. It is difficult to find the resources to focus energy and talents on small markets, even when logic says that they will be big someday. Of course, keeping close to customers is critical for current success. But long-term growth and profit depend upon a very different managerial formula. Quite simply, disruptive technologies are often the catalysts for emerging markets. And finding new markets—and exploiting them—is crucial if a company is to enjoy continued growth well into the future. Companies that demand market data and financial justification before pursuing a new possibility are vulnerable—in fact, their hesitation actually helps faster, more-entrepreneurial companies to catch the next great wave of industry growth.[15]

CASH AND COMMODITIZATION

Moore's Law, Grove's Paranoia, and Christensen's Dilemma combined to weigh heavily on the minds of Intel senior executives. Senior management believed that Intel's almost exclusive focus on chips left it highly vulnerable to a disruptive technology. On top of that, its main microprocessor product line—which made up over 80% of the company's sales and profits—was slowly but surely becoming commoditized by the emergence of serious competitors. After many years of struggling to catch up in product and production technologies, AMD finally began challenging Intel's microprocessor leadership position. A large part of AMD's success came through the acquisition of NexGen, a microprocessor technology company, in 1996. By 1999, AMD's K6 and Athelon chips became recognized by industry commentators and PC makers as real alternatives to Intel's Pentium range in high-end applications where the largest chunk of product margins was to be found. And AMD was not Intel's only competitor: National Semiconductor's Cyrix and Motorola–Apple chips also competed strongly in Intel's prime marketplace.

Nevertheless, through the late 1990s Intel continued to throw off several billion dollars in free cash flow every year. The company's cash generation proved so strong that it had lavish cash for promising investment opportunities. In 1999, the company generated net cash from

---

[14] BusinessWeek, March 3, 1999.

[15] Clayton Christensen. *The Innovator's Dilemma.* Cambridge, MA: Harvard Business School Publishing, 1997.

operating activities of $11.4 billion. It invested only $3.4 billion directly into property plant and equipment, leaving $8 billion for other investment activities. Of this amount, the company spent $4.6 billion buying back its own stock (down from $6.8 billion the previous year), which some observers took to be a sure indication that Intel was finding it hard to generate adequate promising investment opportunities from its internal operations.

In fact, Intel had been trying to foster an entrepreneurial climate within its organization for several years. The company had the goal of developing vibrant new businesses from within. The program called Growing Green Businesses suddenly became an urgent need because of senior management's concern about the commoditization and vulnerability of the company's main product lines. Given its embarrassing cash surplus, Intel senior management also launched a major investment program through its venture capital operation, Intel Capital.

INTEL CAPITAL

Intel Capital's investment strategy proved successful. Its turnover of investments in third-party companies proceeded at a fast pace. The company drove $10 billion into acquisitions and acquiring stock in third-party companies during 1999, while selling $7.2 billion of stock in other firms, leaving a total of $2.8 billion net new investments. By the end of 1999, the company's portfolio of marketable securities was at a carrying value of $9.8 billion, and nonmarketable securities at $1 billion. With the strong bull market continuing for Internet stocks through the first quarter of 2000, Intel's portfolio value continued to grow. By April 1, 2000, the total portfolio was approximately $7.8 billion of appreciation on its marketable securities.[16]

This portfolio comprised investments in 425 companies worldwide. The investments were divided into two broad categories: Internet infrastructure companies including those specializing in client/server products and technologies, networking and communications, and design and manufacturing technologies; and Internet content and service providers. Well known names in the portfolio included companies like Red Hat, Inc., Skystream, Asiacontent.com, and Stamps.com.

GROWING GREEN BUSINESSES

Intel's efforts at growing new businesses internally had been proving tougher going than investing in outside companies. The company had been more successful in acquiring new/existing businesses than in generating its own. Part of the problem, some of Intel's top managers believe, was that the incentive systems, the culture, the mindset, and the climate necessary to generate entrepreneurial start-ups were not appropriate within the organization. Others believed that too many people had become too rich on Intel stock and stock options, to the point that there was simply no incentive either to take risks or push the envelope. While top management believed that success could be had with introducing proper systems and structures to promote entrepreneurial behavior, others believed more radical surgery was required.

Recently, Peter Hake had been appointed as senior vice president in charge of developing the green business side of the company. Hake had a support staff of five managers reporting to him,

---

[16] Intel Web site, June 2000.

and their collective responsibility was to promote entrepreneurship within Intel. Hake saw his central mission as creating a robust portfolio of new initiatives within the organization.

After taking the job, Hake and his team tried valiantly to encourage the young talent in Intel, both engineers and managers, to take some risks and to pursue promising new technologies and businesses. After a year of such activities, their efforts had not shown good results. Hake had learned several features about Intel and its people.

Hake and his team were struck by four distinct problems. First, the best engineering talent aspired to the title "star designer." This was particularly true of engineers working in the core product lines of the company. Hence, the best engineering talent gravitated toward interesting design challenges in the mainstream business of microprocessors.

Second, there was a pronounced bias toward quantifying data and information among the managers of the company. There was tremendous pressure to produce such precise and quantifiable information about all activities, new and old, and anything that could not be measured was not worth thinking about. Unquantifiable information was taken as a sign of ignorance and lack of knowledge. Naturally, such a bias proved hostile to any new business initiative. The company's elaborate planning processes only served to reinforce this bias.

Third, the tremendous success that the company had had in rationalizing the manufacturing process of microprocessors meant that any new activity appeared primitive by contrast. The managers brought the same zeal to solving all problems through a precise, methodical, scientific approach, and some of Hake's staff had come to believe that promoting entrepreneurship in such a climate was impossible. Initiatives that involved imprecision were simply not appealing to the young talent within the company.

Finally, there was a distinct bias toward large size within the company. Used to product lines that generate several billion dollars of revenue a year and working in the shadow of the Intel Capital portfolio of over $10 billion, the managers had difficulty dealing with small volumes and value. Managers were impatient with new businesses that could not ramp up demand or production to a billion-dollar level within a couple of years of start-up. This put considerable pressure on new business managers, and there were few in the organization that wanted to take on such a thankless task.

BACK BY THE VENDING MACHINE

Faced with these idiosyncratic features of Intel, Hake resolved to invite some of the best consultants in the corporate venturing field to help him make progress on Growing Green Businesses. Hake's approach was to invite these consultants to his weekly strategy meeting for a discussion of salient issues.

As Hake leaned against the vending machine, he summarized that he was looking for advice on two specific fronts. First, he wondered how he could bring about change in Intel. Did Growing Green Businesses require radical surgery or would incremental change achieve the purpose?

Second, whichever approach he chose, where and how should he start? What were the three or four most important and crucial things he could do now to create an entrepreneurial firm from this large, but highly successful and somewhat opinionated, organization?

As Hake walked down the corridor toward the meeting room, he took a quick glance over his shoulder and wondered if the consultants might also be able to help him get over his "bear paranoia."

SECTION IV
MANAGING FOR RESULTS

If 80% of your efforts go into following this process to develop a strategic plan, you will receive approximately 20% of the potential benefits. The rest comes from managing the execution, monitoring progress, and leading the organization to the desired results.

CHAPTER 10
ENSURING YOUR STRATEGY IS COMPLETE AND CLEAR

Do you think that mere words are strategy and power for war?

—The Bible: 2 Kings, 18:20

This chapter is really a short introduction to the reading that follows. In recognition that "when executives call everything strategy, and end up with a collection of strategies, they create confusion and undermine their own credibility," Hambrick and Fredrickson (2001, p. 49) offer a practical framework, their *strategy diamond*, to ensure that strategies are complete and clear.

Upon successful completion of this reading you should be able to:

- describe the components of the strategy diamond
- apply the strategy diamond to evaluate the completeness of a strategy's plan

Consider this step in the strategic management process as the "reality check." What is the underlying economic logic for this strategy? Will you have enough resources to implement it stage-by-stage? Where will you employ this strategy? How will you employ this strategy?

Too often, we accept statements like, "our strategy is to reach the Hispanic base," or "our strategy is to be the preferred provider for health care services," or "our strategy is to energize new voters" as true strategies. Remember, a strategy is a plan to create and/or sustain a competitive advantage. It is not a "sound bite." It is a plan that should communicate what is to be done, where, how, and by whom.

It should also be communicated in as simple of terms as possible. "Polysyllabic" is fun to say, but it will obfuscate your intentions. Other unattributed writing tips gleaned from the Internet include:

1. Verbs *have* to agree with their subjects.
2. Prepositions are not words to end sentences with.
3. And don't start a sentence with a conjunction.
4. It is wrong to ever split an infinitive.
5. Also, too, never, ever use repetitive redundancies.

6. No sentence fragments.
7. The passive voice is to be ignored.
8. Never use a big word when a diminutive one would suffice.
9. Use words correctly, irregardless of how others use them.
10. Make sure you proofread to make sure you have not any words out.

Kidding aside, even if your strategy *is* complete, if it is not clear, it will not happen.

Illustration

In its strategic plan, the American Cancer Society (ACS 2010) has a formal mission statement, but it also uses phrases such as "to help create a world with less cancer and more birthdays," humanizing its mission. Its strategies are presented with measurable outcomes and a specific timeframe. From helping people to stay well, helping people to get well, and finding cures, the plan becomes very specific about how those strategies will be executed. For example (p. 12), "Improve quality of life of cancer patients, caregivers, and survivors by assisting primarily with service referral, community mobilization, collaboration, advocacy, and, where appropriate, directly providing services," explains what they will do to address quality of life issues and how they will do it.

As you read the following selection, be reminded that results come from complete and clear plans.

APPLICATION AND REFLECTION

- Do you have a strategy for You, Inc.? If so, what components are missing? Do you have a plan for the staging? The vehicles?

- Select a company, perhaps your employer or its competitors, and evaluate its statements of vision and strategy for clarity. If possible, look for completeness by applying the strategy diamond.

ARE YOU SURE YOU HAVE
A STRATEGY?

Donald C. Hambrick and
James W. Fredrickson

EXECUTIVE OVERVIEW

After more than 30 years of hard thinking about strategy, consultants and scholars
have provided an abundance of frameworks for analyzing strategic situations. Missing,
however, has been any guidance as to what the product of these tools should be—or
what actually constitutes a strategy. Strategy has become a catchall term used to mean
whatever one wants it to mean. Executives now talk about their "service strategy,"
their "branding strategy," their "acquisition strategy," or whatever kind of strategy
that is on their mind at a particular moment. But strategists—whether they are CEOs
of established firms, division presidents, or entrepreneurs—must have a strategy, an
integrated, over arching concept of how the business will achieve its objectives. If a
business must have a single, unified strategy, then it must necessarily have parts. What
are those parts? We present a framework for strategy design, arguing that a strategy has
five elements, providing answers to five questions: arenas, "Where will we be active?"
vehicles, "How will we get there?" differentiators, "How will we win in the marketplace?" staging, "What will be our speed and sequence of moves?" and economic logic,
"How will we obtain our returns?" Our article develops and illustrates these domains
of choice, particularly emphasizing how essential it is that they form a unified whole.

Consider these statements of strategy drawn from actual documents and announcements of
several companies:

"Our strategy is to be the low-cost provider."
"We're pursuing a global strategy."

Donald C. Hambrick and James W. Fredrickson. "Are You Sure You Have a Strategy?" *Academy of Management
Executive* 15, no. 4 (2001): 48–59. Copyright © 2001 by Academy of Management. Reprinted with permission.

"The company's strategy is to integrate a set of regional acquisitions."
"Our strategy is to provide unrivaled customer service."
"Our strategic intent is to always be the first-mover."
"Our strategy is to move from defense to industrial applications."

What do these grand declarations have in common? Only that none of them is a strategy. They are strategic threads, mere elements of strategies. But they are no more strategies than Dell Computer's strategy can be summed up as selling direct to customers, or than Hannibal's strategy was to use elephants to cross the Alps. And their use reflects an increasingly common syndrome—the catchall fragmentation of strategy. After more than 30 years of hard thinking about strategy, consultants and scholars have provided executives with an abundance of frameworks for analyzing strategic situations. We now have five-forces analysis, core competencies, hypercompetition, the resource-based view of the firm, value chains, and a host of other helpful, often powerful, analytic tools.[1] Missing, however, has been any guidance as to what the product of these tools should be—or what actually constitutes a strategy. Indeed, the use of specific strategic tools tends to draw the strategist toward narrow, piecemeal conceptions of strategy that match the narrow scope of the tools themselves. For example, strategists who are drawn to Porter's five-forces analysis tend to think of strategy as a matter of selecting industries and segments within them. Executives who dwell on "co-opetition" or other game-theoretic frameworks see their world as a set of choices about dealing with adversaries and allies.

This problem of strategic fragmentation has worsened in recent years, as narrowly specialized academics and consultants have started plying their tools in the name of strategy. But strategy is not pricing. It is not capacity decisions. It is not setting R&D budgets. These are pieces of strategies, and they cannot be decided—or even considered—in isolation.

Imagine an aspiring painter who has been taught that colors and hues determine the beauty of a picture. But what can really be done with such advice? After all, magnificent pictures require far more than choosing colors: attention to shapes and figures, brush technique, and finishing processes. Most importantly, great paintings depend on artful combinations of *all* these elements. Some combinations are classic, tried-and-true; some are inventive and fresh; and many combinations—even for avant-garde art—spell trouble.

Strategy has become a catchall term used to mean whatever one wants it to mean. Business magazines now have regular sections devoted to strategy, typically discussing how featured firms are dealing with distinct issues, such as customer service, joint ventures, branding, or e-commerce. In turn, executives talk about their "service strategy," their "joint venture strategy," their "branding strategy," or whatever kind of strategy is on their minds at a particular moment.

Executives then communicate these strategic threads to their organizations in the mistaken belief that doing so will help managers make tough choices. But how does knowing that their firm is pursuing an "acquisition strategy" or a "first-mover strategy" help the vast majority of managers do their jobs or set priorities? How helpful is it to have new initiatives announced periodically with the word strategy tacked on? When executives call everything strategy, and end up with a collection of strategies, they create confusion and undermine their own credibility. They especially reveal that they don't really have an integrated conception of the business.

When executives call everything strategy, and end up with a collection of strategies, they create confusion and undermine their own credibility.

Many readers of works on the topic know that strategy is derived from the Greek *strategos*, or "the art of the general." But few have thought much about this important origin. For example, what is special about the general's job, compared with that of a field commander? The general is responsible for multiple units on multiple fronts and multiple battles over time. The general's challenge—and the value-added of generalship—is in orchestration and comprehensiveness. Great generals think about the whole. They have a strategy; it has pieces, or elements, but they form a coherent whole. Business generals, whether they are CEOs of established firms, division presidents, or entrepreneurs, must also have a strategy—a central, integrated, externally oriented concept of how the business will achieve its objectives. Without a strategy, time and resources are easily wasted on piecemeal, disparate activities; mid-level managers will fill the void with their own, often parochial, interpretations of what the business should be doing; and the result will be a potpourri of disjointed, feeble initiatives.

Examples abound of firms that have suffered because they lacked a coherent strategy. Once a towering force in retailing, Sears spent 10 sad years vacillating between an emphasis on hard goods and soft goods, venturing in and out of ill-chosen businesses, failing to differentiate itself in any of them, and never building a compelling economic logic. Similarly, the once-unassailable Xerox is engaged in an attempt to revive itself, amid criticism from its own executives that the company lacks a strategy. Says one: "I hear about asset sales, about refinancing, but I don't hear anyone saying convincingly, 'Here is your future.'"[2]

A strategy consists of an integrated set of choices, but it isn't a catchall for every important choice an executive faces. As Figure 1 portrays, the company's mission and objectives, for example, stand apart from, and guide, strategy. Thus we would not speak of the commitment of the *New York Times* to be America's newspaper of record as part of its strategy. GE's objective of being number one or number two in all its markets drives its strategy, but is not strategy itself. Nor would an objective of reaching a particular revenue or earnings target be part of a strategy.

Similarly, because strategy addresses how the business intends to engage its environment, choices about internal organizational arrangements are not part of strategy. So we should not speak of compensation policies, information systems, or training programs as being strategy. These are critically important choices, which should reinforce and support strategy; but they do not make up the strategy itself.[3] If everything important is thrown into the strategy bucket, then this essential concept quickly comes to mean nothing.

We do not mean to portray strategy development as a simple, linear process. Figure 1 leaves out feedback arrows and other indications that great strategists are iterative, loop thinkers.[4] The key is not in following a sequential process, but rather in achieving a robust, reinforced consistency among the elements of the strategy itself.

The Elements of Strategy

If a business must have a strategy, then the strategy must necessarily have parts. What are those parts? As Figure 2 portrays, a strategy has five elements, providing answers to five questions:

- Arenas: "Where will we be active?"
- Vehicles: "How will we get there?"
- Differentiators: "How will we win in the marketplace?"
- Staging: "What will be our speed and sequence of moves?"
- Economic logic: "How will we obtain our returns?"

This article develops and illustrates these domains of choice, emphasizing how essential it is that they form a unified whole. Where others focus on the inputs to strategic thinking (the top box in Figure 1), we focus on the output—the composition and design of the strategy itself.

Arenas

The most fundamental choices strategists make are those of where, or in what arenas, the business will be active. This is akin to the question Peter Drucker posed decades ago: "What business will we be in?"[5] The answer, however, should not be one of broad generalities. For instance, "We will be the leader in information technology consulting" is more a vision or objective than part of a strategy. In articulating arenas, it is important to be as specific as possible about the product categories, market segments, geographic areas, and core technologies, as well as the value-adding stages (e.g., product design, manufacturing, selling, servicing, distribution) the business intends to take on.

For example, as a result of an in-depth analysis, a biotechnology company specified its arenas: The company intended to use T-cell receptor technology to develop both diagnostic and therapeutic products for battling a certain class of cancers; it chose to keep control of all research and product development activity, but to outsource manufacturing and a major part of the clinical testing process required for regulatory approvals. The company targeted the United States and major European markets as its geographic scope. The company's chosen arenas were highly specific, with products and markets even targeted by name. In other instances, especially in businesses with a wider array of products, market segments, or geographic scope, the strategy may instead reasonably specify the classes of, or criteria for, selected arenas—e.g., women's

Figure 1. Putting Strategy in Its Place

high-end fashion accessories, or countries with per-capita GDP over $5,000. But in all cases, the challenge is to be as specific as possible.

In choosing arenas, the strategist needs to indicate not only where the business will be active, but also how much emphasis will be placed on each. Some market segments, for instance, might be identified as centrally important, while others are deemed secondary. A strategy might reasonably be centered on one product category, with others—while necessary for defensive purposes or for offering customers a full line—being of distinctly less importance.

Vehicles

Beyond deciding on the arenas in which the business will be active, the strategist also needs to decide how to get there. Specifically, the means for attaining the needed presence in a particular product category, market segment, geographic area, or value-creation stage should be the result of deliberate strategic choice. If we have decided to expand our product range, are we going to accomplish that by relying on organic, internal product development, or are there other vehicles—such as joint ventures or acquisitions—that offer a better means for achieving our broadened scope? If we are committed to international expansion, what should be our primary modes, or vehicles—greenfield startups, local acquisitions, licensing, or joint ventures? The executives of the biotechnology company noted earlier decided to rely on joint ventures to achieve their new presence in Europe, while committing to a series of tactical acquisitions for adding certain therapeutic products to complement their existing line of diagnostic products.

The means by which arenas are entered matters greatly. Therefore, selection of vehicles should not be an afterthought or viewed as a mere implementation detail. A decision to enter new product categories is rife with uncertainty. But that uncertainty may vary immensely depending

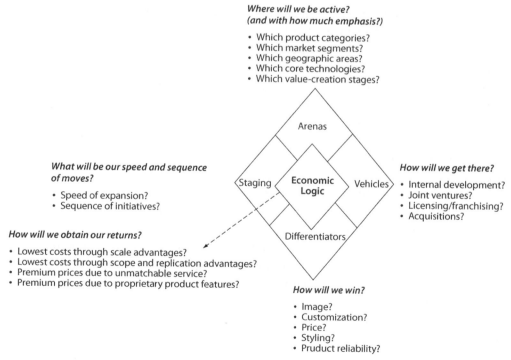

Figure 2. The Five Major Elements of Strategy

on whether the entry is attempted by licensing other companies' technologies, where perhaps the firm has prior experience, or by acquisitions, where the company is a novice. Failure to explicitly consider and articulate the intended expansion vehicles can result in the hoped-for entry's being seriously delayed, unnecessarily costly, or totally stalled.

Failure to explicitly consider and articulate the intended expansion vehicles can result in the hoped-for entry's being seriously delayed, unnecessarily costly, or totally stalled.

There are steep learning curves associated with the use of alternative expansion modes. Research has found, for instance, that companies can develop highly advantageous, well-honed capabilities in making acquisitions or in managing joint ventures.[6] The company that uses various vehicles on an ad hoc or patchwork basis, without an overarching logic and programmatic approach, will be at a severe disadvantage compared with companies that have such coherence.

Differentiators

A strategy should specify not only where a firm will be active (arenas) and how it will get there (vehicles), but also how the firm will win in the marketplace—how it will get customers to come its way. In a competitive world, winning is the result of differentiators, and such edges don't just happen. Rather, they require executives to make up-front, conscious choices about which weapons will be assembled, honed, and deployed to beat competitors in the fight for customers, revenues, and profits. For example, Gillette uses its proprietary product and process technology to develop superior razor products, which the company further differentiates through a distinctive, aggressively advertised brand image. Goldman Sachs, the investment bank, provides customers with unparalleled service by maintaining close relationships with client executives and coordinating the array of services it offers to each client. Southwest Airlines attracts and retains customers by offering the lowest possible fares and extraordinary on-time reliability.

Achieving a compelling marketplace advantage does not necessarily mean that the company has to be at the extreme on one differentiating dimension; rather, sometimes having the best combination of differentiators confers a tremendous marketplace advantage. This is the philosophy of Honda in automobiles. There are better cars than Hondas, and there are less expensive cars than Hondas; but many car buyers believe that there is no better value—quality for the price—than a Honda, a strategic position the company has worked hard to establish and reinforce.

Regardless of the intended differentiators—image, customization, price, product styling, after-sale services, or others—the critical issue for strategists is to make up-front, deliberate choices. Without that, two unfortunate outcomes loom. One is that, if top management doesn't attempt to create unique differentiation, none will occur. Again, differentiators don't just materialize; they are very hard to achieve. And firms without them lose.

The other negative outcome is that, without up-front, careful choices about differentiators, top management may seek to offer customers across-the-board superiority, trying simultaneously to outdistance competitors on too broad an array of differentiators—lower price, better service, superior styling, and so on. Such attempts are doomed, however, because of their inherent inconsistencies and extraordinary resource demands. In selecting differentiators, strategists should give explicit preference to those few forms of superiority that are mutually reinforcing (e.g., image and product styling), consistent with the firm's resources and capabilities, and, of course, highly valued in the arenas the company has targeted.

Staging

Choices of arenas, vehicles, and differentiators constitute what might be called the substance of a strategy—what executives plan to do. But this substance cries out for decisions on a fourth element—staging, or the speed and sequence of major moves to take in order to heighten the likelihood of success.[7] Most strategies do not call for equal, balanced initiatives on all fronts at all times. Instead, usually some initiatives must come first, followed only then by others, and then still others. In erecting a great building, foundations must be laid, followed by walls, and only then the roof.

Of course, in business strategy there is no universally superior sequence. Rather the strategist's judgment is required. Consider a printing equipment company that committed itself to broadening its product line and expanding internationally. The executives decided that the new products should be added first, in stage one, because the elite sales agents they planned to use for international expansion would not be able or willing to represent a narrow product line effectively. Even though the executives were anxious to expand geographically, if they had tried to do so without the more complete line in place, they would have wasted a great deal of time and money. The left half of Figure 3 shows their two-stage logic.

The executives of a regional title insurance company, as part of their new strategy, were committed to becoming national in scope through a series of acquisitions. For their differentiators, they planned to establish a prestigious brand backed by aggressive advertising and superb customer service. But the executives faced a chicken-and-egg problem: they couldn't make the acquisitions on favorable terms without the brand image in place; but with only their current limited geographic scope, they couldn't afford the quantity or quality of advertising needed to establish the brand. They decided on a three-stage plan (shown in the right half of Figure 3): (1) make selected acquisitions in adjacent regions, hence becoming super-regional in size and scale; (2) invest moderately heavily in advertising and brand-building; 3) make acquisitions in additional regions on more favorable terms (because of the enhanced brand, a record of growth, and, they hoped, an appreciated stock price) while simultaneously continuing to push further in building the brand.

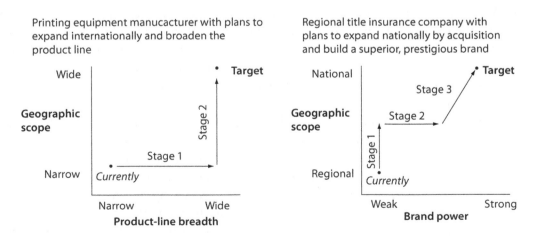

Figure 3. Elements of Strategic Staging

Decisions about staging can be driven by a number of factors. One, of course, is resources. Funding and staffing every envisioned initiative, at the needed levels, is generally not possible at the outset of a new strategic campaign. Urgency is a second factor affecting staging; some elements of a strategy may face brief windows of opportunity, requiring that they be pursued first and aggressively. A third factor is the achievement of credibility. Attaining certain thresholds—in specific arenas, differentiators, or vehicles—can be critically valuable for attracting resources and stakeholders that are needed for other parts of the strategy. A fourth factor is the pursuit of early wins. It may be far wiser to successfully tackle a part of the strategy that is relatively doable before attempting more challenging or unfamiliar initiatives. These are only some of the factors that might go into decisions about the speed and sequence of strategic initiatives. However, since the concept of staging has gone largely unexplored in the strategy literature, it is often given far too little attention by strategists themselves.

Economic Logic

At the heart of a business strategy must be a clear idea of how profits will be generated—not just some profits, but profits above the firm's cost of capital.[8] It is not enough to vaguely count on having revenues that are above costs. Unless there's a compelling basis for it, customers and competitors won't let that happen. And it's not enough to generate a long list of reasons why customers will be eager to pay high prices for your products, along with a long list of reasons why your costs will be lower than your competitors'. That's a sure-fire route to strategic schizophrenia and mediocrity.

It is not enough to vaguely count on having revenues that are above costs. Unless there's a compelling basis for it, customers and competitors won't let that happen.

The most successful strategies have a central economic logic that serves as the fulcrum for profit creation. In some cases, the economic key may be to obtain premium prices by offering customers a difficult-to-match product. For instance, the *New York Times* is able to charge readers a very high price (and strike highly favorable licensing arrangements with online information distributors) because of its exceptional journalistic quality; in addition, the *Times* is able to charge advertisers high prices because it delivers a large number of dedicated, affluent readers. ARAMARK, the highly profitable international food-service company, is able to obtain premium prices from corporate and institutional clients by offering a level of customized service and responsiveness that competitors cannot match. The company seeks out only those clients that want superior food service and are willing to pay for it. For example, once domestic airlines became less interested in distinguishing themselves through their in-flight meals, ARAMARK dropped that segment.

In some instances, the economic logic might reside on the cost side of the profit equation. ARAMARK—adding to its pricing leverage—uses its huge scale of operations and presence in multiple market segments (business, educational, healthcare, and correctional-system food service) to achieve a sizeable cost advantage in food purchases—an advantage that competitors cannot duplicate. GKN Sinter Metals, which has grown by acquisition to become the world's major powdered-metals company, benefits greatly from its scale in obtaining raw materials and in exploiting, in country after country, its leading-edge capabilities in metal-forming processes.

In these examples, the economic logics are not fleeting or transitory. They are rooted in the firms' fundamental and relatively enduring capabilities. ARAMARK and the *New York Times* can charge premium prices because their offerings are superior in the eyes of their targeted customers, customers highly value that superiority, and competitors can't readily imitate the offerings. ARAMARK and GKN Sinter Metals have lower costs than their competitors because of systemic advantages of scale, experience, and know-how sharing. Granted, these leads may not last forever or be completely unassailable, but the economic logics that are at work at these companies account for their abilities to deliver strong year-in, year-out profits.

The Imperative of Strategic Comprehensiveness

By this point it should be clear why a strategy needs to encompass all five elements—arenas, vehicles, differentiators, staging, and economic logic. First, all five are important enough to require intentionality. Surprisingly, most strategic plans emphasize one or two of the elements without giving any consideration to the others. Yet, to develop a strategy without attention to all five leaves critical omissions.

> ### Surprisingly, most strategic plans emphasize one or two of the elements without giving any consideration to the others.

Second, the five elements call not only for choice, but also for preparation and investment. All five require certain capabilities that cannot be generated spontaneously.

Third, all five elements must align with and support each other. When executives and academics think about alignment, they typically have in mind that internal organizational arrangements need to align with strategy (in tribute to the maxim that "structure follows strategy"[9]), but few pay much attention to the consistencies required among the elements of the strategy itself.

Finally, it is only after the specification of all five strategic elements that the strategist is in the best position to turn to designing all the other supporting activities—functional policies, organizational arrangements, operating programs, and processes—that are needed to reinforce the strategy. The five elements of the strategy diamond can be considered the hub or central nodes for designing a comprehensive, integrated activity system.[10]

Comprehensive Strategies at IKEA and Brake Products International

IKEA: Revolutionizing an Industry

So far we have identified and discussed the five elements that make up a strategy and form our strategy diamond. But a strategy is more than simply choices on these five fronts: it is an integrated, mutually reinforcing set of choices—choices that form a coherent whole. To illustrate the importance of this coherence we will now discuss two examples of fully elaborated strategy diamonds. As a first illustration, consider the strategic intent of IKEA, the remarkably successful global furniture retailer. IKEA's strategy over the past 25 years has been highly coherent, with all five elements reinforcing each other.

The arenas in which IKEA operates are well defined: the company sells relatively inexpensive, contemporary, Scandinavian-style furniture and home furnishings. IKEA's target market is young, primarily white-collar customers. The geographic scope is worldwide, or at least all countries where socioeconomic and infrastructure conditions support the concept. IKEA is not only a retailer, but also maintains control of product design to ensure the integrity of its unique image and to accumulate unrivaled expertise in designing for efficient manufacturing. The company, however, does not manufacture, relying instead on a host of long-term suppliers who ensure efficient, geographically dispersed production.

> **IKEA is not only a retailer, but also maintains control of product design to ensure the integrity of its unique image and to accumulate unrivaled expertise in designing for efficient manufacturing.**

As its primary vehicle for getting to its chosen arenas, IKEA engages in organic expansion, building its own wholly owned stores. IKEA has chosen not to make acquisitions of existing retailers, and it engages in very few joint ventures. This reflects top management's belief that the company needs to fully control local execution of its highly innovative retailing concept.

IKEA attracts customers and beats competitors by offering several important differentiators. First, its products are of very reliable quality but are low in price (generally 20 to 30% below the competition for comparable quality goods). Second, in contrast to the stressful, intimidating feeling that shoppers often encounter in conventional furniture stores, IKEA customers are treated to a fun, non-threatening experience, where they are allowed to wander through a visually exciting store with only the help they request. And third, the company strives to make customer fulfillment immediate. Specifically, IKEA carries an extensive inventory at each store, which allows a customer to take the item home or have it delivered the same day. In contrast,

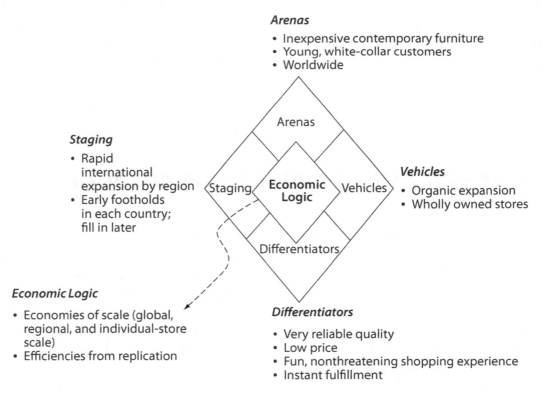

Figure 4. IKEA's Strategy

conventional furniture retailers show floor models, but then require a 6- to 10-week wait for the delivery of each special-order item.

As for staging, or IKEA's speed and sequence of moves, once management realized that its approach would work in a variety of countries and cultures, the company committed itself to rapid international expansion, but only one region at a time. In general, the company's approach has been to use its limited resources to establish an early foothold by opening a single store in each targeted country. Each such entry is supported with aggressive public relations and advertising in order to lay claim to the radically new retailing concept in that market. Later, IKEA comes back into each country and fills in with more stores.

The economic logic of IKEA rests primarily on scale economies and efficiencies of replication. Although the company doesn't sell absolutely identical products in all its geographic markets, IKEA has enough standardization that it can take great advantage of being the world's largest furniture retailer. Its costs from long-term suppliers are exceedingly low, and made even lower by IKEA's proprietary, easy-to-manufacture product designs. In each region, IKEA has enough scale to achieve substantial distribution and promotional efficiencies. And each individual store is set up as a high-volume operation, allowing further economies in inventories, advertising, and staffing. IKEA's phased international expansion has allowed executives to benefit, in country after country, from what they have learned about site selection, store design, store openings, and ongoing operations. They are vigilant, astute learners, and they put that learning to great economic use.

Note how all of IKEA's actions (shown in Figure 4) fit together. For example, consider the strong alignment between its targeted arenas and its competitive differentiators. An emphasis on low price, fun, contemporary styling, and instant fulfillment is well suited to the company's focus on young, first-time furniture buyers. Or consider the logical fit between the company's differentiators and vehicles—providing a fun shopping experience and instant fulfillment requires very intricate local execution, which can be achieved far better through wholly owned stores than by using acquisitions, joint ventures, or franchises. These alignments, along with others, help account for IKEA's long string of years with double-digit sales growth, and current revenues of $8 billion.

The IKEA example allows us to illustrate the strategy diamond with a widely familiar business story. That example, however, is admittedly retrospective, looking backward to interpret the company's strategy according to the framework. But the real power and role of strategy, of course, is in looking forward. Based on a careful and complete analysis of a company's environment, marketplace, competitors, and internal capabilities, senior managers need to craft a strategic intent for their firm. The diamond is a useful framework for doing just that, as we will now illustrate with a business whose top executives set out to develop a new strategy that would allow them to break free from a spiral of mediocre profits and stagnant sales.

Brake Products International: Charting a New Direction

The strategy diamond proved very useful when it was applied by the new executive team of Brake Products International (BPI), a disguised manufacturer of components used in braking and suspension systems for passenger cars and light trucks. In recent years, BPI had struggled as the worldwide auto industry consolidated. Its reaction had been a combination of disparate, half-hearted diversification initiatives, alternating with across-the-board expense cuts. The net result, predictably, was not good, and a new management team was brought in to try to revive performance. As part of this turnaround effort, BPI's new executives developed a new strategic intent by making critical decisions for each of the five elements—arenas, vehicles, differentiators, staging, and economic logic. We will not attempt to convey the analysis that gave rise to their choices, but rather (as with the IKEA example) will use BPI to illustrate the articulation of a comprehensive strategy.

For their targeted arenas, BPI executives committed to expanding beyond their current market scope of North American and European car plants by adding Asia, where global carmakers were rapidly expanding. They considered widening their product range to include additional auto components, but concluded that their unique design and manufacturing expertise was limited to brake and suspension components. They did decide, however, that they should apply their advanced capability in antilock-braking and electronic traction-control systems to develop braking products for off-road vehicles, including construction and farm equipment. As an additional commitment, executives decided to add a new service, systems integration, that would involve bundling BPI products with other related components, from other manufacturers, that form a complete suspension system, and then providing the carmakers with easy-to-handle, preassembled systems modules. This initiative would allow the carmakers to reduce assembly costs significantly, as well as to deal with a single suspension-system supplier, with substantial logistics and inventory savings.

The management team identified three major vehicles for achieving BPI's presence in their selected arenas. First, they were committed to organic internal development of new generations of leading-edge braking systems, including those for off-road vehicles. To become the preferred suspension-system integrator for the major auto manufacturers, executives decided to enter into strategic alliances with the leading producers of other key suspension components. Finally, to serve carmakers that were expanding their operations in Asia, BPI planned to initiate equity joint ventures with brake companies in China, Korea, and Singapore. BPI would provide the technology and oversee the manufacturing of leading-edge, high-quality antilock brakes; the Asian partners would take the lead in marketing and government relations.

BPI's executives also committed to achieving and exploiting a small set of differentiators. The company was already a technology leader, particularly in antilock-braking systems and electronic traction-control systems. These proprietary technologies were seen as centrally important and would be further nurtured. Executives also believed they could establish a preeminent position as a systems integrator of entire suspension assemblies. However, achieving this advantage would require new types of manufacturing and logistics capabilities, as well as new skills in managing relationships with other component companies. This would include an extensive e-business capability that linked BPI with its suppliers and customers. And finally, as one of the few brakes/ suspension companies with a manufacturing presence in North America and Europe—and now in Asia—BPI executives concluded that they had a potential advantage—what they referred to as "global reach"—that was well suited to the global consolidation of the automobile industry. If BPI did a better job of coordinating activities among its geographically dispersed operations, it could provide the one-stop, low-cost global purchasing that the industry giants increasingly sought.

If BPI did a better job of coordinating activities among its geographically dispersed operations, it could provide the one-stop, low-cost global purchasing that the industry giants increasingly sought.

BPI's executives approached decisions about staging very deliberately. They felt urgency on various fronts, but also realized that, after several years of lackluster performance, the firm lacked the resources and credibility to do everything all at once. As is often the case, decisions about staging were most important for those initiatives where the gaps between the status quo and the strategic intent were the greatest. For example, executives decided that, in order to provide a clear, early sign of continued commitment to the major global auto manufacturers, a critical first step was to establish the joint ventures with brake manufacturers in Asia. They felt just as much urgency to gain a first-mover advantage as a suspension-system integrator. Therefore, management committed to promptly establish alliances with a select group of manufacturers of other suspension components, and to experiment with one pilot customer. These two sets of initiatives constituted stage one of BPI's strategic intent. For stage two, the executives planned to launch the full versions of the systems-integration and global-reach concepts, complete with aggressive marketing. Also in this second stage, expansion into the off-road vehicle market would commence.

BPI's economic logic hinged on securing premium prices from its customers by offering them at least three valuable, difficult-to-imitate benefits. First, BPI was the worldwide technology leader in braking systems; car companies would pay to get access to these products for their new high-end models. Second, BPI would allow global customers an economical single source for braking products; this would save customers considerable contract administration and quality-assurance costs—savings that they would be willing to share. And third, through

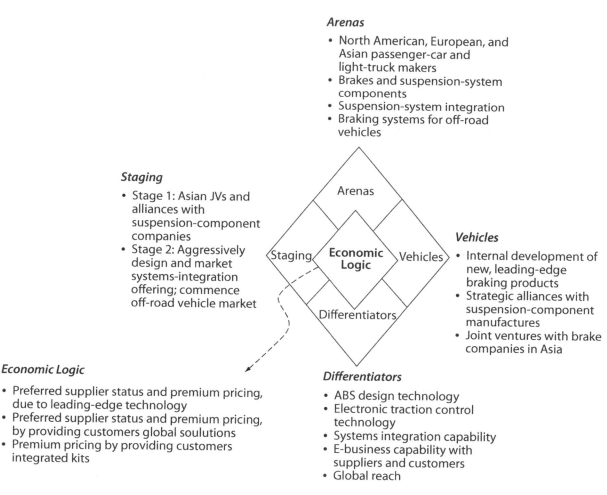

Arenas
- North American, European, and Asian passenger-car and light-truck makers
- Brakes and suspension-system components
- Suspension-system integration
- Braking systems for off-road vehicles

Staging
- Stage 1: Asian JVs and alliances with suspension-component companies
- Stage 2: Aggressively design and market systems-integration offering; commence off-road vehicle market

Vehicles
- Internal development of new, leading-edge braking products
- Strategic alliances with suspension-component manufactures
- Joint ventures with brake companies in Asia

Economic Logic
- Preferred supplier status and premium pricing, due to leading-edge technology
- Preferred supplier status and premium pricing, by providing customers global soulutions
- Premium pricing by providing customers integrated kits

Differentiators
- ABS design technology
- Electronic traction control technology
- Systems integration capability
- E-business capability with suppliers and customers
- Global reach

Figure 5. BPI's Strategy

its alliances with major suspension-component manufacturers, BPI would be able to deliver integrated-suspension-system kits to customers—again saving customers in purchasing costs, inventory costs, and even assembly costs, for which they would pay a premium.

BPI's turnaround was highly successful. The substance of the company's strategy (shown in Figure 5) was critically important in the turnaround, as was the concise strategy statement that was communicated throughout the firm. As the CEO stated:

> We've finally identified what we want to be, and what's important to us. Just as importantly, we've decided what we don't want to be, and have stopped wasting time and effort. Since we started talking about BPI in terms of arenas, vehicles, differentiators, staging, and economic logic, we have been able to get our top team on the same page. A whole host of decisions have logically fallen into place in support of our comprehensive strategic agenda.

OF STRATEGY, BETTER STRATEGY, AND NO STRATEGY

Our purpose in this article has been elemental: to identify what constitutes a strategy. This basic agenda is worthwhile because executives and scholars have lost track of what it means to engage in the art of the general. We particularly hope to counter the recent catchall fragmentation of the strategy concept, and to remind strategists that orchestrated holism is their charge.

But we do not want to be mistaken. We don't believe that it is sufficient to simply make these five sets of choices. No—a business needs not just a strategy, but a *sound* strategy. Some strategies are clearly far better than others. Fortunately, this is where the wealth of strategic analysis tools that have been developed in the last 30 years becomes valuable. Such tools as industry analysis, technology cycles, value chains, and core competencies, among others, are very helpful for improving the soundness of strategies. When we compare these tools and extract their most powerful central messages, several key criteria emerge to help executives test the quality of a proposed strategy. These criteria are presented in Table 1.[11] We strongly encourage executives to apply these tests throughout the strategy design process and especially when a proposed strategy emerges.

There might be those who wonder whether strategy isn't a concept of yesteryear, whose time has come and gone. In an era of rapid, discontinuous environmental shifts, isn't the company that attempts to specify its future just flirting with disaster?

Table 1
Testing the Quality of Your Strategy

Key Evaluation Criteria

1. **Does your strategy fit with what's going on in the environment?**
   Is there healthy profit potential where you're headed? Does your strategy align with the key success factors of your chosen environment?

2. **Does your strategy exploit your key resources?**
   With your particular mix of resources, does this strategy give you a good head start on competitors? Can you pursue this strategy more economically than competitors?

3. **Will your envisioned differentiators be sustainable?**
   Will competitors have difficulty matching you? If not, does your strategy explicitly include a ceaseless regimen of innovation and opportunity creation?

4. **Are the elements of your strategy internally consistent?**
   Have you made choices of arenas, vehicles, differentiators, and staging, and economic logic? Do they all fit and mutually reinforce each other?

5. **Do you have enough resources to pursue this strategy?**
   Do you have the money, managerial time and talent, and other capabilities to do all you envision? Are you sure you're not spreading your resources too thinly, only to be left with a collection off eeble positions?

6. **Is your strategy implementable?**
   Will your key constituencies allow you to pursue this strategy? Can your organization make it through the transition? Are you and your management team able and willing to lead the required changes?

Isn't it better to be flexible, fast-on-the-feet, ready to grab opportunities when the right ones come along?

Some of the skepticism about strategy stems from basic misconceptions. First, a strategy need not be static: it can evolve and be adjusted on an ongoing basis. Unexpected opportunities need not be ignored because they are outside the strategy. Second, a strategy doesn't require a business to become rigid. Some of the best strategies for today's turbulent environment keep multiple options open and build in desirable flexibility—through alliances, outsourcing, leased assets, toehold investments in promising technologies, and numerous other means. A strategy can help to intentionally build in many forms of flexibility—if that's what is called for. Third, a strategy doesn't deal only with an unknowable, distant future. The appropriate lifespans of business strategies have become shorter in recent years. Strategy used to be equated with 5- or 10-year horizons, but today a horizon of two to three years is often more fitting. In any event, strategy does not deal as much with preordaining the future as it does with assessing current conditions and future likelihoods, then making the best decisions possible today.

Strategy is not primarily about planning. It is about intentional, informed, and integrated choices. The noted strategic thinkers Gary Hamel and C. K. Prahalad said, "[A company's] leadership cannot be planned for, but neither can it happen without a grand and well-considered aspiration."[12] We offer the strategy diamond as a way to craft and articulate a business aspiration.

ACKNOWLEDGMENTS

We thank the following people for helpful suggestions: Ralph Biggadike, Warren Boeker, Kathy Harrigan, Paul Ingram, Xavier Martin, Atul Nerkar, and Jaeyong Song.

ENDNOTES

1. M. E. Porter. *Competitive strategy*. New York: The Free Press, 1980, provides an in-depth discussion of the five-forces model. Hypercompetition is addressed in R. A. D'Aveni. *Hyper-competition*. New York: The Free Press, 1994. The resource-based view of the firm is discussed in J. Barney. Firm resources and sustained competitive advantage. *Journal of Management* 17 (1991): 99–120. See M. Brandenburger and R. J. Nalebuff. The right game: Use game theory to shape strategy. *Harvard Business Review* (July–August 1995): 57–71, for a discussion of co-opetition.
2. A. Bianco and P. L. Moore. Downfall: The inside story of the management fiasco at Xerox. *Business Week,* March 5, 2001.
3. A widely applicable framework for strategy implementation is discussed in J. R. Galbraith and R. K. Kazanjian. *Strategy implementation: Structure, systems and process,* 2nd ed. St. Paul: West Publishing, 1986. A similar tool is offered in D. C. Hambrick and A. Cannella. Strategy implementation as substance and selling. *The Academy of Management Executive* 3, no. 4 (1989): 278–285.
4. This observation has been made for years by many contributors, including J. B. Quinn. *Strategies for change: Logical incrementalism.* Homewood, IL: Richard D. Irwin Publishing, 1980; and H. Mintzberg. Strategy making in three modes. *California Management Review* 15 (1973): 44–53.
5. P. Drucker. *The practice of management.* New York: Harper & Row, 1954.
6. J. Haleblian and S. Finkelstein. The influence of organizational acquisition experience on acquisition performance: A behavioral learning perspective. *Administrative Science Quarterly* 44 (1999): 29–56.
7. K. M. Eisenhardt and S. L. Brown. Time pacing: Competing in markets that won't stand still. *Harvard Business Review* (March-April 1998): 59–69, discusses "time pacing" as a component of a process of contending with rapidly changing environments.

8. The collapse of stock market valuations for Internet companies lacking in profits—or any prospect of profits—marked a return to economic reality. Profits above the firm's cost of capital are required in order to yield sustained or longer-term shareholder returns.

9. Galbraith and Kazanjian, op. cit., and Hambrick and Cannella, op. cit.

10. M. E. Porter. What is strategy? *Harvard Business Review,* (November–December 1996): 61–78.

11. See S. Tilles. How to evaluate strategy. *Harvard Business Review* (July–August 1963): 112–121, for a classic, but more limited, set of evaluative tests.

12. See G. Hamel and C. K. Prahalad. Strategy as stretch and leverage. *Harvard Business Review* (March–April 1993): 84–91.

About the Authors

Donald C. Hambrick is the Samuel Bronfman Professor of Democratic Business Enterprise at the Graduate School of Business, Columbia University. He holds degrees from the University of Colorado (B.S.), Harvard University (MBA), and the Pennsylvania State University (Ph.D.). An active consultant and executive education instructor, he also served as president of the Academy of Management. Contact: dch2@columbia.edu. **James W. Fredrickson** is a professor of strategic management and Chevron Oil Centennial Foundation Fellow in the McCombs School of Business of the University of Texas at Austin. He was previously on the Faculties of Columbia University and the University of Pittsburgh, and holds a Ph.D. from the University of Washington. Contact: james.fredrickson@bus.utexas.edu.

Chapter 11
Considering Strategies in a Global Context

It's a global economy, so quit whining ...[1]

—*Om Malik*

Opening Vignette

In his book, *The World Is Flat* (2005), Tom Friedman argues that the proverbial playing field in commerce has been leveled and all competitors have an equal opportunity. He warns that to be competitive in a global market, traditional barriers are becoming increasingly irrelevant, making global positioning a challenge.

One company suceeding in a global context is Coca-Cola Enterprises (CCE). A "first mover," the company first went global during the first world war. Since then, its strategies were not to use cheaper sources of labor to reduce production expense and streamline operations as many manufacturing companies have done. Instead, CCE's global business model has always centered on market expansion.

As such, sensitivity to different cultures, preferences, tastes, and customs has put it way ahead of other U.S. companies trying to go global. Coca-Cola sells over 400 brands in 200 countries. Almost 70% of the company's sales are abroad where Coke is not only a brand, but becomes a way of life due to the strategic involvement of the company in the communities in which it markets its products. For example, the company is expanding into Africa, where distribution is a major obstacle. They are using their sponsorship of the popular pastime of football and linking carbonated soda with spectator tastes.[2]

---

[1] O. Malik. The new land of opportunity. *Business 2.0* (July 2004): 72–78.

[2] R. Irwin. Painting South Africa red. 2001. http://www.brandchannel.com

In this chapter, we add one more dimension to the strategy model. If one dimension is your competitive position and the second dimension is time, then the third dimension is place. In particular, we examine the implications of strategies implemented around the world, i.e., in a global context.

As in mathematics, added dimensions create added complexity. So when we think about "going global," we need new ways of understanding the implications of those strategic choices. This is not to say that you cannot achieve your desired results; rather, you have the opportunity for even greater results (it's a big world out there!), but have to evaluate and execute ever more carefully. Globalization requires awareness, understanding, and response to global development and linkages (Czinkota et. al. 2004).

This chapter does not purport to be an entire course in global management. We will focus on considerations that are largely the purview of strategic management. For example, we do not discuss cultural differences and their marketing implications—which are very important—other than to highlight how those factors may impact your strategic choices. Successful mastery of this material will enable you to:

- extend your understanding of the strategy diamond (Hambrick and Fredrickson 2001) to international business strategies
- evaluate the pros and cons of a host country in terms of distance
- explain the implications of different entry modes
- describe different business configurations for multi-national corporations (MNCs)

INTRODUCTION

Unless you have been in a complete media blackout, you must be aware of how interdependent the world has become. The housing market collapse in the United States has, in an extended chain of events, placed economies around the world on the brink of collapse. Take a common item around your home or office; if it had a transparent supply chain, you might be surprised by its provenance. The t-shirt you are wearing might have been grown in Texas, sewn in China, affected cotton prices in Africa, and created trade imbalances along the way (Rivoli 2005).

Infrastructure improvements and technology advancements have been both enablers and drivers of globalization. Not everyone is in favor of globalization, but the trends seem inexorable. We are experiencing converging market wants and needs, regional economic integration, emerging markets, and competitive pressures for cost reductions and extended lifecycles. These phenomena are all forces pressing us toward globalization.

Some view globalization as threat (due to cultural dilution, resource depletion, and exploitation) and others view globalization as an opportunity (for quality of life improvements and new opportunities). Proponents note that business growth opportunities, particularly in mature industries, tend to be outside of the United States. Labor costs also tend to be lower outside of the United States. However, anti-globalization advocates are concerned about becoming "Westernized," i.e., liberal, materialistic, and/or heretical. And since some developing countries are rich in natural resources and low on regulation, they are in danger of resource depletion. Also, since some of the growth stimulated by globalization creates "sweatshop" jobs, increases pollution, and draws people from the countryside into overcrowded cities and slums, concerns about exploitation are raised. We believe that, whether you are a proponent of globalization or not, you should have the ability to consider strategies in a global context.

In the previous reading, we learned about the importance of a thorough and thoughtful strategy. General business principles apply, but under conditions of greater complexity and uncertainty. Using the Hambrick and Fredrickson (2001) strategy diamond, you learned to consider arenas, vehicles, differentiators, staging, and economic logic, as shown in Figure 2 of their article. While it is fundamentally no different in a global context, the questions become slightly more complex.

It is important to note that business risks increase dramatically for a variety of reasons. Consider that even if you have a good product or service, you might fail because of poor market research or strategy execution, over-extension or over-investment, external forces or operational disruptions, and fraud or corruption. To the questions posed by the strategy diamond, you might add the following as you work through each element of the model:

- How will our offerings fit into the international market?
- Should we enter the market through trade or investment?
- What is the probability of a disruption in supply if we extend our supply chain abroad?
- How do we protect our intellectual, industrial, and other property rights?
- Are we at risk for terrorism, a natural disaster, or government seizure?
- How do we sustain our cash flow?

Staging, or the sequence of events, will be determined as you answer all of the questions.

Economic Logic

For an international expansion to make economic sense, you should be able to generate more revenues or reduce significant costs. On the revenue side, there are "global marketing levers" (Yip 1994) that enable greater:

- market participation,
- product opportunities,
- location of activities, and
- marketing impact

to magnify the impact of competitive moves. Yip acknowledges that all levels of global engagement have coordination costs, but may offer benefits of:

- cost reduction,
- improved quality,
- enhanced customer preference, and
- competitive leverage.

It is interesting to note that these are potential benefits in any market development, one of our grand strategies. An international expansion is, in effect, market development.

Guillen and Garcia-Canal (2009), in their article, "The American Model of the Multinational Firm," suggest that organizations' motivations for foreign direct investment may be more specific, e.g., to:

- create a backward linkage into raw materials,

- achieve forward linkage into foreign markets,
- avoid government curbs in the home country,
- diversify risk,
- move capital abroad,
- follow a home-country customer to foreign markets,
- acquire firm-specific intangibles, or
- leverage firm-specific intangibles.

Again, we can see some correspondence with our grand strategies, e.g., the first two motivations, to create linkages, are essentially vertical integration on a global scale.

Arenas

Deciding where to be active, and what channels of distribution to use, requires a good understanding of the host country's environment. We explained how to use the PESTEL model in Chapter 5; here, we will introduce the CAGE framework (Ghemawat 2003), which examines *distances*, or differences, between the home and prospective host countries according to:

- Cultural distance is created by language barriers and religious differences; social norms can make it especially difficult to market consumer goods, for example. Products with a high linguistic content also suffer.
- Administrative distance is manifest non-normalized relations between governments, different currency valuations, political hostility, and corruption (euphemistically called "institutional weakness" by Ghemawat). Industries with extensive government involvement, e.g., energy, weaponry, agricultural products, and transportation systems, are likely to be tough customers.
- Geographic distance is defined not only in terms of miles apart, but also by remoteness, lack of access, and weak transportation or communication links; even differences in climate can be detrimental to companies wanting to sell fragile or perishable items. Bulky, inexpensive items—like shipping concrete blocks—are also hard to sell into places that are hard to find.
- Economic distance is generally the disparity in consumer incomes but can also be evaluated in terms of a disparity of natural, human, and capital resources. Big-ticket and luxury items are obviously not well-suited to this environment.

Ghemawat suggests considering a strategy of arbitrage (the forgotten strategy) and offers the example of Molson beer in Brazil (2003, p. 78):

> The persistent association of Brazil with football, carnival, beaches and sex—which all resonate powerfully in the marketing of youth-oriented products and services—illustrates the unexploited potential of some countries … to be realized. Witness Molson's recent launch in the Canadian market of A Marca Bavaria, a superpremium beer imported from its Brazilian subsidiary, which uses its association with Brazil's high-energy and sensual image to target primarily 19- to 24-year old men.

Once you have decided where you want to go, then you have to decide how to get there.

Vehicles

There are many different ways to approach global markets. In general terms, they are distinguished by whether the company has an equity position or is paid on a per-product basis. In a non-equity mode, you can choose to export products directly or indirectly (i.e., through a consolidator), or by contractual arrangement. Contracts can range from a specific license for a product or a franchise of the business model to specific functional agreements (such as outsourcing computer programming). With equity investments, you have the option of partial joint ventures or wholly-owned subsidiaries. Of course, with a joint venture, you can be the minority partner, be the majority partner, or opt to go 50/50 (Pan and Tse 2000).

Differentiators

The key question here is whether your existing differentiators will be effective in the new markets. It is also helpful to consider whether, if you do enter a particular country, that will have an impact on other aspects of your business, e.g., are there opportunities for efficiencies?

Bartlett et. al. (2004) suggest different ways to examine these questions, and offer different MNC configurations (i.e., organizational structures) to address the needs, as shown in Table 11-1. In particular, you consider the need for local customization (for differentiation) and the opportunities for efficiencies (for economic logic).

Table 11-1. Differentiation and Configurations

	Weak Opportunities for Efficiencies	Strong Opportunities for Efficiencies
High Need for Localization	MNC CONFIGURATION	TRANSNATIONAL CONFIGURATION
Low Need for Localization	INTERNATIONAL CONFIGURATION	GLOBAL CONFIGURATION

An international configuration can be considered a hub and spoke model, where decisions are centrally controlled and products are sold without localizing the differentiation. This is generally suited to a relatively small operation, in a non-equity mode. Management tends to be biased toward domestic considerations; international opportunities are secondary.

On the other hand, a multinational company (MNC) configuration is more like a radial system, with headquarters at the center providing strategic and administrative support,

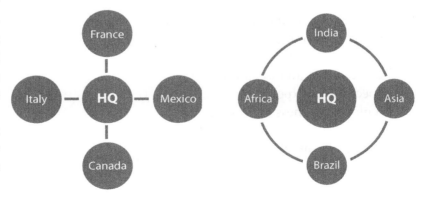

Figure 11-1. International Configuration

Figure 11-2. Multinational Configuration

and countries or regions being fully integrated business entities, customized/localized/differentiated for local markets. For example, The Quaker Oats Company had two main international divisions, Europe and Latin America. Within those two divisions, countries had their own general managers, product mix, marketers, distributors, and computer systems. Of course, some decisions were made at headquarters in Chicago, e.g., when to launch Gatorade® in Italy. And information systems had to provide financial reports for consolidation. There was no effort made to achieve efficiencies among the countries.

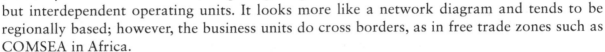

Figure 11-3. Transnational Configuration

A transnational configuration provides both efficiency and customization, requiring dispersed but interdependent operating units. It looks more like a network diagram and tends to be regionally based; however, the business units do cross borders, as in free trade zones such as COMSEA in Africa.

The last configuration is global, which has centralized functions around the world. For example, financial services might be in the United Kingdom. Marketing functions are centralized in the United States. Production is in Thailand. The product or services themselves require little to no change for their differentiation. It, too, looks like a network model but is distinguished from the transnational model by global branding. HP and Nike are two such examples.

THE GLOBAL CONTEXT

An unfortunate reality is that where there are potential rewards, there are potential risks. Some risks can be anticipated with a good PESTEL environmental analysis and mitigated or avoided. Others are harder to predict, e.g., terrorism, although risk signals include poor economic conditions, repression of ethnic groups, and radicalism, according to a study done by the International Monetary Fund (www.imf.org). The Dell Theory of Conflict Prevention says trade partners don't wage war on each other (Friedman 2005).

In summary, consider some sound advice from an international trade lawyer (Travis 2007):

- Take advantage of trade agreements.
- Protect your brand.
- Maintain high ethical standards.
- Stay secure in an insecure world.
- Expect the unexpected.
- All global business is personal.

Be careful out there!

APPLICATION AND REFLECTION

- Think about where globalization fits into your life, e.g., products you use, services you experience, relationships you build.

- Create an example where you might use arbitrage to exploit a CAGE model distance.

- Identify one example for each of the four configurations.

- The following reading focuses on China and India, two enormous markets. What are the key suggestions the authors make?

THE CHINA AND INDIA
STRATEGY

Anil K. Gupta and Haiyan Wang

Far too many companies still spend considerable time and energy debating whether to focus on China or India as their next big market. These are both vast nations with huge population densities—China has 135 people per square kilometer (about 350 people per square mile) and India has two and a half times that, whereas the United States has only 31 people per square kilometer (about 80 per square mile). At first glance, China and India seem overwhelmingly large as well as distinct enough to merit separate strategies.

But that approach is shortsighted. As the two fastest-growing economies in the world, China and India together represent an immediate opening for unparalleled market penetration. The opportunity to tackle them simultaneously cannot be ignored without the real possibility that latecomers will be, well, too late. Other companies will have already staked their claims and raised the barriers to entry. Moreover, economic integration between China and India is proceeding apace. Few people outside these two nations are aware that China is India's number one trading partner and India is among China's top 10 trade relationships. Even if the growth rate in China–India trade slows down to 25% annually from its current rate of about 50%, bilateral trade will reach almost $75 billion in 2010 and $225 billion in 2015 (in USD)—equal to China–U.S. trade just three years ago. And investment between India and China is likely to grow even faster than trade. As these economies become more intertwined, it will be more difficult for outsiders to find an easy path in.

In short, for most Fortune 1000 companies, the right question to consider now is how best to pursue China and India together. The strategic benefits of having a nearly equal presence in both countries, instead of a single focus on one or the other, can be broken down into four categories.

1. Scale. A combined market strategy for China and India is particularly important when a company's cost structure depends on significant economies of scale and when profit margins are razor thin. This is increasingly the case for makers of inexpensive products targeted at the middle- and low-income segments of emerging markets. Take the EC280, a new $335 compact desktop computer with a low-end Intel processor, introduced by Dell, Inc. in March 2007 for first-time buyers in emerging markets. Because this machine would be sold in stores rather than online, Dell would have to share profits with retailers and accept extremely slim margins. In fact, the only way that Dell could make real money on the EC280 was by selling the computer not only throughout the vast Chinese market but also in India and other developing nations.

The rivalry between Cisco Systems, Inc. and China's Huawei Technologies Company offers yet another illustration of the potential downside a company faces if it fails to stretch its core skills across a cohesive China—India market strategy. Huawei is one of Cisco's most aggressive global challengers; indeed, in 2003, Cisco sued Huawei for stealing its source code and using it in competitive routers and switches. The case was dropped nearly 20 months later, after Huawei agreed to discontinue the products. Between 2003 and 2007, Huawei's annual revenue grew from about 20% of Cisco's to nearly half. Huawei's increasing competitive advantage rests heavily on cost leadership, which derives primarily from the fact that the bulk of its R&D and manufacturing operations are based in China. With its lower-cost product portfolio, Huawei is attractive to customers in emerging markets. In fact, in 2007, the Chinese company generated 72% of its revenues from outside China, largely in developing countries.

Huawei is on the record as saying that its goal is to become India's number one supplier of telecom infrastructure equipment. The implications for Cisco are clear. It must develop a counter-strategy that rests on at least three legs: innovating faster than Huawei, drastically reducing its cost structure to match or beat Huawei's low prices, and then riding these gains to attack Huawei in both of its key markets—China and India.

2. Complementary strengths. China is much stronger than India in terms of physical infrastructure and manufacturing efficiency—its manufacturing sector is five times as large as that of India—whereas India bests China in software development, IT-enabled services, and many types of analytical and knowledge-intensive tasks such as legal research, finance and accounting, and advertising.

IBM Corporation provides a near-perfect example of how to leverage the complementary capabilities of manufacturing in China and IT services in India. IBM has built its largest procurement center outside the United States in Shenzhen, China, and two years ago IBM's chief procurement officer relocated there. Sourcing from Asian (primarily China-based) suppliers accounts for about 30% of the company's $40 billion annual purchasing budget; IBM hopes that these moves will make this very busy supply chain more efficient, especially for products destined for Asian markets. But whereas it relies on China for hardware procurement, the company has made India its global center for the delivery of IT services. At the end of 2007, IBM employed more than 70,000 IT professionals in India, about 20% of its global workforce and a group four times the size of its staff in China.

The complementary strengths of China and India extend beyond manufacturing and information technology services. China's chemical industry (particularly specialty chemicals) is significantly more advanced than India's. In addition, certain types of pharmaceutical raw materials are available more abundantly and at lower cost in China than in India. Thus, many India-based pharmaceutical companies turn to China as a primary supplier of pharmaceutical ingredients. In turn, India is emerging as an important source of specialized talent in finance, accounting, and global marketing for many Chinese companies as well as the Chinese units of major multinational corporations. In mid-2007, Chinese computer maker Lenovo Group Ltd. centralized its worldwide advertising activities in Bangalore, to a hub that is responsible for all ads placed outside China.

India's labor costs have been relatively stable, so a company can offset China's higher wages with its Indian presence.

3. **Knowledge transfer.** The fact that China's economy is 12 to 15 years ahead of India's provides many companies with an opportunity to leverage lessons from China. This helps them fine-tune their strategies for the Indian market at a relatively fast pace. Take the case of the PC industry. Dealing with the Chinese and Indian PC markets involves many common factors, such as extremely rapid growth, large proportions of first-time buyers, the need to reach customers not just in the most populous markets but also in smaller ones, the importance of selling through the retail channel, low buying power, few credit cards, and the need for local-language software.

Lenovo has attempted to take advantage of these similarities in the two markets by first putting on paper the essence of the Chinese business model and then "distilling it down to five salient points that we could implement in any country," according to William J. Amelio, Lenovo's president and chief executive. India was picked first for this knowledge transfer, and the company's success with this market entry strategy there has driven Lenovo's wider global sales strategy.

4. **Risk reduction.** Establishing a presence in both India and China can reduce companies' exposure to political risk. Given the rapid transformations in their economies, the Chinese and Indian governments are still trying to determine whether and how to differentiate between domestic and foreign enterprises and what types of policies to adopt for each category of firm. For example, China's new enterprise income tax law eliminates the tax advantages that foreign enterprises historically enjoyed over domestic ones, and a new antimonopoly law may put fresh restrictions on acquisitions within China by foreign firms. Meanwhile in India, the government is often ruled by a coalition of widely disparate partners, populated by incumbents who almost always lose in the next election. With so much uncertainty surrounding future policymaking in both countries, a multinational enterprise with dual operations in China and India stands to do the best job of hedging against political vulnerability.

Economic instability is another concern. From early 2007 to early 2008, manufacturing costs in southern China, where many multinationals have set up shop, have increased by as much as 40%. A rapid increase in the cost of raw materials and energy as well as new labor laws and environmental regulations are the chief reasons. India's labor costs have thus far been relatively stable, so a company can offset China's higher wages with its Indian presence.

For Fortune 1000 companies, the right question to consider now is how best to pursue China and India together.

Finally, intellectual property risk can be mitigated by disaggregating and distributing core research and development and core-component production across China and India as well as other countries. Consider the case of a European manufacturer that sells machinery to construction contractors. Burned by seeing its former Chinese partner produce copycat versions of its products, the company has divvied up the production of subsystems between India and China. Such an approach still permits the company to benefit from low manufacturing costs in each country but minimizes the extent to which the company's design blueprints and manufacturing processes are exposed to local partners or job-hopping local employees.

By 2025, it is highly probable that China–India economic ties (composed of trade, investments, and technology linkages) may be among the five most important bilateral relationships in the world. The rising dragons and tigers from China and India will be one set of beneficiaries.

And multinationals that take advantage now of openings in China and India simultaneously are likely to find themselves equally rewarded.

About the Authors

Anil K. Gupta (agupta@rhsmith.umd.edu), the Ralph J. Tyser Professor of Strategy and Organization at the University of Maryland's Smith School of Business, is coauthor (with Vijay Govindarajan and Haiyan Wang) of *The Quest for Global Dominance: Transforming Global Presence into Global Competitive Advantage,* 2nd ed. (Jossey-Bass 2008). **Haiyan Wang** (hwang@chinaindiainstitute.com) is the managing partner of the China India Institute.

CHAPTER 12
LEADING STRATEGICALLY

Leadership is not magnetic personality that can just as well be a glib tongue. ... Leadership is lifting a person's vision to higher sights, the raising of a person's performance to a higher standard, the building of a personality beyond its normal limitations.

—*Peter F. Drucker*

OPENING VIGNETTE

Does leadership really matter? Can leaders make the tough calls that can turn a flailing company into a market leader? The answer is yes, and the example is Darwin Smith of Kimberly-Clark.

When Smith took responsibility as CEO of Kimberly-Clark, he faced the brutal facts: his company was mediocre and its capital was wastefully tied up in giant paper mills. Smith asked questions. What could Kimberly-Clark be passionate about? What could it be best at in the world? What could improve its economic logic? In his examination of exceptional companies and their leaders, *Good to Great* (2001), Jim Collins noted that the successful ones were willing to face the "brutal facts," just as Smith did.

After decades of Smith's leadership, Kimberly-Clark is the world's number one paper-based consumer products company. Smith did make a difference, and it mattered. He has since been named one of the best CEOs by *Fortune*[1] magazine.

---

[1] J. Collins. "The 10 greatest CEOs of all time." *Fortune* (July 21, 2003). Accessed at http://money.cnn.com

There are always new ideas and good ideas, but have you ever wondered why some companies can leverage good ideas and gain competitive advantage and other companies can't—or don't? Many believe that this critical difference is leadership.

It is leadership that crafts the vision, provides the resources, and mobilizes the workforce toward the common purpose of the strategy. Good leaders enable good ideas to be implemented by providing the commitment of energy and resources to drive the effort. Perhaps more importantly, it is the culture and the visionary tone that strategic leadership sets that makes the critical difference in achieving the desired results.

In this chapter, we examine the importance of leadership in achieving strategic results. Successful mastery of this material will enable you to:

- distinguish between "levels" and qualities of leadership
- understand best practices in strategic leadership
- avoid potential pitfalls
- explain organizational developments that can support strategic change

This chapter ends with a reading entitled "Leading Change," which is, after all, what strategic management for results is all about.

STRATEGIC LEADERSHIP DEFINED

Why is leadership so important? How is it different from management?

Management versus leadership is an ongoing debate, but the most important result is to acknowledge that both are necessary and complimentary to ensure strategic success.

Leadership as defined by Burns (1978) is transformational and is distinguishable from transactional leadership. Transformational leaders are the visionaries who see the potential in the future, are looking to upset the status quo and to engage others in a purposeful direction. This leader is "charismatic" and, according to Burns, is ethically directed in his or her visionary quest. This is different from the transactional leader who is more of a manager and whose role is to guarantee a steady state and to make sure that operations meet the stated goals. As we discussed earlier, the ability to see the desired results, to define the direction, is the first step in the process of strategy development. It is the leader who defines the vision; managers implement this vision, with the leader's support.

Bennis and Nanus (1985) identify the four "Is" of transformational leadership. They are: idealized influence, inspirational motivation, intellectual stimulation, and individual consideration. The key words, ideal, inspiration, intellect, and individual, all are descriptive of a charismatic leader. Also, the concept of what makes a good versus a great leader was the basis of studies at Ohio State in the 1970s. Fiedler (1967) and others also found the importance of individual consideration. Consideration for followers was found to be equally as important as directing the task of work and distinguished an effective leader; that is, a concern for followers further differentiated leaders from more task oriented managers.

Daniel Goleman's work (1998) on emotional and social intelligence has implications for leadership. He asserts that time and time again, individuals with the personality characteristics of self-awareness, self-regulation, motivation, social skill, and empathy lead successful companies. These are the characteristics of emotionally intelligent individuals.

More recently, Jim Collins (2001), in his work on leadership in his book *Good to Great*, showed that the leadership of *great* companies was different from the leadership of *good* ones in a surprising way. In his longitudinal study of companies from 1965–1995, those that were great were designated by their exemplary stock performance. The companies that met the criteria all were led by what Collins designated as Level 5 leaders: leaders who were driven by something more, who were exemplary in "getting the right people on the bus," and in getting their companies to the top by making the hard decisions and acknowledging "the brutal facts." These factors contributed to companies that both sustained and endured.

Maxwell (2010) simplifies the power of leadership as the ability to influence, or get people to do what you want them to do when you want them to do it. Like Goleman and Collins, he suggests that although some individuals are more innately meant to be leaders, leadership can be learned and must be practiced.

LEADERSHIP'S BEST PRACTICES AND PITFALLS

Although we have discussed the individual leaders' characteristics and importance to successful strategies, there are also some "lessons learned" that help leaders to be successful in moving their organizations toward strategic success.

Fundamentally, leadership is manifest by influencing others. The most successful leaders have the trust of their followers. Trusting in a leader can be risky; his or her trustworthiness can be viewed as a function of three broad factors, as perceived by the trustor: the leader's ability and credibility, his/her benevolence (or inclination to want to do what is in the best interests of the trustor), and integrity. Integrity is a complex idea; some consider it synonymous with ethical behavior, but it also means that a leader's words and actions match. Related to this is credibility, where followers believe in the leader. Pagano (2004) suggests nine behaviors that build credibility, including: being overwhelmingly honest, being composed, keeping promises, and delivering bad news well. The idea is to be *transparent*.

Ethical leadership is not easy. Ethical dilemmas are complex, pitting positive values against one another, e.g., short- versus long-term, justice versus mercy, truth versus loyalty, individual versus community (Kidder 1995). With organizations having multiple stakeholders, it is difficult to define "community" or balance between long- and short-term interests.

Ethical leadership is not all about the leader's integrity, either. According to Trevino and Brown (2004, p. 75), "research has found that certain individual characteristics are necessary but not sufficient for effective ethical leadership." It is also a reputational phenomenon, based on external perceptions. They suggest that executives wanting effective ethics management should understand the existing ethical culture, communicate the importance of ethical standards, focus on the reward system, and promote ethical leadership throughout the firm.

Instituting an ethical culture or implementing a business strategy both involve changing the direction of an organization. Many studies have been done that

1. Create a Sense of Urgency

2. Form a guiding coalition

3. Create a Vision

4. Communicate the Vision

5. Empower others to Act on the Vision

6. Create Quick Wins

7. Build on the Change

8. Institutionalize the Change

Figure 12-1. Kotter's Eight Steps for Leading Change

show that getting individuals to change, especially when times are good, can be extremely difficult. Kotter (1996) is highly regarded for his advice on how to make sure that change initiatives are successful. As shown in Figure 12-1, he suggests steps for successful change management that include creating a sense of urgency, developing a powerful coalition, monitoring of results, allowing for short-term wins, and *communicating!*

All change management is oriented toward getting the organization "over the finish line." Lewin (1947) developed a very popular analogy of change as analogous to the melting of an ice cube and the water refreezing in a new shape. Another popular mental model that explains the change process is that of a "journey" that describes the behavior of employees as well as managers in each stage, in which the past is "let go," the change is "explored," and the "new beginnings" are embraced (Bridges 2003).

Probably the most common mistake in change management is the misalignment of the management team and the employees, where employees are back in the "letting go" or endings phase while the leadership team is already in the "new beginnings."

Of the original Forbes 100 in 1917, 61 of these companies were out of business by 1987, and only 18 stayed in the top 100. Seventy-five percent of joint ventures fall apart after the "honeymoon," and 80% of the intended value from mergers and acquisitions fails to materialize (Beer 2002; Gratton 2007). The message is clear: Change is a must, and leading successful change is an imperative for strategies to be successful and achieve the desired future state.

ORGANIZATIONAL DEVELOPMENT

So how do you structure the company to ensure strategic success, and also, how do you know if your strategic change is on track and getting the desired results? One of the most popular tools

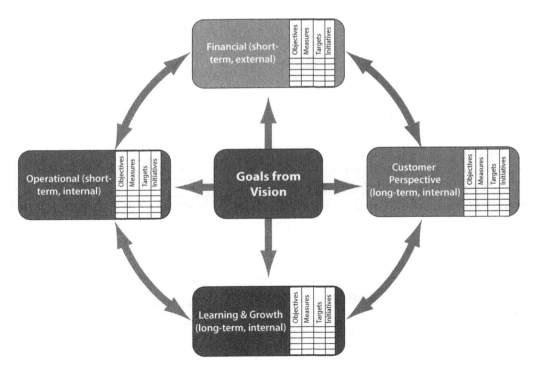

Figure 12-2. Balanced Scorecard

or approaches used to drive an organization toward achieving its strategic goals is the Balanced Scorecard (BSC) developed by Kaplan and Norton (1996).

The BSC provides managers with the instrumentation they need to navigate to the desired results. The BSC translates an organization's mission and strategies into a comprehensive set of performance measures that provides the framework for a strategic measurement and management system. The BSC retains an emphasis on achieving financial objectives but also includes the performance drivers of those financial objectives. Typically, the scorecard measures organizational performance across four perspectives (as shown in Figure 12-1): financial, customers, internal business processes, and learning and growth. In this manner, internal and external perspectives are balanced, as are short- and long-term perspectives. The BSC enables companies to track financial results while simultaneously monitoring progress in building the capabilities and acquiring the intangible assets they need for future growth.

APPLICATION AND REFLECTION

- Think about an individual who has been influential in your life. Describe the qualities they possess and how they affected your behavior and decision-making. Why did you find that person trustworthy?

- Reflect on a change you have tried, either successfully or unsuccessfully, to implement for You, Inc. Relate your efforts to Kotter's suggested steps and see if you agree or disagree with his model for change.

CLOSING CASE

For our closing case, we have selected a familiar organization in what may be an unfamiliar location. As you read about Hong Kong Disneyland, respond to the following:

1. Using the strategy diamond, describe Disney's approach to internationalizing its operations.
2. Compare Los Angeles, California (home), and Hong Kong (host) using the CAGE distance framework. Why would the Tokyo Disneyland be such a success, while the Hong Kong location has been problematic?
3. Evaluate how well Disney's management led the changes needed to adapt to local Hong Kong culture.
4. Identify two issues challenging Hong Kong Disneyland's current operations, and propose solutions. What external factors are involved?
5. What would be some of the foreseeable challenges for Disney if it chooses to enter the China market?

HONG KONG DISNEYLAND

Michael N. Young and Donald Liu

 Ivey Publishing

Richard Ivey School of Business
The University of Western Ontario

September 12, 2006, marked the one-year anniversary of the opening of Hong Kong Disneyland (HKD). Amid the hoopla and celebrations, media experts were reflecting on the high points and low points of HKD's first year of operations, including several controversies that had generated some negative publicity.

At a press conference and interview to discuss the first year of operations, Bill Ernest, HKD's executive vice president, acknowledged that the park had learned a lot from its experiences and that the problems had made it stronger. Ernest also announced that HKD attendance for the year had been "well over" 5 million visitors. Still, this figure was short of the 5.6 million visitors that had earlier been projected by park officials. Ernest stated that the park was on sound financial footing but would not release the details.[1] He also announced the appointment of two non-executive directors; Payson Cha Mou Sing, managing director of HKR International, and Philip Chen Nan Lok of Cathay Pacific would be joining the board of directors in a move calculated to counter charges of a lack of transparency. The criticisms were, in part, coming from members of the Hong Kong Legislative Council as HKD was 57% owned by the Hong Kong Government, which had invested HK$23 billion.[2]

Since plans for the high-profile HKD project were first announced, there had been criticisms of a lack of transparency from Hong Kong government officials, the Consumer Council, and members of the public. The dissatisfaction was reflected in a survey conducted by Hong Kong Polytechnic University in March 2006.[3] Although 56% of the 524 respondents believed the government's HK$13.6 billion (about $1.74 billion) investment to be of a "fair" value, 70% of respondents had a negative impression of the public investment in HKD. This response was a considerably more pessimistic result than previous surveys. It was in the interests of HKD to turn this situation around.

HKD was the third park that Disney had opened outside of the United States, following the Tokyo Disney Resort and Disneyland Resort Paris. The Tokyo Disney Resort was the most successful of all of the Disney parks worldwide, and indeed one of the most successful theme parks in the world; the Disneyland Paris Resort was much less successful.[4] Pundits had begun to wonder whether the outcome of HKD would more closely resemble that of its successful Far Eastern Japanese cousin or whether it would more closely resemble that of the French park. That outcome depended in part on how well Disney would be able to translate its strategic assets, such as its products, practices, and ideologies, to the Chinese context.

COMPANY BACKGROUND

The Walt Disney Company (Disney) was founded in 1923, and was committed to delivering quality entertainment experiences for people of all ages. As a global entertainment empire, the company leveraged its amazing heritage of creativity, fantasy, and imagination established by its founder, Walt Disney. By 2006, Disney's business portfolio consisted of four major segments: Studio Entertainment, Parks and Resorts, Consumer Products, and Media Networks. Exhibit 1 summarizes the details of the company's holdings and their respective financial performance in 2005.

Other Disney Parks and Resorts

Disney opened the first Disneyland, Disneyland Resort, in Anaheim, California, in July 1955. The company's second theme park, Walt Disney World Resort, was opened in Lake Buena Vista, Florida, in 1971. After the establishment of these two large theme parks in the United States, Disney sought to expand internationally. Disney's international expansion strategy was

---

[1] Linda Choy and Dennis Eng. "5 Million Visit Disney Park, Short of Target." *South China Morning Post*, electronic edition (September 5, 2006). Accessed December 3, 2006, at http://scmp.com

[2] In 2006, the Hong Kong dollar was pegged to the U.S. dollar at approximately $1 = HK$7.80.

[3] May Chan. "Disneyland's Image Has Soured Since Its Opening." *South China Morning Post*, p. CITY3.

[4] Mary Yoko Brannen. "When Mickey Loses Face: Recontextualization, Semantic Fit, and the Semiotics of Foreignness." *Academy of Management Review* (October 2004): 593–616.

straightforward, consisting of "bringing the original Disneyland model to a new territory, and then, if feasible, adding a specialty theme park."[5] Tokyo Disney Resort was Disney's first attempt at executing this strategy.

Tokyo Disney Resort

Disney opened its first non-U.S. park in Tokyo, Japan, in 1983. The scope and thematic foundation of the Tokyo park was modeled after the Disney parks in California and Florida. The $1.4 billion cost to develop Tokyo Disney Resort was financed solely by Oriental Land Co., a land-reclamation company formed under a joint-venture agreement between Mitsui Real Estate Development Co. and Keisei Electric Railway Co.[6] Disney did not assume any ownership of Tokyo Disney Resort to minimize risks. The contract signed in 1979 spelled out Oriental Land as the owner and licensee, whereas Disney was designated as the designer and licensor. Although Disney received a $100 million royalty every year, this amount was less than would have been the case if Disney were the sole owner or even a co-owner of Tokyo Disney Resort. By 2006, the 23-year-old Tokyo Disney Resort, along with the addition of Tokyo DisneySea, at an additional cost of $3 billion in 2000[7] was a huge success, with a combined annual attendance of more than 25 million visitors and an operating income of ¥28,957 million (about $245.47 million) generated in 2005 alone.[8]

Tokyo Disney Resort was well received by the Japanese, owing in part to the Japanese interest in Western cultures and the Asian love of fantasy and costume. The secret underlying this success was to provide the visitors with "a slice of unadulterated Disney-style Americana," proclaimed Toshio Kagami, president of Oriental Land Co. Tokyo Disney Resort had attracted wide support from the local Japanese, who accounted for more than 95% of the annual attendance. Moreover, around 15% of the total visitors had visited the park 30 times or more, making Tokyo Disney Resort one of the world's most popular theme parks in terms of annual attendance.[9] The Tokyo Disney Resort also had the highest sales of souvenirs of all the Disney land resorts, in part, because it was the only Disney property to give special admission just for the purpose of purchasing souvenirs.

[5] Sara Bakhshian. "The Offspring." *Amusement Business* (May 2005): 20–21.

[6] Eva Liu and Elyssa Wong. "Information Note: Tokyo Disneyland: Some Basic Facts." Research and Library Services Division of the Legislative Council Secretariat, Hong Kong, 1999. Retrieved March 10, 2006, from www.legco.gov.hk/yr99- 0/english/sec/library/990in02.pdf

[7] Ibid.

[8] Oriental Land Co. 2005 Annual Report. Retrieved March 10, 2006, from http://olc.netir-wsp.com/medias/1656486483_0LCAR2005final.pdf

[9] James Zoltak. "Lots of Walks in the Parks the Past Year." *Amusement Business* (December 2004): 6–7.

Disneyland Resort Paris

France was the largest consumer of Disney products outside the United States, particularly in the area of publications, such as comic books.[10] However, this status did not provide much help to Disneyland Resort Paris (formerly named Euro Disney), Disney's second attempt at international expansion. Disneyland Resort Paris came into operation in 1992, after two-and-a-half years of negotiations with the French Government. Disney was determined to avoid the mistake of forgoing majority ownership and profits as had been the case with Tokyo Disney Resort. Thus, Disney became one of the partners in this project. Under the initial financial arrangement, Disney had a 49% stake in the project. The French Government provided cash and loans of $770 million at interest rates below the market rates, and financed the majority of the $400 million infrastructure.

However, cost overruns pushed overall construction costs to $5 billion—five times the previous estimate of $1 billion. This increase was due to alterations in design and construction plans. This higher cost, coupled with the theme park's mediocre performance during its initial years of operation and other factors, caused the park severe difficulties between 1992 and 1994. The park did not report a profit until 1995, which was largely due to a reduction of interest costs from $265 million to $93 million and the rigorous financial re-engineering efforts in late 1994.[11]

Despite poor results between 1995 and 2001, Disney added a new park, Walt Disney Studios, which brought Hollywood-themed attractions to the French park. At its opening in 2004, the second park attracted only 2.2 million visitors, 5.8 million short of its original projections. At the end of the fiscal year on September 30, 2004, Disneyland Resort Paris announced a loss of €145.2 million (about $190 million).[12]

Part of the problem with the Paris resort was the resistance by the French to what they considered American cultural imperialism. French cultural critics claimed that Disney would be a "cultural Chernobyl," and some stated publicly a desire for the park's failure. For example, critic Stephen Bayley wrote:

> The Old World is presented with all the confident big ticket flimflam of painstaking fakery that this bizarre campaign of reverse-engineered cultural imperialism represents. I like to think that by the turn of the century Euro Disney will have become a deserted city, similar to Angkor Wat [in Cambodia].[13]

Disney had to assure the French government that French would be the primary language spoken within the park. Even the French president, Francois Mitterand, joined in the fray, declining to attend the opening-day ceremony, dismissing the expensive new investment with Gallic indifference as "*pas ma tasse de the*" ("just not my cup of tea").[14]

Robert Fitzpatrick, the first chairman of the Disneyland Resort Paris, was a French-speaking American who knew Europe quite well, in part because of his French wife. Fitzpatrick did not, however, realize that Disney could not approach France in the same way as it had approached

---

[10] Mary Yoko Brannen. "When Mickey Loses Face: Recontextualization, Semantic Fit, and the Semiotics of Foreignness." *Academy of Management Review* (October 2004): 593–616.

[11] James B. Stewart. *Disney War*. New York: Simon & Schuster, 2005.

[12] Jo Wrighton and Bruce Orwall. "Mutual Attractions: Despite Losses and Bailouts, France Stays Devoted to Disney." *Wall Street Journal* (January 26, 2005): A1.

[13] James B. Stewart. *Disney War*, 128. New York: Simon & Schuster, 2006.

[14] Ibid.

Florida when setting up its second theme park. For example, the recruitment process and training programs for its staff were initially not well-adapted to the French business culture. The 13-page manual specifying the dress code within the theme park was apparently unacceptable to the French; the court had even ruled that imposing such a dress code was against the labour laws.

The miscalculations of cultural differences were found in other operational aspects as well. For instance, Disney's policy of banning the serving of alcoholic beverages in its parks, including in California, Florida, and Tokyo, was unsurprisingly extended to France. This restriction outraged the French for whom enjoying wine during lunch and dinner was part of their daily custom. In May 1993, Disney yielded to the external pressure, and altered its policy to permit the serving of wines and beers in the theme park. With the renaming and the retooling of the entire theme park complex to better appeal to European taste, Disneyland Resort Paris finally began to profit in 1995.

Why Such Different Outcomes for Tokyo and Paris?

Why was Disney so successful in Tokyo but largely a failure in Paris? Professor Mary Yoko Brannen maintains that it may in part have been due to the way that Disney's strategic assets—such as products, practices, and ideologies—were translated to and interpreted in the Japanese and French contexts.[15] According to Brannen, the "Americana" represented by Disney was an asset in Japan, where a trip to Disney was seen as an exotic, foreign-like experience. However, this association with the pure form of all things American was a liability in France, where it was seen as a form of reverse cultural imperialism. The result was a "lost-in-translation" effect for many of Disney's most valued icons and established business practices. For example, Mickey Mouse was seen as a squeaky-clean all-American boy in the United States, and he was viewed as conservative and reliable enough to sell money market accounts in Japan. However, in France, he was seen as a street-smart detective because of the popularity of a comic book series, *Le Journal Mickey*.

Likewise, Disney's service training, human resource management (HRM) practices, and training required to achieve the "happiest place on earth" were quite easy to implement in Japan, where such practices represented the cultural norm. In France, however, the same training practices were perceived as invasive and totalitarian. Exhibit 2 summarizes how other strategic assets of Disney were recontextualized to the Japanese and French environments.

In 2006, it remained to be seen how Disney's strategic assets would translate to and be interpreted in the Chinese culture of Hong Kong, the topic to which we turn next.

Mickey Mouse Goes to China

We know we have an addressable market just crying out for Disney products.
—Andy Bird, Walt Disney International president, discussing China's potential[16]

The Chinese "have heard so much about the parks around the world, and they want to experience the same thing," said Don Robinson, the former managing director of HKD. Chinese

---

[15] Mary Yoko Brannen. "When Mickey Loses Face: Recontextualization, Semantic Fit and the Semiotics of Foreignness." *Academy of Management Review* (October 2004): 593–616.

[16] Jeffrey Ressner and Michael Schuman. "Disney's Great Leap into China." *Time* (July 11, 2005): 52–54.

consumers wanted to connect with the global popular culture and distance themselves from their previous collective poverty and communist dictate. Kevin Wong, a tourism economist at the Hong Kong Polytechnic University, remarked that the Chinese "want to come to Disney because it is American. The foreignness is part of the appeal." The Chinese needed Disney, and Disney needed China. For example, Ted Parrish, co-manager of the Henssler Equity Fund, an investment fund house, said, "If Disney wants to maintain earnings growth in the high teens going forward, China will be a big source of that."[17]

Because the Chinese economy was booming, Disney thought it would be a good time to set up a new theme park there. China's infrastructure was still substandard by world standards. In addition, the Chinese currency, the renminbi, was not fully convertible. These and other factors increased the attractiveness of Hong Kong—a Special Administrative Region of China since the handover of sovereignty from the United Kingdom in 1997. Hong Kong had world-class infrastructure and a reputation as an international financial center. Most importantly, Hong Kong had always been a gateway to China. These factors gave Hong Kong an edge as a location for Disney's third international theme park.

THE HONG KONG TOURISM INDUSTRY

> Hong Kong, with its unusual blend of East and West, of Chinese roots and British colonial heritage, of ultramodern sophistication and ancient traditions, is one of the most diverse and exciting cities in the world. It is an international city brimming with energy and dynamism, yet also a place where peace and tranquility are easily found.[18]

Tourism was one of the major pillars of the Hong Kong economy. In 2005, the total number of visitors was more than 23 million, a new record and approximately a 7.1% increase over 2004 (see Exhibit 3). Visitors came from all over the world, including Taiwan, America, Africa, the Middle East, and Macao (see Exhibit 4). Mainland China was the biggest source of visitors, accounting for 53.7% of the total in 2005.[19] The dominance of this group was, in part, supported by the Individual Travel Scheme[20] introduced in 2003.

Local Attractions

Popular tourist attractions in Hong Kong included, but were not limited to, Victoria Peak, Repulse Bay, open-air markets, and Ocean Park. Hong Kong's colonial heritage provided several attractions, such as Cenotaph, Statue Square, and the Government House. Traditional Chinese festivals, such as Tin Hau Festival, Cheung Chau Bun Festival, and Temple Fair, added

---

[17] Paul R. La Monica. "For Disney, It's a Small World after All." CNNmoney.com, September 12, 2005, retrieved March 10, 2006, from http://money. cnn. com/2005/09/12/news/fortune500/hongkongdisney/

[18] Hong Kong Tourism Board. Accessed August 17, 2007, from www.discoverhongkong.com

[19] Hong Kong Census & Statistics Department. "Hong Kong Monthly Digest of Statistics." Hong Kong Census & Statistics Department, Hong Kong, March 2006.

[20] The Individual Travel Scheme was a policy that permitted urban residents from selected cities in Mainland China to apply for visas from the Public Security Department to visit Hong Kong. In 2006, the Scheme covered 38 mainland cities. Until the implementation of this policy, mainlanders could only visit Hong Kong through business or travel groups.

local flavor. Visitors often took part in the celebration of these annual festive events during their stay. The Hong Kong Tourism Board had designated 2006 as "Discover Hong Kong Year" to attract more travelers and encourage them to extend their stay. Furthermore, the AsiaWorld-Expo opened in early 2006, and it was expected to attract more business travelers. Other initiatives included a sky rail to the world's largest sitting Buddha statue and Hong Kong Wetland Park. In addition, the Dr. Sun Yat Sen Museum was being renovated and was scheduled to reopen in early 2007.

Ocean Park

Ocean Park was another prime attraction in Hong Kong and was well-recognized worldwide. Prior to Disney's entry, Ocean Park occupied a quasi-monopoly position as the only local theme park. Founded in 1977, Ocean Park was located near Hong Kong's Central district, the heart of the bustling city. Ocean Park had an annual attendance of more than 4 million visitors and had been ranked recently as one of the top 10 amusement parks in the world by *Forbes* magazine.[21] Ocean Park sought to blend entertainment with educational elements, thus offering the dual experience for its guests termed as "edutainment."

For the 2004/05 fiscal year, Ocean Park's gross revenue was HK$684 million ($87.8 million), which represented a 12% increase over the previous year. The surplus of HK$119.5 million ($15.3 million) was the best performance ever achieved at the Park.[22] In 2006, Ocean Park received necessary financing for a HK$5.55 billion (about $0.71 billion) makeover, including a government-guaranteed portion of HK$1.39 billion (about $0.18 billion).[23] Ocean Park's redevelopment was expected to bring HK$23 billion (about $2.95 billion) to HK$28 billion (about $3.59 billion) over the first 20 years of operation, with visitors projected to increase to more than five million annually by 2011.

HONG KONG'S VERY OWN DISNEYLAND

> Hong Kong Disneyland will be the flagship for the Disney brand in this huge and growing country and play a pivotal role in helping to bring entertainment to this ... part of the world. ... It is our first destination opening in a market where [there] isn't a very deep knowledge of Disney culture and stories.
> —Jay Rasulo, chairman of Walt Disney Parks and Resorts[24]

Disney initiated a conversation with the Hong Kong Special Administrative Region (SAR) government in August 1998 about the possibility of setting up a Disney theme park. To avoid a situation like the one encountered by Disneyland Resort Paris, Disney initially planned to

---

[21] Norma Connolly. "Top 10 Accolade a Boost to Ocean Park." *South China Morning Post*, electronic edition (June 3, 2006). Accessed December 3, 2006, from http://www.scmp.com

[22] The Walt Disney Company. Annual Report, 2005. Retrieved March 10, 2006, from http://corporate.disney.go.com/investors/annual_reports/2005/index.html

[23] Charis Yau. "Ocean Park Eyes $4.1B Loan to Finance Makeover." *South China Morning Post* (April 13, 2006): p. BIZ1. Retrieved May 3, 2006, from WiseNews Database.

[24] Greg Hernandez. "Mickey Gains Recognition in Hong Kong." *Knight Ridder/Tribune Business News* (September 8, 2005): 1. Retrieved March 10, 2006, from Lexis-Nexis Academic Universe Database.

simply run the park on a management fee and licensing contract basis. After extended talks and negotiations, however, Disney agreed to take an ownership stake as well.

HKD was expected to bring a number of economic benefits to Hong Kong. First, approximately 18,400 jobs would be created directly or indirectly at HKD's opening, and this number was expected to increase to 35,800 in 20 years. Plus, 3.4 million visitors, mainly from Hong Kong and Mainland China, would be attracted to the park, and attendance was projected to increase to 7.3 million after 15 years. The additional spending by tourists would amount to HK$8.3 billion (about $1.1 million) in Year 1, rising to HK$16.8 billion (about $2.2 billion) annually by Year 20 and beyond. There would be "soft" benefits as well, such as with the acquisition of first-class technological innovations and facilities and gaining hands-on experience with quality service training. Over a period of 40 years, it was forecast that HKD would generate an economic benefit equivalent to HK$148 billion (about $19 billion). This forecast sounded promising during the 1998/99 period when negotiations were taking place, when Hong Kong was still feeling the effects of the 1997 Asian financial crisis.

The Concluded Deal

This is a happy marriage between a world-class tourism attraction and a world-class tourist destination. We hope that Hong Kong Disneyland will not just bring us more tourists, but also wholesome quality entertainment for local families as well.[25]

After a year of negotiations, the final contract was signed in December of 1999. The theme park and hotels would cost $1.8 billion to construct over six years. In addition, $1.7 billion would be spent for land reclamation as no other suitable location was available in the densely populated territory. The park would be situated on Penny's Bay of Lantau Island, the largest of Hong Kong's outlying islands. The Hong Kong Government and Disney would invest $416 million and $314 million, respectively. In return, Disney held a 43% stake in HKD, and the government held the remaining 57%, which could later be increased to 73% by converting subordinate shares. A further $1.1 billion was put up in the form of government and commercial loans.

Hong Kong International Theme Park Limited (HKITP), the joint venture formed between Disney and the Hong Kong Government in December 1999, oversaw the construction and running of HKD. While the government developed the infrastructure, Disney provided master planning, real estate development, attraction and show design, engineering support, production support, project management, and other development services. Disney also set up a wholly owned subsidiary, Hong Kong Disneyland Management Limited, to manage HKD on behalf of HKITP.

A Rocky Start

There was a palpable excitement when the new Disneyland theme opened, but the skeptics and critics were not so easily impressed. Press reports described the first few months as a "rocky start." Some locals called the park's management policies "absurd."[26]

---

[25] Stephen Ip, Hong Kong secretary for Economic Services. "Hong Kong Disneyland Final Agreement Signed." Press release from Hong Kong government. Accessed August 17, 2007, from www.info.gov.hk/gia/general/99912/10/1210286.htm

[26] "Mousekeeping." *South China Morning Post,* features section (December 28, 2005): 12.

Four weeks prior to the official opening, HKD invited 30,000 selected individuals per day to visit the park to test the rides and other attractions. During the trial period, a thick haze hovered over the whole park, a result of the air pollutants passing down from Mainland China. This problem was well-recognized by Hong Kong authorities and was particularly acute during low wind periods, which trapped all of Hong Kong in smog.[27] Smog virtually engulfed Sleeping Beauty's Castle.

The first problem noticed was that the capacity limit of 30,000 visitors may have been too high. For example, on September 4, 2005, approximately 29,000 local visitors went to the park. The average queuing time was 45 minutes at the restaurants and more than two hours for the rides. The park faced pressure to lower the daily capacity limit. Instead, the park proposed other measures, such as extending the opening time by an hour and encouraging visits during weekdays by offering discounts, as opposed to reducing the actual limit.[28]

The park faced another problem when inspectors from the Hygiene Department were asked to remove their badges and caps prior to carrying out an official investigation of a food-poisoning case. Park officials later apologized and pledged to operate in compliance with all local regulations and customs. But problems continued. The police could not get into the park—even when deemed necessary—unless pre-arranged with the park's security unit.[29]

OPERATIONS

Product Offerings

HKD, like its counterparts in the United States, Japan, and France, symbolized happiness, fantasy, and dreams, and sought to offer an unparalleled experience to its visitors. The admission price was initially set at HK$295 ($38) during the weekdays and HK$350 ($45) on weekends and peak days, the lowest pricing among the five Disney theme parks. A day pass for a child was HK$250 ($32), while it was HK$200 ($27) for seniors aged 65 and older. Tickets were sold primarily via the company's Web site (http://www.hongkongdisneyland.com), which allowed three-month advance bookings. Tickets were sold through travel agencies. These two measures aimed to control the daily number of visitors and avoiding long queues at the entrance. Only a small portion of tickets were available for walk-in customers.

HKD, like other Disney theme parks, was divided into four parts, including Main Street, U.S.A.; Fantasyland; Adventureland; and Tomorrowland. Disney's classic attractions, such as Space Mountain, Mad Hatter Tea Cups, and Dumbo, were included in the park. In Main Street, U.S.A., guests could ride a steam train to tour the park. A large part of Fantasyland was the Sleeping Beauty Castle, which included Dumbo and Winnie the Pooh. Guests could find Mickey,

---

[27] Bruce Einhorn. "Disney's Not-so-magic New Kingdom." *Business Week Online* (September 13, 2005). Retrieved March 10, 2006, from http://www.businessweek.com/bwdaily/dnflash/sep2005/nf2005/nf20050913_9145_db046.htm?chan=search

[28] "HK Disneyland Considers Longer Opening Hours to Beat Long Lines." *The Associated Press*. Retrieved March 10, 2006, from http://english.sina.com/taiwan_hk/p/1/2005/0906/44951.html

[29] Jonathan Hill and Richard Welford. "A Case Study of Disney in Hong Kong." *Corporate Social Responsibility Asia Weekly* (November 16, 2005). Retrieved March 10, 2006, from http://www.csr-asia.com/index.php?p=5318

Minnie, and other popular Disney characters available for photos in the Fantasy Garden, which was unique to HKD. Adventureland was home to Tarzan's tree house, the jungle river cruise, and the Festival of the Lion King show. Tomorrowland featured science fiction and space adventures.

To cater to the time-pressed Hong Kong residents, HKD offered a Fastpass ticketing system, which provided a one-hour window to bypass queues for favored rides. Guests preferring an extended stay could check in to one of the two hotels, HKD Hotel and Disney's Hollywood Hotel, which offered on-site lodging services.

Marketing

HKD collaborated with the Hong Kong Government to jointly promote the theme park. It was estimated that one-third of the visitors would come from Hong Kong, one-third would come from Mainland China, and the remaining third would come from Southeast Asian countries.[30] The free-to-air TV program, *The Magical World of Disneyland,* was broadcast in Hong Kong, and could be received in various regions across Southern China. In each episode, famous pop stars from the region (for example, Jacky Cheung, who was also the official ambassador of HKD) would introduce some behind-the-scene stories about HKD, such as interviews with ride designers. Disney believed that the widespread popularity of Jacky Cheung would connect well with the audience in Asia. HKD also launched a special TV channel on local cable TV. This channel included background stories on founder Walt Disney, information about The Walt Disney Company and its evolution, interesting facts about the company's state-of-the-art animated films, and regular updates on the construction progress of the park.

The theme park also introduced a line of Disney-themed apparel at Giordano, a Hong Kong-based clothing retailer with more than 1,500 outlets in Asia, Australia, and the Middle East.[31] Giordano featured low-price fashionable clothes similar to The Gap in the United States. The Disney line featured adult and children's t-shirts and sweatshirts with popular Disney cartoon characters, such as Mickey Mouse and Nemo. The t-shirts were about HK$80 ($10) at Giordano, much less expensive than comparable items at HKD for HK$380 ($49).

HKD outsourced part of its marketing effort to *Colour Life,* a Guangzhou-based magazine. In September 2005, 100,000 extra copies were printed, featuring the grand opening of HKD that month. It was hoped the extra publicity would increase awareness of the theme park among the residents of Guangzhou, the major metropolitan area of southern China, just north of Hong Kong. The company also donated 200 HKD umbrellas to key newsstands in Guangzhou to provide even more publicity. In addition, HKD partnered with the Communist Youth League of China to run special events for children, such as Mickey Mouse drawing contests.

---

[30] Suchat Sritama. "HK Disneyland to Boost Thai Visitor Numbers." *The Nation* (September 13, 2005). Retrieved March 10, 2006, from http://www.nationmultimedia.com/2005/09/13/business/index. php?news=business_18587589.html

[31] "Hong Kong Disneyland Rolls out Fashions: Hong Kong Disneyland Takes Publicity Blitz to Masses with Fashion Line." *The Associated Press.* Retrieved March 10, 2006, from http://abcnews.go.com/ Business/wireStory?id=963083&CMP=OTC- RSSFeeds0312, archived at http://news.ewoss.com/articles/ D8BFNL1O0.aspx

Human Resource Management

The magical experience of a HKD visit depended upon the quality of service. HKD treated human resource management (HRM) as one of the cornerstones of its competitive advantage. To fill the remaining positions at the park, in April 2005, HKD launched one of the city's largest recruitment events ever. The park screened job candidates according to qualities such as service orientation, language capabilities, passion for excellence, and friendliness. Employees were referred to as cast members because "they are always on stage when interacting with guests, and therefore represent a very important element of the show," said Greg Wann, vice president for HRM at HKD.[32]

In January 2005, HKD sent the first cohort of 500 cultural representatives to Walt Disney World in Orlando for a six-month training program. The cast members would learn about the magical Disney culture and would have a platform to share their Chinese cultural experience with other cast members at Walt Disney World. During their stay at Orlando, the Hong Kong crew was trained according to standards set by The Walt Disney Company worldwide. They also had the opportunity to work in other divisions, including merchandising, food and beverage operations, park operations, custodial services, and hotel operations. In addition to training, HKD provided handbooks to each cast member, which literally detailed the regulations from head to toe. For example, male cast members could not have goatees or beards, and female cast members were not allowed to have fingernails longer than six centimetres.

Local Cultural Responsiveness

Given the cultural *faux pas* that occurred with Disneyland Resort Paris, Disney paid special attention to cultural issues pertaining to HKD. Because the prime target customer segment was the growing group of affluent Mainland Chinese tourists, *feng shui*[33] masters were consulted for advice on the park layout and design. New constructions often began with a traditional good-luck ceremony featuring a carved suckling pig.[34] One of the main ballrooms was constructed to be 888 square meters since eight was an auspicious number in Chinese culture, signifying good fortune. The hotels deliberately skipped the fourth floor because the Chinese associated four with bad luck. Other finer details were incorporated throughout the park to better fit the local culture. For example, the theme park sold mooncakes during the Chinese Mid-Autumn Festival. Phyllis Wong, the merchandising director, stated that green hats were not sold at the park because they were a symbol of a wife's infidelity in Chinese culture.[35]

Cast members at HKD were expected to converse proficiently in English, Cantonese, and Mandarin, and signs in the park were written in both Chinese and English. Another local adaptation was the squat toilets, which were popular throughout China. "These toilets benefit those

---

[32] Based on: Steven Knipp. "The Magic Kingdom Comes to the Middle Kingdom: What It Took for Hong Kong Disneyland to Finally Open in 2005." *Fun World* (February 2005). Retrieved March 10, 2006, from http://www.funworldmagazine.com/2005/february05/features/magic_kingdom/magickingdom.html

[33] Feng shui is the Chinese art and practice of positioning objects in accordance to the patterns of yin and yang, and in flow with chi, the energy source that resides in all matter.

[34] Jeffrey Ressner and Michael Schuman. "Disney's Great Leap into China." *Time* (July 11, 2005): 52–54.

[35] "Disney Uses Feng Shui to Build Mickey's New Kingdom in Hong Kong." *The Associated Press.* Retrieved March 10, 2006, from http://english.sina.com/taiwan_hk/1/2005/0907/45097.html

Mainland Chinese who prefer squatting and those who don't want to see muddy footprints on toilet seats," commented a Hong Kong visitor.[36]

Restaurants offered a wide variety of food, ranging from American-style burgers and French fries to Chinese dim sum and sweet and sour pork. Although some animal activists groups initially protested, shark fin soup was on the menu as "it is what the locals see as appropriate," said Esther Wong, a spokeswoman of HKD.[37]

NEGATIVE PUBLICITY

The Lunar New Year Holiday Fiasco

The park faced several public relations problems during its first year of operations, none bigger than that which occurred during the popular Chinese Lunar New Year holiday period. HKD had introduced a new, discounted, one-day ticket that could be used at any time during a given six-month period. These tickets could not be used on "special days" when the park anticipated an influx of visitors. The first period of special days was the Lunar New Year holidays.[38] In Hong Kong, the 2006 Lunar New Year period started on January 28 (Saturday) and ended on January 31 (Tuesday). However, HKD failed to take into account that the following two days (i.e., February 1 and 2) were still public holidays in Mainland China. Mainland tour agencies had purchased large batches of the discounted tickets and escorted large groups of Mainland tourists to HKD during those two days.

This influx created a major problem for HKD as thousands of mainland tourists clinching their tickets swarmed the front gates of the park. The park could not accommodate the additional guests, and the steel gates were locked shut. Many of these Mainland Chinese tourists had saved all year for this trip and had accompanied their extended families to Hong Kong to experience the Disney magic. Needless to say, they were understandably upset. The crowd turned into an angry mob, and, brandishing their tickets, started shouting profanities and hurling objects at the police and security guards. Some tourists even tried to climb over the gates, which were topped with sharp spikes. The front page of the local paper the next morning showed a Mainland tourist throwing a young child over the closed gates to his parents who had managed to get inside the park. As one disgruntled customer commented from that fateful day, "I won't come again, even if I am paid to."[39]

To China observers, the behavior was not entirely surprising, given that Mainland Chinese consumers can be very vocal when they are dissatisfied with a product or service. For example, in 2001, the dissatisfied owner of a Mercedes Benz SLK230 had his car towed to the center

---

[36] "Disneyland with Chinese Characteristics." Letters from China: China and Independent Travel (July 22, 2005). Retrieved March 10, 2006, from http://voyage.typepad.com/china/2005/07/disneyland_with.html

[37] "HK Disneyland Draws Fire over Soup." Chinadaily.com.cn (May 24, 2005). Retrieved March 10, 2006, from http://www. chinadaily. com. cn/english/doc/2005-05/24/content_445139. htm

[38] The Lunar New Year Holiday, or Chinese New Year, was one of the most important traditional Chinese festivals. A series of celebrations usually took place during the period, starting from the first day of the first month on the Chinese calendar.

[39] Helen Wu. "Queues Take the Magic out of a Crowded Kingdom." *South China Morning Post* (February 4, 2006): CITY1.

of town by a pair of oxen, where workers with sledgehammers demolished the car in front of media crews, creating a publicity nightmare for DaimlerChrysler.[40]

There was plenty of finger-pointing for the fiasco. Fengtan Peiling, the commissioner of the Hong Kong Consumer Council, claimed that Disney had failed to learn about the cultural traditions and consumption habits of Chinese people. Wang Shuxin, from the Shenzhen Tourism Tour Group Centre, blamed HKD of falsely accusing the travel agents for the predicament. His center, which oversaw Mainland tourists traveling to Hong Kong, had more than 300 claims for compensation through travel agencies. Some agencies wanted to sue HKD for a possible breach of contractual terms.[41] Soon afterward, the Hong Kong government released a statement requesting the park to improve its ticketing and guest-entry procedures. Bill Ernest, HKD's executive vice president, later apologized, stating "every market has unique dynamics that must be taken into consideration and must be learned over time," and that Disney was still learning.[42]

Customer Complaints

Customers also complained that the park was too small and that it had too few Hong Kong-themed attractions. HKD had only 22 attractions, 18 fewer than the other Disney theme parks. Other guests claimed that they were mistreated during their stay at the park. Some guests even planned to take legal action against HKD. For example, a park visitor from Singapore alleged negligence and discrimination of Disney's staff because they refused to call an ambulance for her mother who later died of heart failure at an HKD hotel. A spokesperson for HKD denied the allegations, saying that the staff handled the case in the "most appropriate" manner.[43] In another case, a guest and his daughter were in a bakery shop on Main Street, U.S.A., when they were hit by falling debris. The guest stated "the park does not seem to regard customers' safety as its priority" and threatened to take legal action against HKD, adding that they tried to placate him with a Winnie the Pooh for his daughter.[44]

Working Conditions

The character performers at HKD complained that they were overworked and underpaid. The spokesperson of the staff union stated that workdays of more than 12 hours and inadequate rest breaks had overwhelmed many workers, causing work-related injuries, such as joint and muscle strain. In response, Lauren Jordan, the theme park's vice president of entertainment, claimed that "there are a few cast members who have found this work to be less rewarding than others and perhaps more physically challenging than they anticipated."

---

[40] "Luxury Car Under Hammer." *Herald Sun* (December 28, 2001) Retrieved May 3, 2006, from Lexi-Nexis Academic Universe Database.

[41] Meng Chu. "Disneyland Suffers Crowd Problems in Hong Kong." *Voice* (February 10, 2006). Retrieved March 10, 2006, from http://bjtoday.ynet.com/article.jsp?oid=7653476

[42] "HK Disneyland Underestimates Lunar New Year Holiday Potential." *Asia Pulse* (February 6, 2006). Retrieved March 10, 2006, from Lexis-Nexis Academic Universe Database.

[43] Patsy Moy and Ravina Shamdasani. "Call for Inquest into Disney Visitor's Death." *South China Morning Post* (February 20, 2006): CITY1.

[44] May Chan. "Disney's Pooh Unable to Mollify Irate Father." *South China Morning Post* (December 8, 2005): CITY4.

In addition, the character performers who performed in the daily parade and met visitors were petitioning for the same salaries as stage performers. The entry salaries for parade performers averaged about HK$9,000 per month ($1,153) per month compared to about HK$11,000 ($1,409) for stage performers.[45] In response to the staff's concerns, management announced extended breaks of 40 minutes for every 20-minute session with guests during the hot and humid summer season. Cooling vests, designed for the character performers, were also being tested.

Complaints were not limited to the line staff; there was also turnover among the executive staff. As one disgruntled executive complained:

> The Americans make all the key decisions and often the wrong ones. Finance is also king here, and when things go wrong, they look for local scapegoats. The mood and morale is very low here. I know a lot of us are actively looking for jobs [and many of us] are totally disillusioned.[46]

HKD'S RESPONSE

To combat problems highlighted through the media, such as low park attendance, limited attractions, long queues, disgruntled employees, and guests' accounts of rude treatment, HKD implemented several recovery strategies.

New Promotion

To boost attendance, HKD adjusted its pricing strategy. In November 2005, the park offered ticket discounts in which the price for local residents was reduced by HK$50 ($6.41). Moreover, HKD promoted a ticket express package: guests could purchase a one-day rail pass for an extra HK$6.4 over the admission price. This pass gave unlimited rides to and from the park plus a souvenir showcase of the popular Disney characters. Many believed that these new policies were intended to boost attendance, but park spokespersons dismissed such a claim.

In mid-2006, 50,000 taxi drivers were invited to HKD free of charge. Every taxi driver who took up the offer was given free admission to the park between May 15 and June 11, 2006. In addition, a 50% discount was provided to up to three family members or friends who accompanied each driver. The aim of this promotion was to give taxi drivers a personal experience of the park that they could share with others. The Urban Taxi Drivers Association Joint Committee welcomed this scheme but it was not clear whether it was successful.

HKD also introduced a "one-day trip guide" in Chinese during November of 2005.[47] This initiative was intended to explain HKD to local travel guides. Furthermore, special VIP treatment was extended to local celebrities in the form of a Dining with Disney program. Local TV commercials also featured testimonials of previous guests and enticing scenes from inside HKD.

---

[45] Dennis Eng. "Mickey and Friends Call for a Better Work Environment." *South China Morning Post* (April 10, 2006): CITY3.

[46] Dennis Eng. "Two More Executives Quit Disney Park." *South China Morning Post*, CITY1.

[47] Geoffrey A. Fowler and Merissa Marr. "Hong Kong Disneyland Gets Lost in Translation." *The Wall Street Journal Asia* (February 9, 2006): 26.

External Liaison with Mainland Travel Agents

Since Mainland visitors were a primary target of HKD, more proactive and collaborative moves were made with Chinese travel agencies, some of which were reluctant to sell HKD tickets in view of their slim profitability and extensive hassles: "when there are problems, [travel agencies] have to eat the cost and other troubles." To overcome this resistance, HKD offered Chinese travel agents a 50% discount on visits to the park and hotels. Incentives of approximately $2.50 per adult ticket were also given to tour operators who incorporated an HKD visit into their package tours. HKD also changed the sales packages to open-ended tickets, from just fixed-date tickets, which offered greater flexibility for visitors and minimized the number of returned tickets.[48]

SETTING THE COURSE FOR EVENTUAL SUCCESS

The performance of HKD during its first year of operation had not turned out as good as had been hoped with some potentially devastating mistakes. Tour operators further complained that HKD was not big enough to keep the guests occupied for a whole day. Worse still, HKD had faced much negative publicity: from overcrowding, to customer lawsuits, to chaotic incidents during the Chinese Lunar New Year that were front page news in Hong Kong. Further, a survey of current visitors to HKD revealed that 30 per cent of guests opted not to revisit the park, which did not bode well for HKD's future.[49]

Disney had experience in operating parks internationally in both good and bad conditions. Inevitably comparisons had begun being made between HKD and Disneyland Resort Paris in France, which attracted a mere 1.5 million visitors by the end of its second month of operation and nowhere could it match Disney management' s original projection of 15 million in the first year. However, some academics believed that it might take another five years to determine whether HKD could be judged as an economic success or failure.

Although maintaining an optimistic public face, the management team at HKD was facing pressures to turn things around. How could HKD steer through the cultural minefield to ensure Hong Kong Disneyland's success? How well had Disney achieved its goal of translating its strategic assets to the Chinese cultural context? What could HKD do to ensure a successful outcome along the lines of Tokyo Disney and avoid the type of embarrassment experienced with Disneyland Paris? What could the company do to rescue the park from the onslaught of continuing negative publicity? The park's management certainly had its challenges cut out for it.

The initial research and a first draft of this case were completed by Edwina H. S. Chan, Lutricia S. M. Kwok, John C. M. Lee, Jacky W. Y. Shing, and Sally P. M. Tsui as an assignment under the direction of Professor Michael Young.

---

[48] Ibid.

[49] "Feature: Concerns Growing over HK Disneyland's Future." *Knight Ridder/Tribune Business News* (October 20, 2005): 1. Retrieved March 10, 2006, from Lexis-Nexis Academic Universe Database.

Exhibit 1

CURRENT HOLDINGS OF THE WALT DISNEY COMPANY

Business Segments	Performance (2005)
Studio Entertainment	This segment had the greatest decrease of 69%, which the company attributed to the overall decline in unit sales in worldwide home entertainment and at Miramax
Consumer Products	This division reported decrease in operating income of 3% due to lower revenue generated from the sales of Disney goods and merchandise
Media Networks	The higher rates paid by cable operators for ESPN and the Disney Channels and higher advertising revenue at ESPN and ABC were the primary factors driving the 27% growth in revenue at the media network unit.
Parks & Resorts	The Parks and Resorts division also enjoyed a 5% increase in revenue, largely due to the higher occupancy at the resorts, theme park attendance, and guest expenditure.

Source: Annual Report 2005, The Walt Disney Company.

Exhibit 2

HOW DISNEY'S ASSETS AND PRACTICES RECONTEXTUALIZE TO JAPAN AND FRANCE

	United States	Japan	France
Products			
Mickey Mouse	Squeaky-clean, all-American boy representing wholesome American values	Safe and reliable (used to sell money market accounts)	Cunning, street-smart detective epitomized in *Le Journal Mickey* — squeaky clean version is boring
Cowboy	Rugged, self-reliant individualist	Quintessential team player	Carefree, somewhat dim-witted anti-establishment individual
Souvenirs	Fun, part of the experience	Legitimating mementos that fit into the formalized system of gift giving, known as sembetsu	Tacky, waste of money
Practices			
Service Orientation	Hypernormal	Cultural norm	Abnormal
Personnel Management	Hypernormal	Cultural norm	Invasive/illegal
Training	Hypernormal	Cultural norm	Totalitarian
Ideologies			
Disneyland	Modernist theme - fun, clean, wholesome entertainment	Translated modernist theme - fun, clean, safe foreign vacation	Postmodernist theme - resistance to Disney's meta narrative
Foreignness	• Fantasized European roots • Marginalized native and minority others	• Keeping the U.S. exotic • Marginalizing the Asian other	• Politicized repatriation • Schizophrenic relationship with the U.S.

Source: Mary Yoko Brannen, "When Mickey Loses Face: Recontextualization, Semantic Fit and the Semiotics of Foreignness," Academy of Management Review, October 2004, p. 593.

Exhibit 3

ANNUAL VISITOR ARRIVALS IN HONG KONG

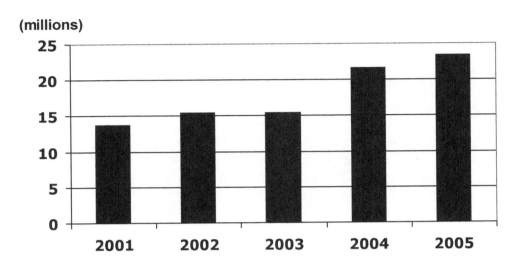

Source: Hong Kong Tourism Board (2006).

Exhibit 4

VISITOR ARRIVALS BY COUNTRY/TERRITORY OF RESIDENCE

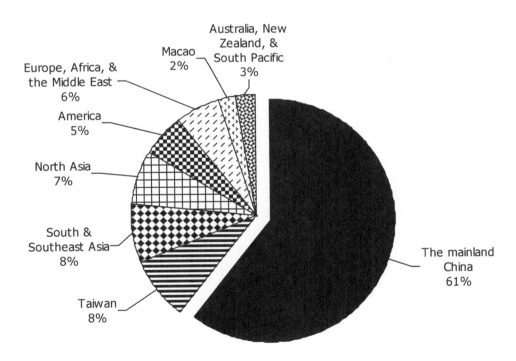

Source: Hong Kong Monthly Digest of Statistics (March 2006).

ABOUT THE AUTHORS

Linda L. Brennan is a professor of management at Mercer University in Macon. Her teaching portfolio includes graduate and undergraduate courses in operations management, leadership, international business, and strategy. She conducts research and consults in the areas of technology impact assessment, process and project management, and instructional effectiveness. Brennan has been published in scholarly and practitioner-oriented journals such as *International Journal of Quality and Reliability Management, Engineering Management Journal, The Journal of Management in Engineering, IEEE Technology and Society,* and *Corporate Governance.* Two of her books, *Computer-Mediated Relationships and Trust: Organizational and Managerial Implications* and *The Social, Ethical, and Policy Implications of Information Systems,* were co-edited with Dr. Victoria Johnson and published by IGI Global. McGraw-Hill published her most recent book, *Operations Management*, in 2010. Dr. Brennan's prior work experience includes management positions at The Quaker Oats Company and marketing and systems engineering experience with the IBM Corporation. A licensed professional engineer, she received her Ph.D. in industrial engineering from Northwestern University, her MBA in policy studies from the University of Chicago, and her B.I.E. in industrial engineering from the Georgia Institute of Technology.

Faye A. Sisk is an associate professor of management in the Stetson School of Business and Economics at Mercer University in Atlanta, where she is the director of executive and professional MBA programs. Dr. Sisk teaches strategic, quality, international, healthcare, and human resource management and brings to the classroom both her corporate and consulting experience. Her clients represent a diverse set of industries, including both for-profit and non-profit organizations, domestically and globally. She also has been involved in executive development for companies and non-profits including BellSouth/AT&T, Alcan Corporation, Susan B. Komen Foundation, and the University Medical Center, Jacksonville, Florida. Prior to her academic appointment, Dr. Sisk held executive positions with HBO & Company (now McKesson HBOC) and was a senior consultant with IMS America and a federal contractor working with agencies such as the FDA, Health & Human Services, and DEA. She has published in academic and practitioner journals on strategy, organizational ethics, quality, and human resource issues, including diversity and gender. She earned her Ph.D. from the University of Florida, where she was a Kellogg Fellow, her MBA from Kennesaw State University, her M.Ed. from the University of North Florida, and her BA from Agnes Scott College.

FEEDBACK? QUESTIONS FOR THE AUTHORS? PLEASE LET US KNOW HOW THIS BOOK IS WORKING FOR YOU, AND WHETHER YOU HAVE SUGGESTIONS FOR ITS IMPROVEMENT. CONTACT BRENNAN_LL@MERCER.EDU.

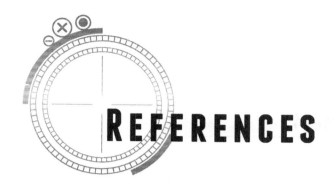

REFERENCES

CHAPTER 1

Carpenter, M. A., & Sanders, W. M. (2009). *Strategic Management, 2/e.* Upper Saddle River, NJ: Pearson Education.

Goldratt, E. M., & Cox, J. (1984). *The Goal: A Process of Ongoing Improvement, 3/e.* Great Barrington, MA: North River Press.

Goodman, R. A., & Lawless, M. W. (1994). *Technology and Strategy: Conceptual Models and Diagnostics.* New York, NY: Oxford University Press.

CHAPTER 2

Baldoni, J. (2006). Steady as you go: Achieving a balanced vision. *Harvard Management Update,* August 2006. Boston, MA: Harvard Business School Publishing.

Collins, J. C., & Portas, J. I. (1991). Organizational vision and visionary organizations. *California Management Review, 50*(2), 117–137.

Crotts, J. C., Dickson, D. R., & Ford, R. C. (2005). Aligning organizational processes with mission: The case of service excellence. *Academy of Management Executive, 19*(3), 54–68.

Daily Technician. (2011). Yahoo: Change at the top. *Daily Technician,* July 10, 2011. Accessed September 18, 2011, at http://www.thedailytechnician.com

CHAPTER 3

Brennan, L. L., & Johnson, V. E. (2003). Strategic responsibility: Technology management for Corporate Social Responsibility. *IEEE Technology and Society, 23*(1).

Grameen Bank. (2011). A short history of the Grameen Bank. Accessed October 19, 2011, at http://www.grameen-info.org/

Starbucks. (2010). Coffee purchasing & farmer support. *Starbucks Global Responsibility Report: Goals & Progress 2010*. Accessed October 19, 2011, at http://www.starbucks.com/responsibility/sourcing

Toffler, B. M. (2003). Five ways to jump-start your company's ethics. *Fast Company, 75*(October), 36.

CHAPTER 4

Blackburn, W. R. (2000). *The Sustainability Handbook*. Environmental Law Institute.

Brundtland Commission. (1987). *Our Common Future*. United Nations Commission on Environment and Development.

Carroll, A. B. (2000). Ethical challenges for business in the new millennium: Corporate social responsibility and models of management morality. *Business Ethics Quarterly*, (January), 33–42.

Elkington, J. (1997). *Cannibals with Forks: The Triple Bottom Line of 21st Century Business*. New Society Publishers.

Friedman, M. (13 September 1970). The social responsibility of business is to increase its profits. *The New York Times Magazine*.

Goleman, D. (2009). *Ecological Intelligence*. New York, NY: Broadway Books.

New, S. (2010). The transparent supply chain: Let your customers know everything about where your products come from—before they discover it first. *Harvard Business Review*, (October), 76–82, reprint #R1010E.

Samuelson, R. J. (9 November 1992). Schumpeter: The prophet. *Newsweek*, 61.

CHAPTER 5

Barker, J. A. (1993). *Paradigms: The Business of Discovering the Future*. New York, NY: HarperBusiness.

Fallows, J. (17 March 2010). How to think about the RMB, "currency manipulation," and trade war. *The Atlantic*. Accessed September 23, 2011, at http://www.theatlantic.com

Gruben, W. C., & Kiser, S. L. (2001). NAFTA and *maquiladoras*: Is the growth connected? *Federal Reserve Bank of Dallas*. Accessed September 23, 2011, at http://www.dallasfed.org

IRS. (2011). 401(k) Resource Guide - Plan Sponsors - General Distribution Rules. Accessed September 16, 2011, at http://www.irs.gov

Johnson, K. (6 November 2008). On concerns over gun control, gun sales are up. *The New York Times*. Accessed September 23, 2011, at http://www.nytimes.com

Shih, C. (2009). *The Facebook Era: Tapping Online Social Networks to Build Better Products, Reach New Audiences, and Sell More Stuff*. New Jersey: Prentice Hall.

SSA. (2011). Medicare. SSA Publication No. 05-10043, June 2011, ICN 460000. Accessed September 16, 2011, at http://www.ssa.gov

CHAPTER 6

Allen, G. B., & Hammond, J. S. (1975). *Note on the Boston Consulting Group concept of competitive analysis and corporate strategy*. Boston, MA: Harvard Business School Publishing. Reprint #9-175-175.

Barney, J. (2001). Is the resource-based "view" a useful perspective for strategic management research? Yes. *Academy of Management Review, 2*(1; January), 41–56.

Brennan, L. L. (2010). *Operations Management*. New York, NY: McGraw-Hill.

Christensen, C. M., & Raynor, M. E. (2003). *The Innovator's Solution*. Boston, MA: Harvard Business School Publishing.

David, F. (1997). *Strategic Management, 6/e*. Upper Saddle River, NJ: Prentice-Hall, Inc.

Gallon, M. R., Stillman, H. M., & Coates, D. (1995). Putting core competency thinking into practice. *Research-Technology Management*, (May–June), 20–28.

Hamel, G., & Prahald, C. K. (1996). *Competing for the Future*. Boston, MA: Harvard Business School Press.

Prahalad, C. K., & Hamel, G. (1990). The core competence of the corporation. *Harvard Business Review*, (May–June), 79–91. Reprint #90311.

Steele, L. W. (1989). *Managing Technology: The Strategic View*. New York, NY: McGraw-Hill.

Wheelwright, S. C., & Clark, K. B. (2003). Creating product plans to focus product development. *Harvard Business Review*, (September). Reprint # 92210.

CHAPTER 7

Brennan, L.L. (2012). The scientific management of information overload. *Journal of Business and Management*, forthcoming.

Liker, J. and Meier, D. (2005). *The Toyota Way Fieldbook*. New York, NY: McGraw-Hill.

Porter, M. E. (2008, 1979) The five competitive forces that shape strategy. *Harvard Business Review*, 86(1):78–93.

Porter, M. E. (1985) How information gives you competitive value. *Harvard Business Review*, 63(4): 149–160.

Porter, M.E. (1985) *Competitive Advantage*. New York, NY: The Free Press.

Womack, J.P., and Jones, D.T. (2005). Lean consumption. *Harvard Business Review*, March 2005. Reprint #R0503C.

CHAPTER 8

Ansoff, I. (1957). Strategies for Diversification. *Harvard Business Review, 35*(5), 113–124.

Bruner, J. (2010). GE, Intel to form new healthcare joint venture. Accessed November 14, 2011, at http://www.intel.com/pressroom/archive/

Buffet, W. E. (2010). Chairman's letter. Berkshire Hathaway's 2010 Annual Report. Accessed November 14, 2011, at http://www.berkshirehathaway.com/2010ar/2010ar.pdf

Cohen, M. (9 November 2011). Borders liquidators get "something" from George Harrison Guitar. *The Wall Street Journal*. Accessed November 16, 2011, at http://online.wsj.com

Foust, D. (14 May 2009). How Delta climbed out of bankruptcy. *BusinessWeek*. Accessed November 16, 2011, at http://www.businessweek.com

Hitt, M. A., Ireland, R. D., & Palia, K. A. (1982). Industrial firms' grand strategy and functional importance: Moderating effect of technology and uncertainty. *Academy of Management Journal, 25*(2), 265–298.

IntelPR. (2011). GE and Intel's telehealth and independent living company is operational today. Accessed November 14, 2011, at http://newsroom.intel.com

Miles, R. E., et. al. (1978). Organizational Strategy, Structure and Process. *The Academy of Management Review, 3*(3), 546–562.

Mulcahy, A. (2006). Behind the scenes of a great turnaround. Interview in the Dean's Innovative Leader Series, Wednesday, November 9, 2006. Accessed November 14, 2011, at http://mitsloan.mit.edu/newsroom/2006-mulcahy.php

PRNewswire. (2011). TiVo and Sony announce strategic alliance. Accessed November 14, 2011, at http://www.prnewswire.com/news-releases/tivo-and-sony-form-strategic-alliance-74295797.html

Radde, L., & Louw, L. (1998), The SPACE Matrix: A Tool for Calibrating Competition. *Long Range Planning, 31*(4), 549–551.

Shih, C. (2010). *The Facebook Era: Tapping Online Social Networks to Market, Sell, and Innovate.* Upper Saddle River, NJ: Prentice Hall.

Tzu, S., & Sawyer, D. (1994). *The Art of War (History and Warfare).* New York, NY: Basic Books.

Ziobro, P. (28 October 2011). P&G says costs will curb current quarter. *The Wall Street Journal.* Accessed online November 16, 2011, at http://online.wsj.com/

CHAPTER 9

Abrahamson, E. (2000). Change without pain: Dynamic Stability. *Harvard Business Review,* (July–August), 75–79. Reprint #R00401.

Anderson, J., & Markides, C. (2007). Strategic innovation at the base of the pyramid. *MIT Sloan Management Review, 49*(1), 83–88. Reprint #49116.

Berry, L. L., Shankar, V., Parish, J. T., Cadwallader, S., & Dotzel, T. (2006). Creating new markets through service innovation. *MIT Sloan Management Review, 47*(7), 56–63. Reprint #47213.

Day, G. S., & Schoemaker, P. J. H. (2011). Innovation in uncertain markets: 10 lessons for green technologies. *MIT Sloan Management Review, 52*(4), 37–45. Reprint #52411.

Drucker, P. F. (1985). *Innovation and Entrepreneurship: Practice and Principles.* New York, NY: Harper & Row Publishers.

Drucker, P. F. (2002). The discipline of innovation. *Harvard Business Review,* (August). Reprint #R0208F.

Eisner, E. W. (1966). A typology of creative behavior in the visual arts, 323–335. In E. W. Eisner and D. W. Ecker, Eds. (1966), *Readings in Art Education.* Waltham, MA: Blaisdell Publishing. Accessed December 7, 2011, at http://people.goshen.edu/~marvinpb/11-13-01/types-of-creativity.html

Hart, S. L., & Christensen, C. M. (2002). The great leap: driving innovation from the base of the pyramid. *MIT Sloan Management Review, 44*(1), 51–56. Reprint #4415.

Harvard Business School Publishing. (2002). Inspiring innovation. *Harvard Business Review,* (August), 78. Reprint #R0208B.

Immelt, J. R., Govindarajan, V., & Trimble, C. (2009). How GE is disrupting itself. *Harvard Business Review,* (October). Reprint #R0910D.

Nidumolu, R., Prahalad, C. K., & Rangaswami, M. R. (2009). Why sustainability is now the key driver of innovation. *Harvard Business Review,* (September), 57–64. Reprint # $0909E.

Prahalad, C. K., & Hammond, A. (2002). Serving the world's poor, profitably. *Harvard Business Review,* (September). Reprint #R0209C.

Prahalad, C. K., & Mashelkar, R. A. (2010). Innovation's holy grail. *Harvard Business Review,* (July–August). Reprint #1007N.

Shellenbarger, S. (27 September 2011). Better ideas through failure. *The Wall Street Journal.* Accessed November 4, 2011, at http://online.wsj.com

Tillman, T. (2011). How sweet the music: Skullcandy IPO prices above the range. *Seeking Alpha.* Accessed January 18, 2012, at http://seekingalpha.com

Chapter 10

ACS. (2010). *Strategic Plan Status Report*. Accessed December 2, 2011, at http://www.cancer.org/acs/groups/content/@nho/documents/document/acspc-026910.pdf

Hambrick, D. C., & Fredrickson, J. W. (2001). Are you sure you have a strategy? *Academy of Management Executive, 15*(4), 48–59.

Chapter 11

Bartlett, C. A., Ghoshal, S., & Birkenshaw, J. (2004). *Transnational Management*. New York, NY: Irwin.

Czinkota, M. R., Ronkainen, P. A., & Moffet, M. H. (2004). *Fundamentals of International Business*. Mason, OH: Thompson South-Western.

Friedman, T. L. (2005). *The World is Flat: A Brief History of the Globalized World in the 21st Century*. New York, NY: Farrar, Straus and Giroux.

Guillen, M. F., & Garcia-Canal, E. (2009). The American model of the multinational firm and the new multinationals from emerging economies. *Academy of Management Perspectives*, (May), 23–35.

Ghemawat, P. (2003). The forgotten strategy. *Harvard Business Review*, (November), 76–84. Reprint #R0311E.

Hambrick, D. C., & Fredrickson, J. W. (2001). Are you sure you have a strategy? *Academy of Management Executive, 15*(4), 48–59.

Pan, Y., & Tse, D. (2000). The hierarchical model of market entry modes. *Journal of International Business Studies, 31*, 535–545.

Rivoli, P. (2005). *The Travels of a T-Shirt in the Global Economy: An Economist Examines the Markets, Power, and Politics of World Trade*. New York, NY: Wiley.

Travis, T. (2007). *Doing Business Anywhere: The Essential Guide to Going Global*. Hoboken, NJ: John Wiley & Sons.

Yip, G. S. (1994). *Total Global Strategy: Managing for World Wide Competitive Advantage*. Upper Saddle River, NJ: Prentice-Hall.

Chapter 12

Beer, M., Eisenstat, R. A., & Spector, B. (1990). Why change programs don't produce change. *Harvard Business Review, 68*(6), 158–166.

Beer, M., & Eisenstat, R. A. (2004). How to Have an Honest Conversation about Your Business Strategy, *Harvard Business Review*, (February).

Bridges, W. (2003). *Managing Transitions: Making the Most of Change*.

Burnes, B. (2004). Kurt Lewin and the Planned Approach to Change: A Re-appraisal. *Journal of Management Studies, 41*(6).

Burns, J. M. (1978). *Leadership*. New York, NY: Harper & Row.

Bennis, W., & Nanus, B. (1985). *Leaders: The strategies for taking charge*. New York, NY: Harper & Row.

Collins, J. (2001). *Good to Great: Why Some Companies Make the Leap ... and Others Don't*. Harper Business.

Fielder, F. E. (1967). *A theory of leadership effectiveness*. New York, NY: McGraw-Hill Book Company.

Garvin, D., Edmonson, A., & Gino, F. (2008). Is Yours A Learning Organization? *Harvard Business Review, 86*(7), 109–116.

Goleman, D. (1998) What Makes a Leader. *Harvard Business Review, 76*(6), 93–102

Gratton, L. (2007), *Hot Spots: Why Some Teams, Workplaces, and Organizations Buzz with Energy—And Others Don't*. Berrett Koehler Publishers.

Kaplan, R., & Norton, D. (1992) The Balanced Scorecard: Measures that Drive Performance. *Harvard Business Review, 70*(1), 71–79.

Kidder, R. (1995). *How Good People Make Tough Choices*. New York, NY: Fireside.

Kotter, J. P. (1996). *Leading Change*. Boston, MA: Harvard Business School Publishing.

Maxwell, J. (2007). *The 21 Indispensable Qualities of a Leader: Becoming the Person Others Will Want to Follow*. Thomas Nelson Publishers.

Pagano, B. (2004). *The Transparency Edge: How Credibility Can Make You or Break You in Business*, Chapter 1. New York, NY: McGraw-Hill.

Trevino, L. K., & Brown, M. E. (2004). Managing to be ethical: Debunking five business ethics myths. *Academy of Management Executive, 18*(4), 69–81.